ESSENTIALS OF
HEALTHFUL
COOKING

WILLIAMS-SONOMA

ESSENTIALS OF
HEALTHFUL
COOKING

RECIPES AND TECHNIQUES FOR WHOLESOME HOME COOKING

TEXT
MARY ABBOTT HESS

RECIPES
DANA JACOBI, MARIE SIMMONS

GENERAL EDITOR
CHUCK WILLIAMS

PHOTOGRAPHY
TUCKER & HOSSLER

Oxmoor
House®

Contents

Sitting down to a delicious meal with people we care about is one of life's great pleasures. Gathered around the table, we share food as well as thoughts, feelings, and experiences. To think of food merely as a carrier for nutrients overlooks a magical transformation: the food we eat truly does become us.

As a young dietitian with a growing family, I discovered that delicious, beautifully presented food is not only a pleasure to eat, but also enjoyable and fulfilling to prepare. I also realized that all my nutrition knowledge meant little if I did not use it to cook food my family and friends looked forward to eating. Thus, I spent the ensuing thirty years keeping pace with breakthroughs in nutrition science and learning how to prepare food that is both delicious and healthful.

I believe that cooking is much more than a means to an end; it is a vital life skill. Eating well, along with other positive lifestyle habits, increases the likelihood of good health and a long life. Research has shown that what we eat can prevent, delay the onset of, or control many medical conditions, such as high cholesterol, hypertension, heart disease, obesity, diabetes, osteoporosis, and some cancers. Although most of us have been trying to eat less fat, many of us have not paid enough attention to eating more fruits, vegetables, legumes, and whole grains—low-fat foods that are overflowing with the vitamins, minerals, fiber, and phytochemicals that people of all ages need to fend off disease and achieve optimal health.

Having served as president of The American Dietetic Association (the world's largest group of nutrition professionals) and as chair of The American Institute of Wine & Food (an organization dedicated to enhancing quality of life by providing education about what we eat and drink), I am intimately familiar with the challenge we face. I also see many opportunities for, and a growing interest in, the seamless blend of good nutrition and good food.

Yes, we might have to make some changes along the way, but that does not mean giving up favorite foods. In fact, with some planning and know-how, all foods can fit into a balanced, healthful diet—even those guilty pleasures high in fat or sugar. Part of the secret rests in learning to eat wisely. This book reveals the rest of the secret: the essentials of healthful cooking.

Mary Abbott Hess

Philosophy of Healthful Cooking

Food plays an important role in everyone's life. In addition to being fuel for the body, food is tied to culture and family traditions. It is not surprising that people find joy in cooking—and in eating. This book is about healthful food that fulfills all these expectations.

Most of us use food not only to nourish our bodies, but also to celebrate, to commemorate, to worship, and even to mourn. How we purchase, prepare, and eat food is influenced by where we live and our religion, ethnicity, family, education, income, and attitudes about promoting health and protecting the environment. Food plays such an intimate role in our lives that it is not surprising many people enjoy it as an expression of friendship and love. The recipes in this book capture another dimension of that joy—the essentials of healthful cooking. Healthful cooking is about much more than good nutrition. It is about good

food—the kind of food that delights all the senses and makes eating one of life's greatest pleasures. The essentials of healthful cooking include choosing fresh, high-quality ingredients; using cooking techniques that maximize nutrition without relying on abundant fat, sugar, or salt for flavor; and creating plate presentations that please the senses.

In the pages that follow, we accentuate the positive by using ingredients that offer the optimal combination of good nutrition and great taste, including well-chosen fats and sugars in reasonable amounts. We maximize the types and amounts of food with health benefits while minimizing foods and preparation techniques that increase health risks. And we encourage you to expand your food horizons by adding new foods and techniques to your cooking repertoire.

Fruits and vegetables, powerhouses of vitamins, minerals, and protective phytochemicals (page 13), are a great place to start. Nowhere is flavor more abundant and freshness more critical. Consider, for example, the crisp sweetness of an apple, the bright green of broccoli and snap peas, and the succulence of a perfectly ripe peach, pear, or apricot. Thanks to air transportation and storage technology, we can buy almost any fruit or vegetable anytime of year. But locally grown seasonal produce served at the peak of freshness typically has the very best flavor. A garden-ripe tomato in midsummer is a world apart from a hothouse tomato sold in midwinter. Root vegetables like parsnips, sweet potatoes, and beets are

sweetest in the autumn. Cherries, strawberries, and blueberries shine in the summer. In-season fresh fruit not only tastes better, but is usually more economical as well.

Many farmers' markets and roadside produce stands offer fruit and vegetable varieties that are chosen especially for their superior flavor and nutrient value. Organic produce—fruits and vegetables certified as grown without the use of chemicals—is often a cut above as well. In contrast, many of the fruits and vegetables sold in supermarkets come from seed varieties selected for efficient harvest, long shelf life, pretty appearance, and uniform size, rather than for taste or nutritional value.

Healthful cooking also includes plenty of full-of-fiber whole grains, calcium-packed low-fat dairy products, and protein-rich legumes, lean meats, seafood, and poultry. And let's face it—the majority of us lust after foods like chocolate, ice cream, salty snacks, and other items high in fat, sugar, or salt. Abstinence only makes the heart grow fonder. If your cooking and eating are based on healthful choices most of the time, you can allow yourself occasional splurges.

A Complete Approach

Choosing the best ingredients, boosting flavor with robust spices and fresh herbs, and using fat strategically are key to making food that is both nutritious and delicious. A complete approach to healthful cooking also encompasses techniques for cooking food and presenting it.

The recipes in this book are proof that healthful food can be beautiful, great tasting, and a joy to prepare, serve, and eat. From appetizers through desserts, breakfast breads to snacks, these recipes are not low-fat, low-calorie imitations but, instead, offer new ideas. The classics are not forgotten, however, with contemporary healthful versions of such favorites as tomato bisque, cannelloni, beef bourguignon, coq au vin, Key lime pie, and chocolate mousse.

The recipes showcase an abundance of grains, vegetables, legumes, fruits, and protein foods that are relatively low in fat, especially saturated fat. A colorful sauce or coulis of fruit replaces a dessert sauce made with lots of refined sugar and cream. Fresh herbs, garlic, onion, ginger, pepper, citrus, and other aromatics add taste and zest to myriad recipes. But that does not mean fat is banned from these pages. We show you how to incorporate heart-healthy monounsaturated fats such as olive oil and canola oil into your diet and how to use fat strategically to add flavor and texture to a variety of preparations.

The cooking techniques we recommend—baking, roasting, grilling, braising, steaming, sautéing, and stir-frying, for example—maximize the natural flavor of foods. Mastering the techniques on pages 20–27 will allow you to create both bold and subtle flavors without depending on too much added fat. You can use the same techniques to make some of your own favorite dishes more healthful.

Although the dishes you will make using this book are glorious, the suggested servings are moderate, in keeping with the portion sizes recommended by health and nutrition experts. The portions served in many American restaurants have become larger and larger. Unfortunately, supersized portions have led to supersized consumers. Elsewhere in the world, portions served in restaurants and at home are much smaller. In homes and many fine restaurants in France, it is considered crass to serve huge portions. The French strive for excellence in food ingredients and appreciate quality, flavor, and cooking technique.

We also cover what you need to know about outfitting your kitchen for healthful cooking (pages 28–31). Every kitchen needs the right equipment, from roasting pans, grill pans, and steamers to a blender, a food processor, and a food mill.

You will find three other useful resources. The first is a list of healthful food choices (pages 10–11). The second is a produce guide arranged by color category (page 15). For a variety and abundance of nutrients, use fruits and vegetables from all the color categories. Lastly, the per-serving nutritional content of each recipe has been calculated. These nutritional values are presented on pages 290–97. NOTE: If you have any food intolerances or special dietary requirements, consult with a nutrition professional for information on how to manage your diet and how to modify these recipes and others to meet your needs. Also note that pregnant women, very young children, and individuals with poor immune responses are advised to avoid eating raw seafood or uncooked eggs.

Ingredients for a Healthful Kitchen

Although a healthful diet can include any food, as long as you watch the frequency of consuming it and portion size, some foods are smart choices all the time. When purchasing fruits and vegetables, select seasonal produce for best flavor and maximum nutrients.

GRAINS

Complex carbohydrates, B vitamins, iron, fiber, phytochemicals

Bagels: especially pumpernickel, rye, seeded, whole wheat (wholemeal)

Baked chips: corn, tortilla

Breads: multigrain and whole grain, bread sticks, crisp breads, flat breads, whole-grain English muffins, whole-wheat pita

Cereals: ready-to-eat multigrain and whole grain

Cookies: fig bars, gingersnaps, oatmeal raisin

Grains: barley, bulgur, couscous, kasha, millet, oats, polenta, quinoa

Pastas: artichoke, spinach, whole grain

Popcorn: without butter

Pretzels: unsalted or lightly salted

Rice: brown, wild

Tortillas: corn, flour

Wheat germ

FRUITS*

Carbohydrates, fiber, vitamins and minerals (especially potassium), phytochemicals

Berries: blackberries, blueberries, gooseberries, raspberries, strawberries

Citrus: clementines, grapefruits, lemons, limes, oranges, tangelos, tangerines

Dried: apricots, cherries, cranberries, dates, figs, plums, raisins

Fruit juices and ciders: freshly squeezed or pressed, unsweetened

Melons: cantaloupe, casaba, Crenshaw, honeydew, watermelon

Orange and red fruits: apricots, mangoes, papayas, persimmons, red grapefruits

* All fresh fruits and vegetables are healthful. This list includes particularly healthful produce.

VEGETABLES*

Fiber, vitamins and minerals, phytochemicals

Avocados

Bell peppers (capsicums): green, red, yellow

Cabbage family: bok choy, broccoli, broccolini, brussels sprouts, cauliflower, napa cabbage, red and green cabbage

Eggplants (aubergines)

Herbs: fresh and dried

Leafy greens: beet greens, broccoli rabe, chard, collard greens, kale, red and green leaf lettuce, romaine (cos) lettuce, spinach

Onion family: leeks; red, yellow, and white onions; scallions; shallots

Roots and tubers: beets, carrots, garlic, fresh ginger, potatoes, radishes, rutabagas, sweet potatoes, turnips, baked root-vegetable chips

Seeds and pods: corn, *edamame*, green beans, long beans, snow peas (mangetouts), sugar snap peas

Shoots, stalks, and stems: asparagus, celery, fennel

Squash: winter, including acorn, butternut, pumpkin, turban; summer, including crookneck, pattypan, zucchini (courgette)

Tomatoes and tomato products

Vegetable salsas

* All fresh fruits and vegetables are healthful. This list includes particularly healthful produce.

LEGUMES, NUTS, AND SEEDS

Protein, carbohydrates, fiber, vitamins and minerals

Legumes: dried and canned

Lentils

Nut butters: cashew, peanut, and other varieties

Nuts: almonds, cashews, chestnuts, pine nuts

Peas: dried, canned, and frozen

Seeds: flaxseed, pumpkin, sesame, squash, sunflower

Soybean products: soy beverages, soy cheese, soy nuts, tempeh, tofu

FISH, POULTRY, AND EGGS

Protein, vitamins and minerals, omega-3 fatty acids (fatty fish)

Anchovies: canned

Eggs: whole and yolks, 5 per week; whites as desired

Poultry: ground (minced)

Poultry and game birds: skin removed before eating

Sardines: canned

Sausage: poultry

Shellfish and finfish: fresh, flash frozen, or canned

Tuna: canned, 2 times a week

MEATS

Protein, B vitamins, iron, zinc

Beef, buffalo, lamb, pork, veal, and venison: lean and extra lean, ground, and well trimmed

Liver: calves' and chicken, occasionally

Sausage: reduced fat

DAIRY

Protein, vitamins and minerals (especially calcium and vitamin D)

Buttermilk: low fat, fresh and dried

Cheese, hard: cheddar, Parmesan, and other strong-flavored cheeses in small amounts

Cheese, soft: cottage, farmer, goat, part-skim mozzarella, pot, ricotta

Milk: low fat and nonfat fresh, nonfat dry, nonfat evaporated and condensed

Sour cream: nonfat and light

Yogurt: low fat and nonfat; frozen

FATS AND OILS**

Monounsaturated fat, omega-3 fatty acids

Bacon: preservative free

Butter

Chicken fat

Cream cheese: reduced fat and Neufchâtel

Mayonnaise: reduced fat

Oils: canola, flaxseed, nut, olive, peanut

** Used in moderation.

SWEETS**

Simple carbohydrates

Fruit sorbets and Italian ices

Honey

Jams, jellies, and preserves

Maple syrup: pure

**Used in moderation.

OTHER INGREDIENTS

Broths: reduced sodium, fat free

Capers

Cocoa powder: Dutch process, unsweetened

Mustards

Salt: kosher, sea**

Soy sauce: reduced sodium**

Spices and seasonings

Teas: especially green tea

Vinegars

Water: plain, flavored, sparkling

Wine, spirits, and liqueurs**

** Used in moderation.

TOP IT OFF

A simple topping can make a good dish look and taste even better.

Low-fat toppings for savory dishes

Caramelized onions (pages 149 and 164)

Chopped roasted red bell peppers (capsicums) (page 277) or sun-dried tomatoes

Chopped toasted nuts, in small amounts

Gremolata (page 272)

Preserved lemons (page 272)

Low-fat toppings for desserts

Chopped sun-dried fruits

Coarsely crushed meringue cookies

Dusting of unsweetened cocoa powder

Finely chopped candied citrus peel (page 275) or candied ginger

Pomegranate seeds

Legumes and Grains

The high nutritional value, hearty flavor, and long shelf life of legumes make them a staple of healthful cooking. Likewise, grains—notably whole grains such as whole wheat (wholemeal), oats, and brown rice—are must-have ingredients in any healthy kitchen.

Like produce, legumes are nutrition superstars. Legumes are, by definition, the seeds of plants with pods that split open when dried—in other words, peas, beans, lentils, and peanuts. They are rich in fiber, protein, complex carbohydrates, and phosphorus and also have some iron. Most legumes have little or no fat; exceptions are peanuts and soybeans, which contain heart-healthy monounsaturated fat.

In addition to earning high marks for nutritional value, legumes are economical, have a long shelf life, and contribute lots of flavor, texture, and color to meals. Most are sold dry and must be soaked before cooking. To save time, you can use canned legumes such as chickpeas (garbanzo beans), cannellini beans, black beans, and kidney beans or frozen varieties such as black-eyed peas or limas.

The soybean, one of the most versatile members of the legume family, is available in a variety of forms, including canned and frozen soybeans, frozen *edamame* (young soybeans), tofu, miso, tempeh, soy milk, soy yogurt, soy cheese, and soy nuts.

Grains are an important part of the diet that we tend to take for granted. Bread, cereal, pasta, and rice deserve a closer look, especially the whole-grain varieties.

A whole grain has three parts, each of which provides different nutrients. Bran, the hull or outer coating of the whole grain, delivers vitamins as well as fiber that aids elimination, lowers blood cholesterol levels, and reduces the risk of colon cancer. In refined grains, such as white flour, semolina, and white rice, the fiber has been removed, leaving the interior part of the grain, the endosperm, which is mostly starch and some protein. Milling also removes the third part of the whole grain, the germ (as in wheat germ), which contains unsaturated fat, protein, iron, and many vitamins and minerals. Although refined grains (and white flour) are often enriched with a few nutrients that have been removed in milling, important components, like fiber and protective phytochemicals, are not replaced.

In 1992 the U.S. Department of Agriculture (USDA) introduced the Food Guide Pyramid, which places all grain-based foods together and encourages people to consider this group as the foundation of a healthful diet. Many health experts, however, believe that highly refined breads, cereals, pastas, and grains are much like refined sugar and should be limited. Refined carbohydrates do, in fact, raise blood sugar and are a problem for people with insulin resistance.

Other pyramids have been recommended for specific age groups and for the foods of regional and ethnic groups. In 2001, Walter Willett, MD, and the Harvard Medical School published the Healthy Eating Pyramid, which, like all the other pyramids, emphasizes the importance of fruits and vegetables. This pyramid, however, distinguishes whole grains from refined grains, highlights legumes and nuts, promotes the benefits of heart-healthy fats, and recommends daily exercise. A new USDA pyramid is scheduled for release in 2005.

In the Healthy Eating Pyramid, white potatoes are in the same category as refined grains, because, like refined grains, they raise blood sugar. Keep in mind, however, that the potato is a good source of vitamin C, some minerals, and fiber. Certainly french fries, which add considerable fat, are not a healthful choice, but a baked potato can be. It all depends on what you eat on it or with it.

Fruits and Vegetables

Their beautiful colors, sculpted shapes, and varied tastes make fruits and vegetables versatile ingredients. They also contain an abundance of nutrients and phytochemicals. Reap all the benefits fruits and vegetables have to offer by including a variety of produce in your daily diet.

Fruits and vegetables have always been nutrition superstars. Although we are eating more of them, we are not necessarily making the best choices.

Now there is more reason than ever to increase the variety and frequency of our produce consumption. In addition to supplying vitamins, minerals, and fiber, fruits and vegetables are rich in phytochemicals, beneficial compounds found in plants. These bioactive compounds are the next frontier in nutrition science. Likely numbering in the thousands, protective phytochemicals—working alone and in combination with one another and with nutrients—have the potential to slow aging, enhance immunity, prevent and slow cancer, enhance communication among cells, repair DNA damaged by smoking and other toxins, and protect the heart and circulatory system.

So far, researchers have studied only a few hundred phytochemicals intensively, including isoflavones and phytosterols in soy, lignans in flaxseed, lycopene in red fruits, and catechins and quercetin in tea and wine.

In 1997, the USDA established a Phytonutrient Laboratory. The next several decades promise to be as rich in phytochemical discoveries as the early to mid-twentieth century was in the discovery of vitamins and minerals.

Research has found that phytochemicals protect against disease by various physiologic mechanisms. For example, phytochemicals in soybeans have estrogen-like effects. Some women use tofu and other soy products as a natural form of estrogen replacement after menopause. Other phytochemicals act as antioxidants, which protect the body by neutralizing unstable oxygen molecules (free radicals) that damage cells and promote disease. Regularly eating foods rich in phytochemicals can help reduce the incidence of various cancers, heart disease, impaired vision, and other health problems.

There are thousands of phytochemicals, many of which have yet to be identified. And we still have much to learn about how phytochemicals interact with one another and with the nutrients in fruits and vegetables. Thus, the best way to benefit is to eat a wide variety of fruits and vegetables—and plenty of them. Protective phytochemicals are also found in chocolate, wine, coffee, and tea, foods that are not considered fruits or vegetables but are all made from plants.

Guide to Produce by Color*

Choose produce from a range of color categories, both for visual interest and for maximum nutrition. The fruits and vegetables in each category carry varying amounts of phytochemicals that offer valuable health benefits. Use produce as soon as possible after purchase.

COLOR GROUP	CHOICES	PHYTOCHEMICALS/BENEFITS
Blue/purple	**FRUITS:** blackberries; black currants; blueberries; elderberries; plums, fresh and dried; purple figs; purple grapes; raisins **VEGETABLES:** purple asparagus; purple bell peppers (capsicums); purple cabbage; purple eggplants (aubergines); purple potatoes	Contain anthocyanins and phenolics that lower the risk of some cancers; promote urinary tract health; help memory function; and promote healthy aging
Green	**FRUITS:** avocados; green apples; green grapes; green pears; honeydew melon; kiwifruits; limes **VEGETABLES:** artichokes; asparagus; bok choy; broccoli; broccoli rabe; brussels sprouts; celery; collard greens; cucumbers (with skin); curly endive; green beans; green bell peppers; green cabbage; green (spring) onions; kale; leeks; lettuces; mustard greens; napa cabbage; okra; peas; spinach; turnip greens; zucchini (courgettes)	Contain indoles, lutein, monoterpenes, phenethyl isothiocyanate, sulforaphane, and zeaxanthin that lower the risk of breast, prostate, lung, and other cancers; promote eye health; help build strong bones and teeth; and boost immunity
White/tan/brown	**FRUITS:** bananas; Bosc pears; dates; tan figs; white nectarines; white peaches **VEGETABLES:** cauliflower; garlic; ginger; jicama; mushrooms; onions; parsnips; shallots; soybeans; turnips; white-fleshed potatoes	Contain allicin, genistein, phenethyl isothiocyanate, and phytosterols that promote heart health; help maintain healthful cholesterol level; lower the risk of breast, lung, and other cancers; and slow cholesterol absorption
Yellow/orange	**FRUITS:** apricots; cantaloupe; golden apples; grapefruits; lemons; mangoes; oranges; papayas; persimmons; tangerines; yellow nectarines; yellow peaches; yellow pears **VEGETABLES:** acorn squashes; butternut squashes; carrots; pumpkins; rutabagas; sweet corn; sweet potatoes; yellow beets; yellow bell peppers; yellow potatoes; yellow summer squashes; yellow tomatoes	Contain bioflavonoids, carotenoids, and limonoids that promote heart health; promote eye health; lower the risk of some cancers; and boost immunity
Red	**FRUITS:** blood oranges; cherries; cranberries; pomegranates; pink/red grapefruits; raspberries; red apples; red grapes; red pears (with skin); strawberries; watermelon **VEGETABLES:** radicchio; radishes; red beets; red bell peppers; red onions; red potatoes; red tomatoes; rhubarb	Contain anthocyanins, catechins, chlorogenic acid, and lycopene that promote heart health; help memory function; lower the risk of some cancers; promote urinary tract health; and boost immunity

*Adapted from educational materials of the Produce for Better Health Foundation

Tips for Healthful Cooking

The recipes in this book take advantage of an array of strategies to make foods both healthful and appealing, such as using fats in moderation and topping finished dishes with flavorful garnishes. You can apply these same strategies to all of your cooking.

APPEALING TO ALL OF THE SENSES

Keep in mind that the enjoyment of food is multidimensional. Technically, flavor is the combination of taste and aroma, but in reality we also perceive flavor through what we see, hear, and feel. For example, bright green, orange, and red fruits and vegetables suggest freshness; grill marks on a serving of meat, fish, or vegetables hint of a smoky taste; and a juicy-looking piece of poultry promises a succulent experience. A sizzling steak and the fizz of Champagne delight the sense of hearing. Likewise, mouth-feel—as in the heat of chiles, the cool of mint, the chill of sorbet, or the crunch of fennel—is part of the total flavor experience.

When planning meals, think about how shapes and colors will complement one another on the plate. Serve foods of different temperatures and textures to stimulate the taste buds. Edible garnishes such as chopped nuts, shavings of cheese, or a sprinkle of confectioners' (icing) sugar or unsweetened cocoa powder over dessert adds interest to the plate and often boosts nutrition, too.

FOCUSING ON FAT

Removing fat from recipes is the most obvious way to make foods more healthful, but it is by no means the only way nor always the best choice. By using fat strategically and cooking with naturally low-fat ingredients, you can create deliciously healthful and satisfying dishes. For example, you can apply a light coating of oil and a sprinkling of herbs to vegetables before roasting. Vegetables can be given a thin film of flavored oil, such as lemon, pepper, walnut, basil, or garlic, before or after they are cooked. A full-flavored extra-virgin olive oil combined with sherry or wine vinegar makes a great salad dressing, and a little goes a long way. Try swirling a tablespoon of butter into a sauce to add gloss and richness, or place a dab of butter on top of soup before serving to make it glisten.

Flavoring with Meat and Cheese

Just a small amount of prosciutto, pancetta, or smoked salmon can add flavor to otherwise meatless pasta and rice dishes. Likewise, spicy low-fat turkey or chicken sausages give soups and stews a satisfying heartiness. You can use grilled eggplant (aubergine), grilled firm tofu, or grilled cremini, portobello, or shiitake mushrooms as meat alternatives in salads, sandwiches, and stir-fries.

Dry cheeses such as feta, sharp cheddar, Parmigiano-Reggiano, and pecorino are particularly full flavored, which means you can use less of them than you can of other cheeses and still create a robust taste. Just a few tablespoons of shredded hard cheese contain a good measure of calcium, too. For pizza, use half the amount of cheese called for by grating fontina for flavor with part-skim mozzarella for creamy texture. Instead of making mashed potatoes with butter and whole milk, use evaporated skim milk or light sour cream and Parmigiano-Reggiano.

Making Healthful Substitutions

When you see cream or milk in a savory recipe, consider using fat-free, low-sodium chicken or vegetable broth in its place with just a tablespoon or so of cream for color and texture. Depending on the recipe, try low-fat buttermilk or nonfat evaporated skim milk instead of cream. To thicken sauces and soups, use puréed or shredded potato, or puréed cooked dried beans or chickpeas (garbanzo beans). All of these substitutes also enhance the nutrient value of a recipe.

Citrus juice or a flavored vinegar can stand in for most of the oil in a marinade. You can also forgo butter-rich sauces on vegetables and add a sprinkling of lemon, lime, or orange zest or a scattering of chopped toasted nuts in their place. Instead of a butter-rich pastry pie crust, try a filo crust, a graham cracker or gingersnap cookie crust, or a meringue shell. Puddings can be made with low-fat or nonfat milk, with nutmeg, cinnamon, or another aromatic spice used to boost flavor.

ADDING NUTRITION AND FLAVOR

It is easy to get so caught up in cutting the fat from recipes that we forget to add ingredients that are naturally low in fat. There are many ideas you can implement to boost flavor and nutrition without increasing fat.

By using puréed peaches, apricots, plums, or prunes; unsweetened applesauce; or mashed bananas to replace some of the fat in baked goods, you also add fiber, vitamins, minerals, and phytochemicals. Like fat, fruit purées hold moisture in baked goods, promote browning, and help tenderize.

Some items, such as muffins, fruit breads, and cakes, are better candidates for fat reduction than others. Start by replacing half the fat with half as much fruit purée. Then, each time you make the recipe, reduce the fat more until you find the smallest amount that still gives satisfactory results.

When making a recipe with vegetables, prepare some extra. For example, if the recipe calls for chopping half of a bell pepper (capsicum), chop the whole vegetable. Add more to the recipe for increased flavor, or freeze the extra in a zippered plastic bag and use later to enrich soups, sauces, stir-fries, and pasta.

Edamame (soybeans in their pods) are a colorful and interesting addition to a plate of crudités. Use puréed silken tofu to replace some of the full-fat sour cream in dips, and soy milk instead of sour cream or cow's milk in salad dressings or cream soups.

Try to cook with whole grains like rolled oats, cracked wheat, millet, and brown rice most of the time. Use whole-grain bread for sandwiches and toasted whole-wheat (wholemeal) pita chips to accompany dips. Whole-grain pasta or brown or wild rice makes an excellent addition to some salads and soups.

Enhancing Flavor

We tend to appreciate food more when our sense of taste is stimulated and surprised. When we get bored, as often happens when restricting any part of our usual diet, we crave flavor, which can lead to bingeing on foods high in fat or sugar. Artfully flavoring food is an easy way to keep cravings under control.

You can grow your own fresh herbs year-round in a sunny window. Snipped leaves add fresh flavor and eye appeal to almost every recipe. When adding herbs and spices to cold recipes, such as dressings and dips, allow the flavors to blend, in the refrigerator, for a brief period before serving.

Add fresh herbs to cooked recipes as close to serving time as possible. Dried herbs and spices can be added earlier in the cooking process. Just before serving the dish, taste it and adjust the seasoning.

In addition to herbs and spices, here are other flavor boosters to have on hand:
- Lemons or oranges for sprinkling finely grated zest on steamed or roasted vegetables or over tuna or chicken salad.
- A selection of vinegars—such as cider, red and white wine, rice wine, herb, sherry, and balsamic—for marinating meats and vegetables before grilling and for making salad dressings.
- Pineapple, tomato, and apricot juices for salsas and sauces.
- Dried fruits, such as apricots and cranberries, for adding flavor, sweetness, and color.
- Nuts and seeds to toast and sprinkle over salads, vegetables, main dishes, and desserts.

Remember that flavor is as much about aroma as it is about taste. When steaming vegetables or seafood, add flavorings to the water such as strong-scented herbs (rosemary, lemongrass, or basil); balsamic vinegar; walnut or sesame oil; fresh ginger; or horseradish.

To heighten the flavor of grilled foods, add aromatics to the coals, including grapevines; nut shells; branches of rosemary or other herbs; fennel stalks; or citrus peel. Also try herb and spice blends such as Greek seasoning, Cajun seasoning, and seasoned cracked pepper to punch up the flavor of grilled foods.

Top It Off (page 11) offers additional suggestions for low-fat toppings.

SERVING HEALTHFUL FOOD

Presenting food so that it appeals to all the senses has become important in this era of "supersizing," a phenomenon that has distorted our perception of what a sensible serving of food looks like. Reasonable portions now look meager, especially when served on the over-sized tableware found in many restaurants.

Appealing Presentations

You can use several strategies for controlling portion size but still offer a meal that does not seem skimpy. One is to serve food on smaller plates. A standard dinner plate used to measure 10 inches (25 cm) in diameter. Some restaurants now use plates that are 11 or 12 inches (28 or 30 cm) in diameter.

You might also want to check the volume of your individual serving bowls. Using a measuring pitcher, pour 1 cup (8 fl oz/ 250 ml) of water into one of your soup bowls. Once you see the result, you may want to buy smaller bowls. Pasta served in small bowls makes each portion look generous.

Another approach is to use a ¹/₂-cup (4–fl oz/ 125-ml) scoop as an easy measure for single servings of mashed potatoes, tuna salad, or any soft food. Have scoops in several sizes and shapes to vary the presentation of food. For a serving of meat, thinly slice it and fan it on the

plate. This presentation makes a 3- to 4-ounce (90- to 125-g) portion look more generous. Arrange protein salads such as tuna or chicken salad on a bed of greens. The portion will look more generous, and the greens will boost the nutrient level of the meal.

Dishes that call for cream or cheese, such as eggplant Parmesan, can be prepared in individual ramekins to create an attractive presentation and to limit portion size. Desserts such as fruit crisps and puddings can be served in stemmed glasses to create a beautiful but portion-controlled presentation.

Attractive healthful additions such as thinly sliced apples or pears, citrus segments, lightly cooked green beans, cherry tomatoes, or baby radishes can be used to garnish plates. Make the plate look "full" with fruits and vegetables that add panache.

Whole-grain bread can be sliced thinly and then toasted to use for *crostini* or to accompany dips. Also toast thinly sliced fruit-and-nut breads and serve like biscotti or with a small amount of low-fat cheese as a simple dessert.

Slices of tomatoes and part-skim mozzarella, along with herbs and roasted vegetables can be stacked to add visual interest and let you create appealing flavor combinations.

You can cut bar cookies into squares, then cut them on the diagonal to make triangles. A serving of one triangular cookie is visually interesting and also has half the calories.

STANDARD PORTION SIZES

The chart below offers visual images that will help you gauge healthful portion size.

FOOD	SERVING	LOOKS LIKE
Chopped raw vegetables	¹/₂ cup (2–2¹/₂ oz/60–75 g) vegetables	¹/₂ baseball or rounded handful of an average adult
Raw leafy vegetables	1 cup (1 oz/30 g)	1 baseball or fist of an average adult
Fresh fruit	1 medium piece ¹/₂ cup (2–3 oz/60–90 g) chopped	1 tennis ball ¹/₂ baseball or handful of average adult
Cooked pasta and rice, dried cereal	¹/₂ cup (3 oz/90 g)	¹/₂ baseball or rounded handful of average adult
Cooked, boneless, meat, poultry, seafood	3 ounces (90 g)	Deck of cards
Cooked dried beans	¹/₂ cup (3¹/₂ oz/105 g) cooked	¹/₂ baseball or rounded handful of average adult
Nuts	¹/₃ cup (1¹/₂ oz/45 g)	Level handful of average adult
Cheese	1¹/₂ ounces (45 g)	Computer disk or 2 dominos

A Nutrition Primer

Nutrition science has evolved dramatically, and the future promises to be equally exciting. Research has shown that as we grow older—and live longer than ever before—eating healthfully will lower the chance of developing the chronic diseases commonly associated with aging.

Although belief in the healing power of food is as old as civilization itself, the science of nutrition is a relatively new discipline. At the turn of the twentieth century, infectious diseases were the primary cause of death in the United States. With improved sanitation, the development of antibiotics, and better nutrition, illnesses such as tuberculosis, influenza, and pneumonia were able to be controlled. The discovery of vitamins allowed deficiency diseases such as scurvy and pellagra to be conquered. As a result, average life expectancy in the United States has increased from less than fifty years in the early 1900s to almost eighty in 2000.

Now we live long enough to develop chronic diseases such as cardiovascular disease, cancer, diabetes, and osteoporosis—conditions that are influenced by genetics but may be delayed or even prevented by making changes in diet and lifestyle. Faced with this challenge, nutrition researchers have made great strides in understanding the complicated biochemistry of the human body and how nutrients work at the cellular level. Over the last decade, knowledge of the antioxidant effects of certain vitamins and minerals has grown tremendously. This progress is especially significant in light of the air and chemical pollution and tobacco smoke that permeate the environment, creating free radicals that attack healthy cells. Antioxidants such as vitamins C and E and beta-carotene help protect cells from this damage.

Scientists also have uncovered a wealth of plant compounds known as phytochemicals (page 15) whose positive effects include fighting cancer, building bones, protecting vision, and boosting the immune system, as well as antibacterial and antiviral activity.

What is the next frontier in nutrition science? Thanks to sequencing of the human genome, we will soon be able to screen for genetic susceptibility or resistance to various diseases. That technology, coupled with an increasing understanding of how nutrition affects health, will one day lead to diets customized to an individual's unique genetic profile. We already know, for example, that people with high triglycerides (high levels of fat in the bloodstream) do better on low-carbohydrate diet, and that people with insulin resistance may benefit from a diet lower in carbohydrates and higher in protein. As we mover further into the era of "nutragenomics," such recommendations will become much more individualized.

LIQUID PLEASURES

Water is a vital nutrient. You can live many days without food, but only a few days without water. The body uses water for many life-supporting functions, such as carrying nutrients, lubricating joints, eliminating waste, and regulating body temperature. You need about 8 cups (64 fl oz/2 l) of water or other beverages daily, and even more when you are exercising vigorously.

Although alcoholic beverages supply calories with few or no nutrients, they may offer some heart-health benefits when used

in moderation, such as one or two glasses of wine daily. These benefits most likely come from phytochemicals in wine such as resveratrol and catechins. In small amounts, alcohol can relieve stress and promote relaxation and decreases in blood pressure. Consumed in excess, it causes poor judgment and creates safety and health risks. Alcohol has also been linked to a rise in breast cancer risk, due perhaps to the interaction of alcohol with estrogen.

Whether or not you choose to drink alcohol is a personal decision that should be based on your family history, your health profile, the medications you take, and your personal preferences. There is much to be said for the pleasures of pairing food and wine, but the experience is not necessarily for everyone.

Alcohol can also be used as a flavoring. When you cook with beer, wine, or spirits, much of the alcohol will evaporate, leaving its flavor behind. The amount of alcohol remaining depends on temperature and length of cooking time. If you would rather not cook with alcohol, replace it with fruit juice or alcohol-free wine or beer. Instead of using almond-, orange-, or mint-flavored liqueurs to season food, use a few drops or more of concentrated flavoring extract (essence).

Healthful Cooking Techniques

Many techniques that you probably use in your everyday cooking are sound methods for healthful cooking. As you prepare the recipes in this book and master the various techniques, you will develop the skills required to make all of your meals healthful.

The nine methods here are well suited to the healthful kitchen. Baking, roasting, sautéing, stir-frying, and grilling are excellent choices because they need little fat for a successful result. Steaming and poaching are good options, because they call for no fat and the cooking liquid is often used to make a companion sauce, thereby retaining the foods' nutrients. Braising and stewing, sometimes mistakenly regarded as producing only rich, fattening dishes, can be healthful, especially because all the flavors and nutrients are captured in a single pot. The foundation of healthful cooking, regardless of method, is fresh, high-quality ingredients, which should be prepared as close to mealtime as possible and watched with care to avoid overcooking. Refer to the chart below for doneness temperatures for meat and poultry.

FAT AND COOKING

As discussed on page 16, dealing with fat is one of the biggest challenges in healthful cooking. In deciding to limit the amount of fat you use or to substitute another type of fat, you will want to consider three key factors that determine the type of fat called for in recipes. One is whether a solid fat or liquid oil is needed. This choice often comes into play when making baked goods. In selected recipes like the cookies on page 221, the fat can be reduced and replaced with fruit purée without a sacrifice in taste and texture.

The second factor is whether the particular flavor of a fat or oil is desired. Whereas a distinctively aromatic nut oil such as walnut is appreciated in a salad dressing, it may not be appropriate for other recipes, where a more neutral-tasting oil or a small amount of butter is preferred because it will not compete with the dominant flavors.

The final factor is the temperature to which an oil or a fat will be heated before it begins to break down and smoke. This is known as the oil's smoke point. Sautéing and stir-frying use particularly high heat and therefore require an oil, such as canola or peanut, with a high smoke point.

DONENESS TEMPERATURES FOR MEAT AND POULTRY

TYPE	RARE	MEDIUM-RARE	MEDIUM	MEDIUM-WELL	WELL
Beef	125°–130°F (52–54°C)	130°–135°F (54°–57°C)	140°–150°F (60°–65°C)	150°–160°F (65°–71°C)	above 160°F (71°C)
Lamb	125°–130°F (52–54°C)	130°–135°F (54°–57°C)	140°–150°F (60°–65°C)	150°–160°F (65°–71°C)	above 160°F (71°C)
Pork	——	——	140°–150°F (60°–65°C)	150°–160°F (65°–71°C)	above 160°F (71°C)
Poultry	——	——	——	——	above 160°F (71°C)

BAKING AND ROASTING

The term *baking* is commonly linked with breads, cakes, pies, and the like, but when applied to meats, poultry, seafood, and vegetables, the terms *baking* and *roasting* are often used interchangeably. Both refer to cooking in the dry heat of an oven. Baking foods are sometimes covered; roasting foods are always uncovered and typically exposed to relatively high temperatures. This high heat releases the natural sugars in vegetables and fruits, leaving them tender on the inside and caramelized and sometimes even crisp on the outside. All meats, but especially lean meats, demand a watchful eye when roasting, as they can easily dry out. When done properly, both roasting and baking produce a moist and juicy finish and concentrated flavors.

Pan roasting calls for searing, or quickly browning, food in a little oil in a heavy-bottomed sauté pan or frying pan on the stove top over high heat and then finishing the dish in a hot oven. The pan must also be oven-proof, unless you plan to transfer the food to an ovenproof vessel. It is important to select an oil with a high smoke point (the temperature at which the oil breaks down and begins to smoke), such as canola, olive, or safflower, and to use a minimum amount, which is often applied directly to the food rather than to the pan. When searing, allow space between the foods, or the temperature will drop and the foods will steam, rather than brown.

How to Roast

1 Choose the right pan, such as a roasting pan or baking dish (page 28) or an ovenproof frying pan (page 29). There should be room for the food to fit comfortably and the air to circulate freely. A rack is sometimes useful for elevating large items in a roasting pan.

2 Some recipes call for tying or trussing whole poultry or roasts into a compact shape for encasing seasonings or making an attractive presentation when carving at the table.

3 For foods that will cook relatively briefly, or when pan roasting, sear the food in a small amount of hot oil to give it a flavorful, browned crust. Longer-cooked foods will develop a crisp, golden exterior without this extra step.

4 Roast according to recipe guidelines, then check for doneness using a visual cue or an instant-read thermometer (refer to the chart on page 20 for the ideal doneness temperatures).

The temperature will rise 5° to 10°F (3° to 6°C) if the food is allowed to rest before serving, equalizing the temperature and moistness.

5 If making a pan sauce, skim the fat from the pan juices, and place the pan on the stove top over medium heat. Pour in the liquid of choice, then deglaze the pan, stirring the liquid with a wooden spoon and scraping up the browned bits from the pan bottom.

6 To finish the sauce, cook until reduced to the desired consistency, or stir in a small amount of cornstarch (cornflour) mixed with water and cook, stirring, until lightly thickened.

BRAISING AND STEWING

These two classic techniques, which call for cooking in liquid, are ideal ways to prepare large and often tough cuts of meat and sturdy vegetables, such as carrots, celery, and leeks. The results are comforting, hearty, flavorful dishes that retain the nutrients of all their ingredients and rely on little added fat.

For braising, foods are slowly cooked in a relatively small amount of liquid in a covered pot on the stove top or in the oven. Stewing is closely related, although it usually incorporates a larger amount of liquid and smaller pieces of food, and can be done in an uncovered pot. The braising or stewing liquid can be water or a more flavorful liquid, such as stock or wine. The addition of onions, garlic, herbs, or other aromatic ingredients contribute flavor.

Large saucepans (page 29) are ideal for braising. The versatile Dutch oven (page 29) can be used on the stove top and in the oven.

Contrary to the general rule that healthful foods should be prepared as close to mealtime as possible, braised and stewed dishes are frequently better when made the day before you plan to serve them. The waiting period allows the flavors to develop more fully. In addition, when these dishes are refrigerated, any fat congeals on the surface, from which it can be easily removed before reheating.

Braised or stewed dishes are often served with rich side dishes such as cream-laden mashed potatoes or potato gratin, or heavily buttered noodles. To keep the entire meal healthful, pair braises and stews with low-fat vegetable or grain accompaniments.

How to Braise

1 Start with sturdy cuts of meat or fibrous vegetables (tender foods will fall apart during the long cooking process) and season them well. If desired, marinate the ingredients.

2 If cooking meats or poultry, first brown on all sides in a small amount of oil and then transfer to a plate. This will give the finished dish appealing color and flavor.

3 Add any aromatics, such as onion, carrot, and celery, and/or other ingredients, such as tomato paste or wine. Cook them according to the recipe instructions.

4 If using meat or poultry, return it to the pan. Pour in the cooking liquid, generally about halfway up the height of the food for a braise and more for a stew. Bring the liquid to a boil, then reduce the heat to low to maintain a steady, gentle simmer.

5 Cover the pan, if directed in the recipe, and cook over low heat, or cover and cook in a medium-low oven. If necessary, turn the ingredients periodically to ensure even cooking.

6 Check the food for doneness. If too much liquid remains at the end of cooking, uncover the pan, remove the solids, if desired, raise the heat, and cook briskly until the liquid reduces and thickens to the desired consistency.

GRILLING

Grilling, or the cooking of food over a charcoal or gas fire, is suited to a healthful regimen because little added fat is used. The recipes in this book call for direct-heat grilling, a high-heat method used for cooking small or thin foods in a short amount of time. Foods are placed directly over the hot coals of a charcoal grill or the preheated heat elements of a gas grill. The high heat sears and caramelizes the surface and seals the juices inside.

One key to successful grilling is to season or marinate food before it goes on the fire. In the past, recipes warned cooks against salting meat before cooking, or it would dry out. In today's thinking, salt, pepper, herbs, and other seasonings applied before grilling not only contribute flavor, but also form a savory, caramelized crust that keeps foods juicy and tender. If a sauce contains sugar, brush it on toward the end of cooking, to prevent burning.

Always begin with a clean grill rack (consult your owners' manual for the preferred way to clean your grill) and oil both it and the food, especially when cooking fish and shell-fish, most vegetables, and lean meats and poultry. Use a pastry brush, an oil-saturated, rolled-up paper towel, or a nonstick cooking spray to oil the grill rack. Most of the oil will burn off during the cooking, so you do not need to worry about added fat.

How to Grill

1 Prepare a fire in a charcoal grill, or ignite the fuel jets on a gas grill. For a charcoal grill, let the coals burn until they have a light coating of ash, about 30 minutes. If using a gas grill, pre-heat the grill for about 15 minutes. If necessary, clean the grill rack using a wire grill brush (page 29) when the fire is hot.

2 Use an oil-saturated paper towel, a pastry brush, or a nonstick cooking spray (away from the fire) to oil the grill rack lightly.

3 Place the food, presentation side down if indicated in the recipe, on the rack. (The first side grilled often has the best-looking grill marks, so it is wise to start with the side you plan to show when the food is plated.)

4 If attractive crosshatch marks are desired, cook undisturbed for a minute or two, then pick up the food, rotate 45 degrees, return it to the grill, and cook until done on the first side.

5 Turn the food and continue to cook to according to recipe guidelines, again rotating for crosshatch marks if desired. Check for done-ness using a visual cue or an instant-read ther-mometer (refer to the chart on page 20 for the ideal doneness temperatures).

6 If you do not have a grill, you can use a broiler (grill) to achieve similar results. The heat comes from above, rather than below, but the timing is about the same. Foods are placed 4 to 8 inches (10 to 20 cm) away from the heat source, with thicker cuts at greater distances. If food is too close to the heat, the outside will char before the inside cooks.

POACHING

Poached foods are partially or fully immersed in not-quite-simmering liquid. This technique is ideal for cooking fish, eggs, chicken, fruits such as pears, and other delicate foods that need careful treatment to prevent them from breaking apart or overcooking. Foods are usually poached whole, such as whole chickens and fish, or in large pieces, such as chicken breasts and fish fillets.

Always keep the heat very low when poaching. Even small bubbles can tighten protein fibers, causing the food to toughen. Poached foods are usually removed from the cooking liquid as soon as they are done to avoid over-cooking. Sturdy items, like whole chickens or pears, can remain in the cooking liquid, which can further flavor the flesh.

The poaching liquid can be water to which fresh herbs, spices, and aromatics are added, or it can be a flavorful broth or wine for cooking savory dishes, or a flavored syrup for poaching fruits for dessert. Vegetables and eggs are usually poached in salted water or water with a little vinegar. Fish is commonly poached in a court bouillon, a briefly cooked broth made from water, aromatic vegetables, vinegar or lemon juice, and herbs and spices.

Poaching is an excellent addition to a healthful cooking repertory because it calls for no additional fat and leaves even lean foods moist and juicy. Although some of the foods' nutrients leach out into the poaching liquid, the liquid can often be reduced and used to make a sauce for the finished dish.

You will not need specialized cooking equipment for poaching, although some manufacturers sell products, such as egg poachers and fish poachers, which are customized to certain types of food.

How to Poach

1 Select a pan not much larger than the food to be poached. The poaching liquid should be able to flow easily around all sides of the food.

2 Use water, stock, wine, sugar syrup, or other liquid that complements the food you are poaching. If appropriate, season it with herbs, spices, aromatics (carrot, celery, onion), or other flavor enhancers.

3 Bring the liquid to a boil, then reduce the heat to very low so that it barely simmers and adjust the heat so that the surface of the liquid moves only slightly. Monitor the heat closely; only a few small bubbles should break the surface. For an accurate test, insert an instant-read thermometer into the liquid; it should read 160°–180°F (71°–82°C).

4 To keep the food submerged in the poaching liquid, and to aid in even cooking, place a small, heatproof plate over the food while it cooks.

5 Follow the cooking times given in individual recipes. Use the tip of a small knife to check that the food is poached until tender.

6 If directed in the recipe, strain the poaching liquid and reduce it in a clean saucepan to make a companion sauce.

SAUTÉING

Sautéed foods are quickly cooked, usually over medium or medium-high heat, in a small amount of fat. Foods are turned, tossed, or stirred in the pan, cooking the outside evenly without overcooking the inside, and then are promptly served. Sautéed foods have a nutritional advantage over most foods that are cooked and held before serving.

Foods for sautéing should be naturally tender, portion sized or smaller, and relatively thin. To sauté thicker pieces of meat or poultry, first pound them with a meat mallet to flatten them to a uniform thinness. If you want the foods to brown lightly, make sure that they are relatively free of moisture, and do not crowd them in the pan. Tightly packing the pieces in a pan that is too small will cause the temperature to drop, trapping moisture that will result in steaming rather than browning.

Patience is also important when sautéing. Resist the urge to move the food before it has taken on color, or you could tear or otherwise mar the surface. If the food appears to be sticking to the pan, do not worry. When it is sufficiently browned, it will release easily.

How to Sauté

1 Choose the correct size pan (page 29). The pieces of food should fit easily in the pan with about 1 inch (2.5 cm) of space on all sides. More space could cause the oil to burn. Packing the food too tight could trap moisture, resulting in steaming rather than browning.

2 Preheat the pan over medium-high heat or the heat level specified in the recipe. This ensures that a nice crust will form on the food when it is added to the pan.

3 When the pan is hot, add a small amount of oil. The more natural fat present in the food, such as oil-rich fish, the less oil will be needed. Well-seasoned or nonstick pans may not need added fat. When the oil is hot—rippling will be visible on the surface—add the food to the pan, starting presentation side down if indicated in the recipe.

4 Let the food sit undisturbed for 30 seconds or so, depending on its size and thickness. Larger pieces of food are usually ready to turn when they are golden brown on the underside. Turn them and continue to cook until done as directed in the recipe. For the best appearance, generally turn large pieces only once; you can turn smaller pieces more often.

5 As foods are sautéed, they release their natural juices into the pan. You can make an easy pan sauce by adding liquid and deglazing the pan (page 21, steps 5 and 6).

6 Searing, a variation of sautéing, calls for browning foods quickly over medium-high or high heat. It has two main uses in a healthful cooking repertory: to develop a flavorful, caramelized surface on foods that will be sautéed, braised, stewed, or roasted and to cook foods, such as salmon (shown above) or tuna (pages 118 and 163), that are meant to be served rare. When searing meat or fish, it is advisable to pat it dry with paper towels; this removes moisture that will hinder browning. Also be sure to use a heavy pan such as a cast-iron frying pan.

STEAMING

Steaming involves the cooking of food over boiling or simmering water in a covered pan. The same term is used for cooking some foods, such as mussels and clams, in a small amount of simmering liquid in a covered pan. Water is the most common steaming liquid, sometimes with the addition of herbs, spices, onion, garlic, or other aromatics.

Because it is a gentle cooking method, steaming is well suited to such delicate foods as seafood and certain vegetables. It helps a food to retain its shape, color, flavor, and texture better than boiling, simmering, or even poaching. Steaming is also the most healthful of all cooking techniques, as it uses no added fat and preserves more nutrients.

You can use a steamer (page 29), or a collapsible, footed steamer basket, which will turn almost any saucepan into a steamer. In a pinch, you can also use a metal colander. In all cases, the steaming water in the pan must never touch the bottom of the rack or basket. If the food must steam for a long time, check periodically to make sure that the water has not boiled dry, adding more boiling water as needed. Also, steam can burn you, so take care when uncovering the pan.

How to Steam

1 If you are using a collapsible steamer basket or a colander, fill a saucepan with water to a depth of about 1/2 inch (12 mm). If you are using a steamer pan, fill the pot with at least 3 inches (7.5 cm) of water. Bring the water to a boil over high heat.

2 If using a collapsible steamer basket or a colander, set it in the pan, taking care not to burn yourself with the hot water or steam.

3 Place the food in the basket, allowing enough room for the steam to circulate freely. You will need to arrange pieces such as fish fillets or potatoes in a single layer and not touching for efficient cooking.

4 Cover the pan tightly and adjust the heat so that the food cooks at a moderate, steady pace. Check occasionally to make sure that the liquid is not bubbling too fast or too slow.

5 Starting at the earliest point indicated in the recipe, check the food for doneness, following the cues provided. If the food is not ready, replace the lid and continue to steam. Note that removing the lid will cause the temperature in the steamer to drop, extending the cooking time, so check only as often as necessary.

6 Cooking in a parchment (baking) paper packet—known as cooking *en papillote*—is a perfect way to steam fish, vegetables, and other delicate items in the oven. The foods, encased in the paper, are cooked by trapped steam, which forms when the liquid inside the packet heats up. The packet captures the foods' juices, which become a natural sauce for the finished dish. This technique allows you to cook an entire meal (protein, vegetables, and sauce) in one step, facilitating cleanup. Another feature is that, when opened at the table, the packets release their fragrant steam, making a particularly dramatic presentation.

STIR-FRYING

A popular Asian cooking method, stir-frying calls for rapidly cooking small pieces of food in a little oil in a wok placed over high heat. The wok, which has a rounded bottom and high, slightly sloped sides, is the perfect implement for stir-frying, as it exposes the food to the maximum cooking surface while keeping it from escaping over the rim as you stir.

Stir-frying generally calls for smaller pieces of food and higher heat than sautéing. In addition, stir-fried foods are kept in constant motion during cooking, and ingredients are generally placed in the pan in a specific sequence, with those requiring the longest cooking times added first and quick-cooking items added at the last moment. The sauce for a stir-fry, like that of a sauté, is made or finished in the pan, thus retaining the nutrients of all the ingredients.

Although Asian-style dishes are the most obvious candidates for stir-fries, you can also fashion stir-fries from pantries in other parts of the world, such as a simple Italian mix of sun-dried tomatoes, basil, and fresh vegetables for topping pasta or serving as a side dish.

Stir-fried dishes are traditionally finished with a sauce that is thickened with cornstarch (cornflour)—a good option for a healthful meal. There are other, less healthful aspects of stir-frying to keep in mind, however. Avoid excessive use of cooking oil and high-sodium soy sauce and other salty ingredients.

How to Stir-Fry

1 Before you begin cooking, prepare all ingredients and place them within easy reach of the stove. (Stir-frying is a fast cooking method, and you will need everything close at hand.) Cut foods into bite-sized pieces, marinating or seasoning them as directed in individual recipes.

2 Preheat a wok (page 30) or large, deep frying pan or sauté pan (page 29) over high heat until hot. It is important that the pan is hot before you begin cooking to ensure that the food cooks quickly without sticking.

3 Add oil to the pan as directed in the recipe. Carefully tilt and rotate the pan so that the oil is distributed over most of the pan's surface.

4 When the oil is ready—rippling will be visible on its surface—add the ingredients to the pan in the order indicated in the recipe. Usually the meat, poultry, or seafood portion of the stir-fry is added to the pan first. Using 2 wooden or metal spatulas (or similar implements), toss and stir the ingredients rapidly, being sure to push them up the sides of the pan to expose them evenly to the heat.

5 Some recipes call for cooking the ingredients in stages and transferring each ingredient to a plate as it is done. Add a little more oil to the wok between batches if needed, being sure to heat it until very hot before adding the next ingredient, usually the vegetable component.

6 Return all the ingredients to the pan, if you have stir-fried them in stages. Add the sauce mixture and continue to stir-fry until all the ingredients are heated through and they are lightly coated with sauce.

Equipment for Healthful Cooking

Preparing healthful foods requires only few specialized tools or utensils. As this guide illustrates, you can make the recipes in this book with a well-chosen selection of equipment, from roasting pans and sauté pans to a food processor and blender.

General Cooking Tools

Easy to use, blunt-tipped TONGS are manipulated by squeezing together the two long arms. They are handy for handling hot food, picking up pieces of meat without piercing them (and losing juices), tossing salad greens, and arranging food on plates. Many longer tongs are outfitted with a locking device that keeps them closed during storage—a space saver for a crowded utensil drawer.

Also called a hamburger or pancake turner, a SPATULA measures 2 to 4 inches (5 to 10 cm) wide and has thin edges for slipping under food and a short or long handle. Some spatulas are solid; others have slots through which cooking juices can slip. Spatulas are useful for many cooking tasks: turning roasts, stirring aromatics when braising, flipping food on the grill, and tossing ingredients when sautéing or stir-frying. Be sure to use heat-resistant nylon or wooden spatulas on nonstick surfaces to avoid scratches; metal spatulas are fine for grills and heavy-duty frying pans.

Roasting and Baking Pans

A large, rectangular ROASTING PAN has a handle at either end and is sometimes fitted with a removable rack to elevate meat or poultry above the pan bottom. Look for a roasting pan made of stainless steel or anodized or nonstick aluminum.

Used for a wide variety of cooking needs, deep ovenproof glass or porcelain BAKING DISHES come in all shapes and depths. Two highly versatile sizes are a 9-by-13-by-2-inch (23-by-33-by-5-cm) baking dish and an 8- or 9-inch (20- or 23-cm) square dish with 2-inch (5-cm) sides.

Small, round porcelain or ceramic baking dishes, RAMEKINS are usually 3 to 4 inches (7.5 to 10 cm) in diameter and are used for making individual servings of sweet or savory dishes. Ramekins are especially useful in a healthful cooking repertoire when regulating portion size is an important consideration. Custard cups or individual soufflé dishes can be used in place of ramekins.

Baking Sheets and Broiling Pans

Rectangular metal BAKING SHEETS with shallow, slightly sloping sides can be used for roasting or baking small pieces of meat, poultry, seafood, or vegetables.

Similar to baking sheets, insulated COOKIE SHEETS have an air pocket between two sheets of metal and a low rim or no rim on one or two ends, a feature that allows you to slide baked goods off easily. These specialty cookie sheets are ideal for baking delicate items that may otherwise darken too much on the bottom, such as meringues.

Before baking, it is a good idea to line baking sheets or cookie sheets with parchment (baking) paper, which provides a nonstick surface, prevents the need to use extra fat or oil, and makes cleanup easy. Parchment can withstand the high heat of the oven, but it must never be used in the broiler or directly on a burner, or it could cause a fire.

A two-part rectangular BROILING PAN, which fits under the broiler (grill) unit in an oven, has a perforated upper pan, or rack, that allows the fat to drip into the lower, deeper pan. To prevent sticking and for easy cleanup, spray the rack with nonstick cooking spray (away from the heat source) and line the lower pan with heavy-duty aluminum foil.

Left to right: GENERAL COOKING TOOLS; ROASTING AND BAKING PANS; BAKING SHEETS AND BROILING PANS

Simmering and Braising Pans

Round pans with straight or sloping sides, SAUCEPANS range from 1 to 5 quarts (1 to 5 l), with a 2-quart (2-l) pan the most versatile size. Anodized aluminum and aluminized steel are the best materials.

Used for braising or stewing on top of the stove or in the oven, a DUTCH OVEN is a large, round or oval, heavy-bottomed pot with a tight-fitting lid and usually two loop handles. Look for pots with a nonreactive surface, such as enameled cast iron, so that wine or other acidic ingredients can be used as braising or stewing liquids. Dutch ovens come in a wide range of sizes; an 8- or 9-quart (8- or 9-l) pot is recommended for most home kitchens.

Steaming Equipment

STEAMERS are large pots fitted with a perforated basket or rack (or sometimes a pair of tiered racks) and a lid. Many pasta pots come with a smaller, lighter steamer basket as well as the perforated pasta basket.

Collapsible STEAMER BASKETS, made of a series of pierced, overlapping, folding leaves attached to a perforated round base, can transform almost any saucepan or stockpot into a steamer. The basket has feet that keep its base above the level of the water, and sometimes a ring for lifting it out of the pan. Many also have a removable central post.

In the absence of a steamer basket, a metal COLANDER or a sieve (page 30) can be set inside a large saucepan or a stockpot. For best results, be sure that there is about an inch (2.5 cm) of space between the edge of the colander and the wall of the saucepan.

Top to bottom: SIMMERING AND BRAISING PANS; STEAMING EQUIPMENT; GRILLING EQUIPMENT; SAUTÉING AND STIR-FRYING PANS

Grilling Equipment

Outdoor GRILLS come in two common types: a charcoal grill, fueled by charcoal briquettes or hardwood charcoal chunks, and a gas grill, fueled by natural gas or propane. For indoor use, various models of electric grills are available. The timing for cooking foods on indoor grills is usually longer than that of outdoor grills, as they generally do not get as hot.

A long-handled, stiff-bristled GRILL BRUSH is essential for cleaning the grill, preventing the need to coat the grill with excess fat to keep food from sticking. Use it while the grill is hot, before or after cooking, to scrape off food particles stuck to the rack.

Sautéing and Stir-Frying Pans

A SAUTÉ PAN has a high, angled handle and relatively high, straight sides that prevent oil from splattering and also keep foods from escaping over the rim during cooking. The sides, usually 3 to 4 inches (7.5 to 10 cm), also make the pan useful for cooking some braised or stewed dishes that include substantial liquid. Sauté pans, usually sold with lids, come in a range of sizes, with $2^1/2$ to 4 quarts (2.5 to 4 l) the most useful for most home cooks. Pans with ovenproof handles can also be used for oven roasting small items.

A FRYING PAN, also known as a skillet, is often confused with a sauté pan, but traditionally differs in two ways: the sides are shorter and flare slightly, and the pan does not have a lid. Frying pans are particularly useful for cooking foods that must be stirred or turned out into a bowl or onto a plate. Although nonstick pans are popular, be sure you have at least one frying pan without a protective surface to use for deglazing, as when making a pan sauce (page 21). Ovenproof pans may also be used for roasting (page 21).

The distinctive Asian WOK has a rounded bottom that allows small pieces of food to be rapidly tossed and stirred, while the high, gradually sloping sides help keep the food inside the pan. Woks are available in carbon steel, stainless steel, aluminum, and even non-stick finishes, although the last reduces the ability to achieve nicely browned meats. Woks with flat bottoms are made for use on electric stoves. A large, deep, heavy sauté pan or frying pan is a good substitute.

Mixers

Mixers are of two basic types: the HEAVY-DUTY STAND MIXER and the HANDHELD MIXER. The stand mixer, which usually comes with wire whip, dough hook, and paddle attachments, makes quick work of whole-grain bread and pizza doughs, other stiff doughs, and heavy batters. Handheld, or portable, mixers, which have less powerful motors, are good for most other tasks. Both types are useful in making fat-free desserts, which rely heavily on whipped egg whites. Stand mixers, however, free your hands for other tasks.

Blending Equipment

STANDING BLENDERS are ideal for puréeing soups and blending cold drinks such as fruit smoothies.

IMMERSION BLENDERS, also called hand or handheld blenders, are tall units with a handle at one end and rotary blades at the other. They are particularly handy for puréeing food in the container in which it was mixed or cooked, which means that they can handle larger amounts than what will fit in a standing blender. Always make sure the blades are fully immersed in the food or mixture to be processed before engaging the motor, or you will have a spattered kitchen.

The healthful kitchen relies heavily on the FOOD PROCESSOR for its notable versatility. It can turn out purées, blend mixtures, and slice, chop, and shred ingredients. All models come with an S-shaped metal blade. Other attachments are a disk for shredding, grating, and slicing; a plastic blade for kneading dough; and a disk for julienning. If you do not own a food processor, look for a well-regarded brand for the best quality and value.

Puréeing Equipment

In addition to a food processor and blender, a handy tool for puréeing cooked or soft foods is a FOOD MILL. Usually made of stainless steel or plastic, it consists of a panlike receptacle with a perforated base, a crank-shaped handle, and sometimes arms for securing the mill over a bowl. A paddle-shaped blade sits on top of the perforated base. As you turn the handle of the food mill, the blade rotates and forces food through the holes in the base into a bowl or other container, and also traps any peels, seeds, or coarse bits. Some food mills are sold with a single fixed disk. Other mills have three or more interchangeable disks with holes of different sizes, to produce purées of varying coarseness.

Also called a strainer, a SIEVE is a bowl-shaped device used to purée soft foods and to strain out solids from liquids. Wire-mesh sieves come in a variety of sizes and gauges of mesh, including fine, medium, and coarse. The best sieves have a long handle and metal hooks that help secure them on a bowl or other receptacle. Look for sieves with stainless-steel mesh and sturdy frames, and long wooden or heatproof plastic handles that feel comfortable in your hand.

Top to bottom: MIXERS; BLENDING EQUIPMENT; PURÉEING EQUIPMENT

A RICER is extremely useful for turning nonfibrous vegetables like potatoes into fine-textured purées. A ricer looks like a small pot with holes in the bottom and has a plunger attached to the handle. Cooked vegetables are put in the pot, then are forced through the holes with the plunger to form soft ricelike bits. A ricer makes quick work of puréeing vegetables to use in place of fat-rich thickeners.

spray bottle and fill it with oil. The only caveat is that the nozzle must be cleaned after each use to keep it from clogging.

Seasoning Tools

Freshly ground pepper is a must in the healthful kitchen, where its natural piquancy heightens the flavors of foods to which it is added. Look for a PEPPERMILL made of wood

The sharp blades of the flat, rectangular MANDOLINE also cut vegetables and fruits quickly and with precision and uniformity. Mandolines are available in stainless-steel or plastic; some must be steadied by hand, while others have foldaway legs. An assortment of blades makes a variety of cuts possible. Look for a mandoline with a hand guard that keeps your fingers clear of the cutting edge as you

Left to right: SEASONING TOOLS; CUTTING TOOLS; MEASURING TOOLS

Fat-Reducing Tools

PASTRY BRUSHES, made from natural or nylon bristles, are used to spread oil, butter, or similar ingredients sparingly on foods to help reduce the fat content in recipes. They are also handy for brushing sauces or glazes on roasted or grilled foods. Reserve one brush for savory foods and another for sweet foods.

COOKING SPRAY is canned oil packed under pressure, dispersed by a propellant, and used to grease pots and pans. Cooking spray is especially appreciated in the healthful kitchen because it disperses the oil lightly and evenly, allowing the cook to use less oil than other methods of coating pans. Look for refillable bottles that employ a pumping mechanism to build enough pressure to spray oil without the use of propellants or other added chemicals. If you prefer, you can use a clean conventional

or heavy plastic and outfitted with a sturdy hardened-steel grinder and a knob at the top for adjusting the coarseness of the grind.

Aromatic spices, another wonderful addition to the healthful pantry, can add potent flavor to dishes. For the most flavorful results, spices should be ground in small quantities in a MORTAR AND PESTLE or a small electric COFFEE MILL reserved just for that purpose.

Cutting Tools

Because the healthful kitchen depends on supremely fresh ingredients prepared as close to serving time as possible, it is important to have a good set of KNIVES. Invest in the best-quality knives you can afford—a chef's knife and a paring knife to start—as they will last a lifetime if sharpened regularly and stored where the blades will not be nicked.

move the ingredient across the blade. For small quantities, good results can be achieved with a VEGETABLE PEELER or the slicing surface of a BOX GRATER-SHREDDER.

Measuring Tools

Careful measuring not only will ensure that the recipes you try in this book are successful, but will also help you follow nutritional recommendations. Every kitchen should have a good set of MEASURING SPOONS and both dry and wet MEASURING CUPS, the former made of stainless steel or heavy-duty plastic, and the latter of clear glass or plastic.

To help you measure correct portion sizes, it is a good idea to weigh ingredients on a KITCHEN SCALE. The most practical scales allow you to weigh ingredients by placing them in any bowl or container.

Appetizers

About Appetizers

Small, light, and flavorful, appetizers stimulate the appetite for the dishes to follow. Vegetables, in the form of fillings, bases, dips, and salsas, are the stars of this opening course, delivering big doses of fiber, phytochemicals, vitamins, and other nutrients along with fresh, bright flavors.

For many people, cooking is about sharing, and the recipes in this chapter are ideally suited to doing just that. A menu that includes appetizers, which can be either hors d'oeuvres passed on a tray or a plated first course, usually means that guests are coming for dinner.

Many of the most popular hors d'oeuvres are enclosed in a pastry wrapper or placed on a pastry base. But pastry typically relies on fats like butter or vegetable shortening, which can add lots of calories (kilojoules). Excellent alternatives are the tartlet shells created from layers of filo dough and baked until crisp for Goat Cheese Tartlets with Cranberry–Red Onion Compote (page 37). The pastry is kept within healthful guidelines by spraying the filo layers with canola oil, a monounsaturated fat, rather than brushing them with less heart-healthy butter.

Vegetables can also serve as the base for finger foods, as in the stuffed potatoes on page 42. Spring or early summer's young, just-harvested potatoes are called for here, but the herb-laced creamy filling would be equally delicious with other vegetables: halved and seeded cherry tomatoes, Belgian endive (chicory/witloof) leaves, hollowed-out radishes, or slices of summer squash.

HEALTHFUL DIPS AND SALSAS
Bean-based dips, such as Red Bean Purée with Pita (page 43), are easy to make, nearly fat free, and rich in protein and fiber. If you are short on time, you can use good-quality canned beans, rinsed to remove any excess sodium. The mayonnaise or sour cream found in creamy dairy-based dips can be replaced with puréed silken tofu, as in Creamy Herb Dip with Crudités (page 41), cutting the fat and boosting nutritional value.

Many salsas are naturally fat free, such as the mix of tomato, cucumber, and protein-rich quinoa that accompanies plump grilled shrimp (prawns) on page 49. Since the vegetables used in salsas are uncooked, all the flavor, texture, and nutrients remain intact. It is easy to create your own salsas, and making them at home means that you avoid the sodium and preservatives in many commercial products. To prepare a salsa, combine two parts diced vegetable such as tomatoes or red bell peppers (capsicums) or fruit such as orange, pineapple, or mango; one part diced sweet onion such as Maui or Vidalia; one part chopped fresh leafy herb such as cilantro (coriander), flat-leaf (Italian) parsley, or basil; and lemon or lime juice to taste. To heighten the flavors, add minced fresh chile, such as jalapeño or serrano, and garlic to taste.

Dips and salsas demand accompaniments, and the ones presented here continue the low-fat, high-fiber theme. Among them are a rainbow of crudités, lean protein, strips of toasted whole-grain bread, and wedges of whole-wheat (wholemeal) pita.

Cooked vegetables are also great building blocks for a wide variety of healthful appetizers. Grilled mushrooms, artichokes, and bell peppers splashed with a bold vinaigrette make a nutritious antipasto (page 38). Baby zucchini (courgettes) and eggplants (aubergines) can be prepared the same way. Arrange the various vegetables on a bed of salad greens for a simple, yet highly appealing first course. Or cut the vegetables into smaller pieces, thread them onto small bamboo skewers, grill them, and serve them as hors d'oeuvres.

A TRIO OF SEAFOOD IDEAS
Raw, cured, and lightly steamed fish and shellfish are popular starters on many restaurant menus. They are also easy to make at home and can be part of a sound dietary plan if prepared with care. Tuna Tartare (page 46) is a high-protein, low-cholesterol, heart-healthy appetizer suitable for even the fanciest dinner party. Be sure that the tuna is impeccably fresh and kept well chilled. To maintain the appetizer's healthful profile, use only small amounts of soy sauce and sesame oil.

Smoked Salmon with Mustard-Horseradish Sauce (page 45) is high in protein and low in fat, plus the recipe is a time-saver for the busy cook. The sauce takes just minutes to make, and the purchased salmon and accompanying black bread need no additional preparation. A heaping bowl of Mussels with Fresh Herbs (page 44) is an impressive first course for guests who probably will not realize how easy these shellfish are to prepare. Cooking the mussels in wine and herbs rather than the cream sauces so often found in restaurant versions ensures that the dish has far fewer calories without sacrificing taste.

Everyone at your table will appreciate these dishes for their superb flavors, yet few, if any, will miss the rich sauce. What they will recognize is that the dishes are light and satisfying and do exactly what they are supposed to do—spark the appetite while leaving plenty of room for the meal to come.

Goat Cheese Tartlets with Cranberry–Red Onion Compote

The combination of creamy cheese, crisp filo, and a tangy compote makes this an hors d'oeuvre that guests will remember. All of the elements can be made at least 1 day in advance, and the assembled tartlets will hold for up to 3 hours. There will be leftover compote, which makes a delicious low-fat condiment for poultry and pork, like a chutney or relish. Sheets of filo pastry are typically brushed with butter as they are layered. Using a high-quality oil cooking spray instead helps reduce the fat.

To make the cranberry–red onion compote, place the onions in a small Dutch oven or heavy saucepan. Add the olive oil and toss well to coat the onions with the oil. Place the pan over medium-high heat and sauté the onions until they start to wilt, 2–3 minutes. Add 2 tablespoons water, stir in $^1/_2$ teaspoon salt, and continue sautéing the onions, stirring occasionally, until the onions are limp, about 8 minutes. Cover the pan tightly, reduce the heat to medium, and cook the onions, adding more water, 2 tablespoons at a time, to prevent scorching, until the onions are very moist and soft, about 15 minutes.

Add the brown sugar and stir until it dissolves. Add the cranberries, sherry, vinegar, and thyme and season generously with pepper. Simmer, stirring occasionally, until the cranberries are very soft and the compote has the consistency of jam, 25–30 minutes. Scoop the compote into a bowl and let cool to room temperature. You will have $1^3/_4$ cups (14 oz/440 g). If not using the compote immediately, cover tightly and refrigerate.

To make the filo cups, preheat the oven to 325°F (165°C). Have ready a muffin pan with miniature (sometimes called gem) cups; you will need 15 cups. Working quickly to prevent the filo from drying out, spread out 1 filo sheet on a work surface and coat lightly with cooking spray. Lay a second sheet of filo on top of the first. Coat it lightly with cooking spray. Top with the third sheet, coating it lightly with spray, and then with the fourth sheet, coating it lightly with spray. Using a sharp knife, cut the stacked filo into $3^1/_2$-inch (9-cm) squares. You should have 15 squares. Gently fit each filo square into a muffin cup, pressing the dough layers gently but firmly into place. The corners of the dough will stick up in points above the pan.

Bake the filo cups until golden brown, 8–10 minutes. Transfer the pan to a wire rack and let the filo cups cool partially in the pan for about 10 minutes. Transfer the cups to the rack and let cool completely. (The cups can be made up to 3 days in advance; store in an airtight container at room temperature.)

To make the cheese filling, in a bowl, mix together the goat cheese and buttermilk. Stir in $^1/_4$ teaspoon salt, or more to taste, and a generous amount of pepper. You will have about $^2/_3$ cup (5 oz/155 g) filling.

To assemble the tartlets, spoon 2 teaspoons of the cheese filling into each filo cup. Top with a generous teaspoon of the compote and serve.

For the Cranberry–Red Onion Compote

3 large red onions, halved lengthwise and thinly sliced crosswise

1 tablespoon extra-virgin olive oil

Kosher salt

$^1/_2$ cup ($3^1/_2$ oz/105 g) firmly packed brown sugar

$^1/_2$ cup (2 oz/60 g) dried cranberries

$^1/_2$ cup (4 fl oz/125 ml) dry sherry

1 tablespoon balsamic vinegar

$^1/_2$ teaspoon dried thyme

Freshly ground pepper

For the Filo Cups

4 sheets filo pastry

Canola-oil cooking spray

For the Cheese Filling

$^1/_4$ lb (125 g) fresh goat cheese

2 tablespoons low-fat buttermilk

Kosher salt and freshly ground pepper

MAKES 15 TARTLETS

Grilled Vegetable Antipasto

6 baby artichokes

4 large portobello mushrooms, about 5 oz (155 g) each, brushed clean and stems removed

2–3 teaspoons extra-virgin olive oil

For the Vinaigrette

Juice of ¹/₂ lemon (about 2 tablespoons)

2 teaspoons balsamic vinegar

1 teaspoon extra-virgin olive oil

Kosher salt and freshly ground pepper

1 large red bell pepper (capsicum)

1 bunch arugula (rocket)

MAKES 4 SERVINGS

Bring a saucepan three-fourths full of water to a boil. While the water is heating, using a sharp knife, slice off the top ¹/₂ inch (12 mm) of the leaves of each artichoke. Starting at the base, pull off and discard the tough outer leaves until you reach the pale inner leaves. Cut off all but ¹/₂ inch (12 mm) of the stem and peel its tough outside flesh (page 278).

Add the artichokes to the boiling water, reduce the heat so the water is at a gentle boil, cover, and cook until a knife inserted just above the base of an artichoke meets only slight resistance, about 15 minutes. Using tongs, transfer the artichokes, stem end up, to a colander and drain well. When the artichokes are cool enough to handle, cut each in half lengthwise, then cut each half in half again. Using a teaspoon, scoop out and discard any prickly chokes. Set aside.

Prepare a CHARCOAL or GAS GRILL for direct-heat grilling over medium-high heat. Oil the grill rack. Liberally brush the artichoke quarters and mushroom caps with the olive oil.

To make the vinaigrette, in a bowl, whisk together the lemon juice, vinegar, and olive oil until blended. Stir in ¹/₄ teaspoon salt, or more to taste, and season with pepper. Set aside.

BY CHARCOAL GRILL: Using tongs, place the bell pepper over the hottest part of the fire and grill, turning as needed, until the skin is blistered and charred black on all sides, 6–8 minutes. Transfer to a paper bag, close loosely, and let steam for about 15 minutes. Place the artichoke quarters, with a cut side down, directly over the fire and grill until grill marks are visible, 1–2 minutes. Turn to the other cut side and grill until grill marks are visible, about 1 minute. Transfer the artichokes to a plate. Place the mushrooms directly over the heat, gill sides up, and grill until grill marks are visible, 2–3 minutes. Rotate the

BY GAS GRILL: Using tongs, place the bell pepper directly over the heat elements and grill, turning as needed, until the skin is blistered and charred black on all sides, 6–8 minutes. Transfer to a paper bag, close loosely, and let steam for about 15 minutes. Place the artichoke quarters, with a cut side down, directly over the heat elements and grill until grill marks are visible, 1–2 minutes. Turn to the other cut side and grill until grill marks are visible, about 1 minute. Transfer the artichokes to a plate. Place the mushrooms directly over the heat elements, gill sides up, and grill until grill marks are visible, 2–3 minutes. Rotate the mushrooms

Grilling sweet red peppers, meaty portobello mushrooms, and tender artichokes infuses them with a satisfying smoky taste. While still warm, the vegetables are dressed with a piquant vinaigrette.

mushrooms 90 degrees and continue to grill until cross-hatching is visible, about 2 minutes longer. Turn the mushrooms gill sides down and grill until tender in the center when pierced with a knife, about 1 minute longer. Transfer the mushrooms to the plate with the artichokes.

90 degrees and continue to grill until cross-hatching is visible, about 2 minutes longer. Turn the mushrooms gill sides down and grill until tender in the center when pierced with a knife, about 1 minute longer. Transfer the mushrooms to the plate with the artichokes.

Remove the bell pepper from the bag, peel away the charred skin, then halve the pepper lengthwise and remove the stem, seeds, and ribs. Cut each pepper half lengthwise into 4 strips.

Cover a platter with a bed of arugula. Arrange the artichokes, mushrooms, and bell pepper strips on the greens. Stir the vinaigrette, spoon over the vegetables and greens, and serve at once.

Creamy Herb Dip with Crudités

Inspired by the green goddess salad dressing popular since the 1920s, this dip is enriched with tofu as a way to reduce the fat and add the nutrition of soy. The soft cake form of tofu gives the dip a creamier texture than would silken tofu, but if silken is the only type available, use one with a firm texture. Anchovies are an optional addition; if you like, rinse 3–5 oil-packed fillets and blend with the other ingredients for the dip. You can also use your choice of fresh vegetables as dippers.

Peel the carrots. Peel the daikon and then cut into strips ¹/₄ inch (6 mm) thick. Cut the bell pepper lengthwise into strips ³/₄ inch (2 cm) thick.

BY FOOD PROCESSOR: Combine the parsley, onion, and garlic in a food processor and pulse to chop finely. Add the mayonnaise, sour cream, and tofu and process until well blended. Add the vinegar and tarragon and process until smooth. Pour into a bowl. Stir in ¹/₄ teaspoon salt, or more to taste. Season with pepper.

BY BLENDER: Combine the mayonnaise, sour cream, and tofu in a blender and process until well blended. Add the parsley, onion, garlic, and tarragon, and process until smooth. Pour into a bowl, stir in the vinegar and ¹/₄ teaspoon salt, or more to taste. Season with pepper.

You will have about 2 cups (16 fl oz/500 ml) dip. (The dip will keep in the refrigerator for up to 4 days. Bring to room temperature before serving.) To serve, arrange the carrots, daikon strips, and bell pepper strips in bowls. Serve at once with the dip.

8 baby carrots

1 small daikon

2 large red bell peppers (capsicums), seeded

1 cup (1 oz/30 g) loosely packed fresh flat-leaf (Italian) parsley leaves

3 tablespoons chopped yellow onion

1 clove garlic, quartered

¹/₂ cup (4 fl oz/125 ml) *each* low-fat mayonnaise, nonfat sour cream, and soft tofu

2 tablespoons tarragon vinegar

1 tablespoon chopped fresh tarragon

Kosher salt and freshly ground pepper

MAKES 16 SERVINGS

New Potatoes Stuffed with Fines Herbes

¹/₃ cup (¹/₂ oz/15 g) snipped fresh chives

¹/₃ cup (¹/₃ oz/10 g) loosely packed fresh flat-leaf (Italian) parsley leaves

³/₄ cup (6 oz/185 g) fat-free fromage blanc

4 fresh basil leaves

1 shallot, very finely minced

Kosher salt and freshly ground pepper

6 new potatoes, each about 1¹/₂ inches (4 cm) in diameter, preferably 2 red, 2 white, and 2 purple

MAKES 4 SERVINGS

Finely chop the chives and parsley. Transfer to a bowl, add the cheese, and stir well to combine. Stack the basil leaves, roll up lengthwise into a cylinder, and then, using a very sharp knife, cut crosswise into a fine chiffonade (page 279). Chop the chiffonade and add it to the cheese mixture along with the shallot. Stir to mix well and season with ¹/₄ teaspoon salt and a generous amount of pepper.

Place the potatoes in a large saucepan with water to cover by 2 inches (5 cm). Bring to a boil over high heat, reduce the heat to medium-low, cover, and simmer until the potatoes are tender when pierced with a knife, 12–15 minutes.

When the potatoes are just cool enough to handle, halve them crosswise. Using a melon baller, scoop out about half of the flesh from each half, leaving a shell about ¹/₂ inch (12 mm) thick. Using a sharp knife, cut a thin slice off the bottom of each half. Stand each potato half, hollow side up, on a serving plate.

Using a small spoon, fill each potato half with about 1 tablespoon of the cheese mixture, mounding it generously. Serve immediately.

Fines herbes is a mixture of finely chopped fresh herbs often used for seasoning egg and vegetable dishes. Typically, it includes parsley, chives, chervil, and tarragon, but you can compose your own blend, as with this trio of chives, parsley, and basil. When the herbs are added to tangy fromage blanc, a soft, fresh cheese available fat free, they color it a lovely pale green. Using three different colored potatoes adds even more visual appeal.

Red Bean Purée with Pita

This bean purée boasts a strong Southwestern accent. Toasted pita bread triangles make good accompaniments, as would reduced-fat, baked tortilla chips. If desired, rub one side of each pita triangle with a garlic clove.

Soak and drain the beans as directed on page 278. Place the soaked, drained beans in a saucepan and add water to cover generously. Bring to a boil over high heat, reduce the heat to low, cover partially, and simmer gently until very soft, 1–1 1/2 hours. Drain well and set aside to cool.

Finely chop the onion and place in a food processor with the beans, cumin, oregano, chile powder, tomato sauce, and cilantro. Process until smooth. Pour into a bowl and stir in 1/2 teaspoon salt, or more to taste. Season with pepper. You will have about 2 cups (16 fl oz/500 ml).

Preheat the oven to 400°F (200°C). Lightly brush 1 side of the pita breads with olive oil and place on a baking sheet. Bake until crisp, 6–8 minutes. Remove and transfer the pita breads to a wire rack to cool.

Cut each pita bread into 8 equal wedges. Place the bowl of dip on a platter, arrange the pita wedges around the bowl, and serve.

1 cup (7 oz/220 g) dried pinto beans

1 small red onion

1 teaspoon ground cumin

1/2 teaspoon dried oregano

1/8 teaspoon chipotle chile powder

1/4 cup (2 fl oz/60 ml) tomato sauce

1/4 cup (1/4 oz/7 g) firmly packed fresh cilantro (fresh coriander) leaves

Kosher salt and freshly ground pepper

2 pita breads

Olive oil for brushing

MAKES 8 SERVINGS

Mussels with Fresh Herbs

2 tablespoons chopped fresh flat-leaf (Italian) parsley

8–10 fresh thyme sprigs

2 large fresh rosemary sprigs

1 cup (8 fl oz/250 ml) bottled clam juice

3 lb (1.5 kg) mussels, scrubbed and debearded

4 lemon wedges

MAKES 4 SERVINGS

Place the parsley in a small bowl. Pull enough leaves from the thyme sprigs to measure 1 teaspoon. Add to the parsley. Place the remaining thyme in a deep pot with a tight-fitting lid. Pull enough leaves from the rosemary sprigs and then mince to measure 1 teaspoon. Add to the parsley and thyme. Place the rest of the rosemary in the pot. Set the mixed herbs aside. Pour the clam juice into the pot.

Place the pot over high heat and bring the liquid to a boil. Add the mussels, discarding any that fail to close to the touch. Cover and return the liquid to a boil. Cook until the mussels open, 4–5 minutes. Remove the pot from the heat and, using a slotted spoon, divide the cooked mussels among warmed wide, shallow bowls, discarding any that failed to open. Spoon the broth remaining in the pot into the bowls, dividing it evenly.

Sprinkle one-fourth of the mixed herbs over each serving. Garnish each serving with a lemon wedge, squeezing it over the mussels, and serve.

The chef at Don Camillo in Sicily uses an abundance of fresh herbs to prepare aromatic mussels. Medium-sized blue mussels (actually a deep blue-black) are the best type to use for this dish, which echoes the one at Don Camillo. Serve with slices of crusty bread for soaking up the accompanying broth. This generous dish has fewer than 100 calories per serving.

Smoked Salmon with Mustard-Horseradish Sauce

While Americans like to eat smoked salmon on bread and bagels, Europeans tend to prefer it sliced paper-thin and served on a plate, accompanied by thin slices of black bread or pumpernickel. This recipe is somewhat high in sodium; keep that in mind when planning the rest of the day's meals.

Arrange 2 or 3 slices (2 oz/60 g) of the salmon on a salad plate, overlapping the edges of the slices and covering the plate. Repeat to make 4 portions in all.

In a small bowl, whisk together the mustard, sour cream, horseradish, and milk to make a sauce that resembles a thick, creamy salad dressing. Stir in $1/4$ teaspoon salt and season with pepper.

Cover each salmon portion with about 2 tablespoons of the sauce, spreading it like a glaze. There will be some bare spots. Sprinkle one-fourth of the dill and one-fourth of the capers evenly over each serving. Serve at once.

$1/2$ lb (250 g) smoked salmon, thinly sliced

2 tablespoons *each* whole-grain mustard, nonfat sour cream, and prepared horseradish, squeezed dry

$1/4$ cup (2 fl oz/60 ml) 1-percent-fat milk

Kosher salt and freshly ground pepper

2 tablespoons minced fresh dill

4 teaspoons capers

MAKES 4 SERVINGS

Tuna Tartare

1 English (hothouse) cucumber

2 tablespoons reduced-sodium soy sauce

2 tablespoons rice vinegar

1 tablespoon wasabi powder, or 2 teaspoons wasabi paste

2 teaspoons canola oil

$1/2$ lb (250 g) sushi-grade tuna fillet, in a single piece

$1/2$ teaspoon peeled and grated fresh ginger

$1/8$ teaspoon Asian sesame oil

Kosher salt and freshly ground pepper

Black sesame seeds

MAKES 4 SERVINGS

Using a sharp knife, and holding it at a 45-degree angle to the cucumber, cut 12 slices each $1/4$ inch (6 mm) thick from the center of the cucumber, forming long ovals. Place the slices on a plate, cover with plastic wrap, and refrigerate for up to 4 hours. Reserve the remaining cucumber for another use.

In a small bowl, stir together the soy sauce and vinegar. In another small bowl, whisk together the wasabi powder and 4 teaspoons water until smooth. If using wasabi paste, add only 3 teaspoons water. Whisk in the canola oil until the mixture resembles a creamy salad dressing.

Using a very sharp, thin-bladed knife that will cut the fish cleanly, trim away any dark areas and any white, fibrous membranes. Cut the tuna across the grain into slices $1/8$ inch (3 mm) thick. Cut each slice lengthwise into strips $1/8$ inch (3 mm) wide, then cut the strips crosswise into $1/8$-inch (3-mm) cubes. Place the diced tuna in a small bowl. Using a fork, gently mix in the ginger, sesame oil, $1/2$ teaspoon salt, and 3 or 4 grinds of pepper, distributing the seasonings evenly.

To assemble, top each cucumber slice with about 1 tablespoon of the tuna. Arrange 3 tuna-topped cucumber slices on each individual plate. Using a small spoon, drizzle one-fourth of the soy mixture on each plate between the cucumber slices. Using the tines of a fork, drip 3 or 4 drops of the wasabi mixture over the soy mixture, then dab a bit of the wasabi mixture on top of each mound of tuna. Sprinkle sparingly with sesame seeds and serve at once.

Nearly anyone on a high-protein diet will appreciate this glistening tuna, subtly seasoned with ginger and wasabi. It can be the hors d'oeuvre or the first course at a dinner party, or a light meal on its own. Ask your fishmonger to cut the fish from the eye of an impeccably fresh tuna loin to avoid any tough membranes. Buy the tuna the day it will be served and keep it well chilled until just before cutting. The soy and wasabi drizzled on each plate serve as both decoration and dipping sauce. Use only the highest-quality soy sauce for this dish. This recipe calls for raw fish; refer to the note on page 9.

Grilled Shrimp with Tomato-Quinoa Salsa

Shrimp grilled in the shell are exceptionally succulent and full of flavor. Peeling them is messy but worth the effort. Quinoa, a protein-packed grain, gives the mildly hot salsa unexpected flavor and a pleasant crunch. You will not need all the quinoa you cook for the salsa. Add the leftover to soups or sprinkle it over salads. Cooked quinoa will keep, in the refrigerator, for up to three days. If you can find them, use shrimp with the heads still intact for a striking presentation.

To make the tomato-quinoa salsa, in a small saucepan, bring 1 cup (8 fl oz/ 250 ml) water to a boil over high heat. Add the quinoa, reduce the heat to low, cover, and simmer until the quinoa is cooked but still slightly crunchy, about 15 minutes. Drain and let cool.

In a small bowl, combine the tomato, cucumber, jalapeño, onion, and orange and lime juices. Mix in $^1/_3$ cup (3 oz/90 g) of the cooled quinoa, reserving the rest for another use (see note). Add the parsley and toss with a fork to distribute evenly. Stir in $^1/_4$ teaspoon salt, or more to taste, and season with pepper. Set aside.

Prepare a CHARCOAL or GAS GRILL for direct-heat grilling over medium-high heat. Oil the grill rack. Brush the shrimp with the olive oil.

BY CHARCOAL GRILL: Using tongs, place the shrimp over the hottest part of the fire and grill until they begin to curl and are bright pink on the bottom, about 3 minutes. Turn the shrimp and grill until they are bright pink all over, 2–3 minutes longer. They should be firm to the touch at the thickest part.

BY GAS GRILL: Using tongs, place the shrimp directly over the heat elements and grill until they begin to curl and sare bright pink on the bottom, about 3 minutes. Turn the shrimp and grill until they are bright pink all over, 2–3 minutes longer. They should be firm to the touch at the thickest part.

Set the bowl of salsa in the center of a platter. Arrange the grilled shrimp around the bowl. Diners peel the shrimp, then top them with the salsa.

For the Tomato-Quinoa Salsa

$^1/_4$ cup (1$^1/_2$ oz/45 g) quinoa, rinsed thoroughly in a sieve and well drained

1 large, ripe tomato, seeded and chopped

2-inch (5-cm) piece English (hothouse) cucumber, peeled, seeded, and cut into $^1/_4$-inch (6-mm) cubes

1 small jalapeño chile, seeded and minced

$^1/_2$ small red onion, finely chopped

2 tablespoons fresh orange juice

Juice of $^1/_2$ lime (about 1 tablespoon)

$^1/_3$ cup ($^1/_3$ oz/10 g) loosely packed fresh flat-leaf (Italian) parsley leaves

Kosher salt and freshly ground pepper

16 large shrimp (prawns), $^3/_4$–1 lb (375–500 g) total weight

1–2 teaspoons extra-virgin olive oil

MAKES 4 SERVINGS

Soups
and Stews

About Soups and Stews

A healthful soup or stew usually starts with a low-sodium, fat-free stock, followed by the addition of dried beans or other vegetables or seafood. Even rich-tasting puréed soups take on a healthful profile when prepared with ingredients and cooking methods that eliminate the need for cream.

Soups and stews are generally thought of as comfort foods: hearty, rustic, slow-cooked dishes. This chapter demonstrates that they are far more varied than what is suggested by that simple description. A soup can be a light starter or a substantial main dish, a silky-smooth purée or a chunky mix of greens and potato, a course served piping hot or well chilled. Stews are almost as versatile, turning up loaded with beans and squash, pieces of fish fillet, or myriad shellfish. The soups and stews here are all good examples of how easy and appealing healthful cooking can be.

A successful soup often begins with a good-flavored stock or broth. Two recipes for stocks are included (page 270), one made from chicken, the other from roasted vegetables. If you do not have time to tend a simmering stock, you will find many good-quality commercial broths on market shelves. The best choices are low-sodium, fat-free broths, preferably organic, sold in cans or aseptic packages. Some specialty-food stores sell frozen broths. Read the labels carefully to make sure any product you purchase is low in fat and low or moderate in sodium.

NUTRITION SUPERSTARS

Soups and stews made from dried beans are rich in fiber, complex carbohydrates, B vitamins, protein, and phosphorus. Simply put, dried beans are nutrition superstars. They are widely sold, but farmers' markets and some stores usually carry so-called new crop dried beans, many of them heirloom varieties. These recently harvested legumes, available especially in autumn, ensure an appealing texture and superior bean flavor for such dishes as Tuscan Bean Soup (page 56) and Black Bean Stew (page 58).

Beans also star in Kale and Potato Soup (page 64), an adaptation of the classic Portuguese caldo verde that includes linguiça or chorizo (spicy pork sausages) for flavor. This version of the hearty soup uses low-fat turkey kielbasa in place of the traditional sausages. Old-fashioned Corn Chowder (page 63) is made more healthful by substituting puréed silken tofu for the usual milk or cream. The soup's smoky flavor comes from a garnish of crisply fried and crumbled preservative-free bacon, which replaces the salt pork or fatback used to flavor many chowders.

Nearly every national cuisine has its own fish or shellfish stew, dishes that have an important role in a healthful diet. Both fish and shellfish are good sources of vitamins, minerals, and protein, and several types are high in desirable omega-3 fatty acids. Many health experts recommend eating fish at least three times per week, and serving seafood in soups and stews is an excellent place to start. This chapter includes Italian Shellfish Stew (page 69), a rich mix of shrimp (prawns), scallops, squid, and clams, and Fish Stew with Fennel and Saffron (page 66), a heady combination built on white fish fillets. Both recipes can be adapted to your taste or pocketbook by substituting different types of fish or shellfish, or changing the amounts.

HEALTHFUL PURÉED SOUPS

Many soups here are partially or completely puréed, which gives them body and richness without the use of cream or butter. Chilled Potato and Leek Soup (page 54) calls for puréeing Yukon gold potatoes, whose silky texture and buttery flavor mimic the heavy (double) cream used in vichyssoise. Classic bisques are also known for their lavish use of cream. In Roasted Tomato Bisque (page 61), however, the soup's substantial body and intense flavor are achieved by roasting tomatoes to concentrate their natural sweetness and reduce their moisture content.

Puréeing soups is easily accomplished with a food mill, a food processor, or a standing or immersion blender. If using a food mill, set it securely on the rim of a saucepan or flat-bottomed bowl before passing batches of hot food through it. If puréeing in a standing blender or food processor, process the hot mixture in small batches, holding the lid of the blender or the plunger (stopper) of the food processor securely in place while processing to prevent splatters. If using an immersion blender, submerge the blade completely in the soup to avoid splashes and burns.

Nearly every type of soup benefits from a garnish. Choose garnishes carefully, however, staying away from lots of butter, mounds of grated cheese, or swirls of heavy cream. The garnishes in this chapter, including chopped fresh herbs, nonfat or light sour cream, and dry-fried mushrooms, all follow this rule.

Keeping soups healthful and flavorful starts with choosing wholesome ingredients and ends with a sensible garnish. Between these two points, always select thickeners and flavorings wisely to ensure a result that is both delicious and nutritious.

Chilled Potato and Leek Soup

4 leeks, white part only, chopped

4 large green (spring) onions, white part only, chopped

3 cups (24 fl oz/750 ml) Rich Chicken Stock (page 270) or reduced-sodium, fat-free chicken broth

1 lb (500 g) yellow-fleshed potatoes such as Yukon gold, peeled and diced

1 1/2 tablespoons unsalted butter

Kosher salt and freshly ground pepper, preferably white

2 tablespoons snipped fresh chives

MAKES 4 SERVINGS

In a Dutch oven or large, heavy saucepan over medium-high heat, combine the leeks, green onions, and ¹/₂ cup (4 fl oz/125 ml) of the stock. Bring to a boil, reduce the heat to low, cover, and cook the vegetables until they have wilted and begin to soften, about 8 minutes. Add the potatoes and the remaining 2¹/₂ cups (20 fl oz/625 ml) stock, re-cover, and cook until the vegetables are very soft, 25–30 minutes.

Remove the pan from the heat, uncover, and let the soup stand for 15 minutes to cool slightly. Stir in the butter.

Using an immersion blender, purée the soup until it is very smooth, 3–4 minutes. Alternatively, working in batches, carefully purée in a standing blender until very smooth. Stir in ¹/₄ teaspoon salt, or more to taste, and season with pepper. Let the soup cool to room temperature. Cover and refrigerate until well chilled, 3–4 hours or up to overnight. The soup will thicken, becoming very creamy.

Just before serving, taste the soup and adjust the seasoning. Divide it among soup bowls and garnish with the chives. Serve at once.

Vichyssoise, the classic chilled soup of potatoes, leeks, cream, and sometimes butter, is rich and delicious—and high in fat. This low-fat version delivers the buttery flavor of the original by using yellow-fleshed potatoes and just a small amount of butter. Homemade stock will enrich the flavor and keep the sodium content modest. To avoid visible flecks of pepper, season the soup with white pepper, rather than black.

Butternut Squash Soup

Smooth as velvet, this soup, right down to its dry-sautéed mushroom garnish, shows how good low-fat cooking can be. The addition of a sweet apple and orange juice concentrate heightens the flavorful, deep orange-yellow flesh of the butternut squash. The soup is packed with vitamins and phytochemicals, and is perfect for everyone, including vegetarians.

Cut the squash in half. Remove and discard the seeds, then peel and dice the flesh. In a Dutch oven or large, heavy saucepan over medium-high heat, combine the squash, apple, shallots, broth, oregano, and cayenne. Bring to a boil, reduce the heat to medium-low, cover, and simmer until the vegetables are very soft, 25–30 minutes. Remove from the heat, uncover, and let the soup stand for about 15 minutes. Using an immersion blender, purée the soup in the pan until it is very smooth, 3–4 minutes. Alternatively, working in batches, carefully purée in a standing blender until smooth, then return to the pan. Stir in the orange juice concentrate and $1/4$ teaspoon salt, or more to taste. Season with black pepper.

Remove the stems from the mushrooms and discard. Cut the caps into 1-inch (2.5-cm) cubes. Heat a large frying pan over medium-high heat. (Do not use a pan with a nonstick coating.) When it is hot, add the mushrooms to the dry pan and sauté, tossing and stirring them with a wooden spoon. When the mushrooms release their liquid, after about 3 minutes, continue to cook and stir until they are dry and well browned, 4–5 minutes. Transfer to a plate.

Reheat the soup over medium heat, stirring occasionally. Divide it among warmed wide, shallow bowls and spoon one-fourth of the mushrooms into the center of each bowl. Serve at once.

**1 butternut squash,
about 1$^1/_4$ lb (625 g)**

**1 Fuji apple, halved, peeled,
cored, and diced**

2 shallots, chopped

**2 cups (16 fl oz/500 ml)
reduced-sodium, fat-free
vegetable broth**

$^1/_2$ teaspoon dried oregano

**Pinch of ground cayenne
pepper**

**2 tablespoons thawed, frozen
orange juice concentrate**

**Kosher salt and freshly
ground black pepper**

**2 large portobello
mushrooms, brushed clean**

MAKES 4 SERVINGS

Tuscan Bean Soup

1 cup (7 oz/220 g) dried
borlotti or cranberry beans,
soaked and drained
(page 278), or 3 cups
(21 oz/655 g) shelled fresh
borlotti or cranberry beans
(about 4 lb/2 kg unshelled)

1/2 head savoy cabbage,
about 1 lb (250 g), or
1 small bunch *cavolo nero*
(see note)

2 tablespoons extra-virgin
olive oil

1 large yellow onion, chopped

2 cloves garlic, minced

1 large carrot, peeled and
chopped

1 celery stalk, thinly sliced

1 can (28 oz/875 g) diced or
chopped tomatoes

1 bay leaf

Pinch of red pepper flakes
(optional)

Kosher salt and freshly
ground black pepper

8 slices day-old coarse
country bread, each 1 inch
(2.5 cm) thick (optional)

MAKES 8 SERVINGS

If using dried beans, place the soaked, drained beans in a saucepan, and add water to cover generously. Bring to a boil over high heat, reduce the heat to low, cover partially, and simmer gently until tender, 1–1 1/2 hours. Remove from the heat and drain, reserving the beans and liquid separately. If using fresh beans, set them aside.

If using savoy cabbage, cut the half head in half again, to form 2 wedges, then cut the wedges crosswise into strips 1/2 inch (12 mm) wide. If using *cavolo nero*, remove the center rib from each leaf, then cut the leaves crosswise into strips 1/2 inch (12 mm) wide. Set aside.

In a large Dutch oven or other deep, heavy pot over medium-high heat, warm the olive oil. Add the onion, garlic, carrot, and celery and sauté until the onion and celery are translucent, about 6 minutes. Add the cabbage or *cavolo nero* strips, and stir until they wilt, about 5 minutes. Add the tomatoes and their liquid and stir to combine.

If using cooked dried beans, measure the bean cooking liquid and add water as needed to total 4 cups (32 fl oz/1 l). Add the beans and liquid to the pan along with the bay leaf and red pepper flakes, if using. Bring to a boil over medium-high heat, reduce the heat to medium-low, cover, and simmer until the beans are heated through, about 10 minutes. Stir in 1/4 teaspoon salt, or more to taste, and season with black pepper.

If using fresh beans, add them to the pan along with the bay leaf and red pepper flakes, if using. Pour in 4 cups (32 fl oz/1 l) cold water and bring to a boil over high heat. Reduce the heat to medium-low, cover, and simmer until the beans are tender but not soft, about 20 minutes. Stir in 1/4 teaspoon salt, or more to taste, and season with black pepper.

If using the bread, place a slice in each warmed wide, shallow bowl. Remove the bay leaf from the soup and discard. Ladle the soup into the bowls and serve.

Tuscans call this hearty soup minestrone on the day it is made, and *ribollita* the next day, when they add stale bread to thicken and stretch it. In Italy, fresh or dried borlotti beans, which are pinkish beige with burgundy markings, are used. If you cannot find them, cranberry beans, which are similar, are excellent substitutes. Italian cooks also traditionally add *cavolo nero*, literally "black cabbage," which has green-black, crinkled leaves and a mildly bitter taste. Sometimes called lacinato or dinosaur kale, it can be used in place of, or along with, the savoy cabbage.

Black Bean Stew

1 cup (7 oz/220 g) dried black beans

1 large yellow onion, chopped

2 cloves garlic, minced

1 small butternut squash, about 1 lb (500 g)

1 green bell pepper (capsicum), seeded and diced

1 teaspoon dried oregano

¹/₄ teaspoon caraway seeds

¹/₂ cup (4 fl oz/125 ml) lager beer

Kosher salt and freshly ground pepper

MAKES 4 SERVINGS

Soak and drain the black beans as directed on page 278. Place the drained beans in a large saucepan and add 4 cups (32 fl oz/1 l) water. Bring to a boil over high heat, reduce the heat to low, cover, and simmer gently until almost tender but still quite firm, about 1 hour.

Add the onion and garlic to the beans, re-cover, and continue to cook over low heat until the beans are tender, about 30 minutes longer.

Cut the squash in half. Remove and discard the seeds, then peel the flesh. Cut the flesh into 1-inch (2.5-cm) cubes. Add the squash, bell pepper, oregano, caraway seeds, and beer to the pan, raise the heat to medium, and cook, uncovered, until the squash and beans are soft but still hold their shape, about 30 minutes. Stir in ¹/₂ teaspoon salt, or more to taste, and season with pepper.

Ladle the stew into warmed soup bowls and serve at once.

Butternut squash is rich in beta-carotene and protective phytochemicals. Both squash and black beans are good sources of dietary fiber. The nutty taste of the squash is complemented by the caraway seeds and beer used to season this hearty vegetarian stew.

Sweet Green Pea Soup

VARIATION

Chilled Green Pea Soup

Prepare the soup as directed and let cool completely after puréeing. Cover and refrigerate until chilled but not ice-cold, about 3 hours. Just before serving, stir in the juice of ½ lime (about 1 tablespoon) and ladle the soup into bowls.

All peas are members of the legume family. Some are grown to be eaten fresh, removed from their pods, like English peas. The frozen petite peas used here are ideal, since fresh peas have a short season. But when fresh peas are available, use them in place of the frozen. The starch provided by Arborio rice adds body and creaminess to the soup without dulling the flavor of the peas.

In a large saucepan over medium-high heat, warm the canola oil. Add the leek, onion, and zucchini and stir to coat with the oil. Reduce the heat to low, cover tightly, and cook until the vegetables are very soft, about 10 minutes. Add the rice and 3 cups (24 fl oz/750 ml) water, raise the heat to medium, and bring to a boil. Reduce the heat to maintain a simmer, cover, and cook for 10 minutes. Add the peas, re-cover, and cook until the peas are very tender, about 10 minutes. Remove from the heat, uncover, and let stand for 15 minutes to cool slightly.

Using an immersion blender, purée the soup until it is very smooth. Alternatively, working in batches, carefully purée the soup in a standing blender until smooth; return it to the pan. Reheat the soup over medium heat to serving temperature. Divide the soup among warmed soup bowls, garnish with the chives, and serve.

1 tablespoon canola oil

1 leek, white part only, chopped

1 white onion, chopped

1 small zucchini (courgette), trimmed and chopped

1 tablespoon Arborio rice

2 cups (10 oz/315 g) frozen petite green peas

About 6 whole fresh chives, cut into 1½-inch (4-cm) lengths

MAKES 4 SERVINGS

Roasted Tomato Bisque

Roasting tomatoes concentrates their flavor, giving this bisque a full-bodied taste without the use of cream, except for a dollop of light sour cream used as a garnish. This soup is smooth and elegant enough to serve at a dinner party. Or accompany it with Tomato, Onion, and Goat Cheese Sandwiches (page 164), Vegetable Melts on Garlic Toast (page 155), or whole-grain crackers.

Preheat the oven to 425°F (220°C). Cover 1 large or 2 medium-sized baking sheets with aluminum foil. Arrange the tomatoes, cut side up, on the prepared sheets. Sprinkle evenly with 1 teaspoon salt and several grinds of pepper. Roast the tomatoes until they are soft, but still hold their shape, about 30 minutes.

In a Dutch oven or large, heavy saucepan over medium-high heat, warm the olive oil. Add the onion and garlic and sauté until translucent, about 3 minutes. Reduce the heat to low, cover, and cook until the onion releases its juices, about 8 minutes. Stir in the paprika. Raise the heat to medium-high and add the tomatoes, along with any juices collected on the pan(s), then pour in 1 cup (8 fl oz/ 250 ml) water. Reduce the heat to medium, cover, and simmer until the vegetables are very soft, about 25 minutes.

Remove from the heat and, working in batches, carefully pass the soup through a food mill fitted with the medium disk placed over a bowl. Alternatively, pass the soup through a fine-mesh sieve placed over a bowl, pressing against it with the back of a wooden spoon.

Rinse the pan and return the soup to it. Stir in $1/4$ teaspoon salt, or more to taste, season with pepper, and then reheat over medium heat. Divide the soup among warmed soup bowls and place 1 teaspoon sour cream in the center of each bowl, swirling it slightly. Garnish with the parsley and serve.

2¹/₂ lb (1.25 kg) plum (Roma) tomatoes, halved lengthwise

Kosher salt and freshly ground pepper

1 teaspoon extra-virgin olive oil

1 small yellow onion, chopped

1 small clove garlic, minced

1 teaspoon sweet paprika

4 teaspoons light sour cream

4 teaspoons chopped fresh flat-leaf (Italian) parsley

MAKES 4 SERVINGS

Corn Chowder

For the best flavor, make this soup at the height of summer, using just-picked local corn, yellow or white, or a combination. The cobs are simmered to make a broth, which is then puréed with silken tofu, resulting in a rich-tasting soup without the cream or milk typically added to corn chowders. Another change from the classic version: a garnish of crumbled crisp bacon replaces the salt pork or fatback usually cooked with the corn. If you make the soup in advance and refrigerate it, it will take on a grainy look. When it is reheated, the graininess will disappear.

Husk the corn ears and carefully remove all the silk. Hold 1 ear upright, stem end down, in the center of a wide, shallow bowl. Using a sharp knife, slice straight down between the kernels and the cob, rotating the ear a quarter turn after each cut. Then, using the dull side of the knife blade, run the blade down the length of the ear to extract the "milk" and bits of corn remaining on the ear, again rotating the ear a quarter turn after each stroke. Repeat with the remaining 3 ears. Put all of the corn and the corn cobs in a Dutch oven or large saucepan.

Add 6 cups (48 fl oz/1.5 l) water to the pan and place over high heat. Bring to a boil, reduce the heat to medium-low, and boil gently, uncovered, until the corn is tender, 10–20 minutes; the timing depends on the tenderness of the corn. Remove and discard the cobs. Pour the contents of the pan through a sieve, reserving both the corn and the corn broth. Return half of the broth to the pan. Set half of the cooked corn aside.

In a blender, carefully combine the remaining broth, remaining cooked corn, and tofu, and purée until a creamy mixture forms, about 2 minutes. Set aside.

Add the yellow onion, potato, bell pepper, and cayenne to the pan holding the broth and bring to a boil over high heat. Reduce the heat to maintain a simmer and cook, uncovered, until the potato is tender, about 10 minutes. Pour in the corn-tofu mixture, stir in the reserved corn and the green onion tops, and heat through. Add 1 tablespoon lemon juice (the lemon juice eliminates any tofu "bean flavor"), then stir in 1/4 teaspoon salt, or more to taste, and season with black pepper and with more lemon juice, if needed.

While the soup is cooking, in a frying pan over medium heat, fry the bacon, turning the slices as needed, until crisp, about 5 minutes. Transfer to paper towels to drain. Ladle the chowder into warmed soup bowls. Cut the bacon slices in half, then crumble 1/2 slice into the center of each bowl. Serve at once.

4 ears corn

1 cup (8 oz/250 g) silken tofu

1 yellow onion, cut into 1/2-inch (12-mm) cubes

1 boiling potato, about 6 oz (185 g), peeled and cut into 1/2-inch (12-mm) cubes

1 red bell pepper (capsicum), seeded and cut into 1/2-inch (12-mm) pieces

Pinch of ground cayenne pepper

1/2 cup (1 1/2 oz/45 g) chopped green (spring) onion tops

1–2 tablespoons fresh lemon juice

Kosher salt and freshly ground black pepper

3 slices preservative-free bacon

MAKES 6 SERVINGS

Kale and Potato Soup

1 cup (7 oz/220 g) dried cannellini beans, soaked and drained (page 278), or 1 can (15 oz/470 g) cannellini beans

1 bunch kale, about ³/₄ lb (375 g)

1 yellow-fleshed potato such as Yukon gold, about ¹/₂ lb (250 g)

2 teaspoons extra-virgin olive oil

1 large yellow onion, chopped

4 cloves garlic, chopped

2 oz (60 g) low-fat turkey kielbasa, sliced

¹/₈ teaspoon red pepper flakes

Kosher salt

MAKES 6 SERVINGS

If using dried beans, place the soaked, drained beans in a saucepan and add water to cover generously. Bring to a boil over high heat, reduce the heat to low, cover partially, and simmer gently until tender, 1–1¹/₂ hours. Drain well, measure out 2 cups (14 oz/440 g), and set aside; reserve any remaining beans for another use. If using canned beans, drain well, rinse under running cold water, drain well again, and set aside.

Remove the tough stems from the kale leaves and cut the leaves crosswise into strips ¹/₂ inch (12 mm) wide. You will have about 5 cups (10 oz/315 g). Cut the potato into 1-inch (2.5-cm) pieces.

In a Dutch oven or other large, heavy saucepan over medium-high heat, warm the olive oil. Add the onion and sauté until translucent, about 4 minutes. Add the garlic and cook for 1 minute. Stir in the kale, potato, kielbasa, red pepper flakes, and ¹/₂ teaspoon salt, or more to taste. Pour in 8 cups (64 fl oz/2 l) water. Bring to a boil, reduce the heat to medium-low, and simmer, uncovered, until the kale is almost tender, about 20 minutes.

Add the beans and cook until heated through, about 5 minutes. Ladle the soup into warmed soup bowls and serve at once.

Generous measures of kale and beans make this soup filling enough to serve as a main course, accompanied by whole-grain bread. Using a modest amount of sausage deepens the soup's flavor; vegetarians can replace the meat with smoked tofu. Portuguese linguiça or chorizo is traditional, but using low-fat turkey kielbasa imparts the same smoky, spicy flavor with less fat and cholesterol.

Fish Stew with Fennel and Saffron

1/2 teaspoon saffron threads

4 teaspoons extra-virgin olive oil

1/4 cup (1 oz/30 g) chopped shallot

1/2 jalapeño chile, chopped

1 cup (8 fl oz/250 ml) bottled clam juice

1 cup (8 fl oz/250 ml) dry white wine such as Sauvignon Blanc

3 fresh thyme sprigs or 1/2 teaspoon dried thyme

1 bay leaf

1 orange zest strip, 3 inches (7.5 cm) long by 1 inch (2.5 cm) wide

1/2 teaspoon fennel seeds

1 fennel bulb

1 red bell pepper (capsicum)

1 red onion, chopped

Kosher salt and freshly ground pepper

1 firm white fish fillet such as halibut, scrod, or cod, about 1 lb (500 g), cut into 4 equal portions

1/2 cup (4 oz/125 g) nonfat sour cream

2 tablespoons chopped fresh mint

MAKES 4 SERVINGS

In a small bowl, combine the saffron threads and 2 tablespoons hot water. Set aside for 20 minutes to soften the saffron and release its color.

In a Dutch oven or large, heavy saucepan over medium-high heat, warm 2 teaspoons of the olive oil. Add the shallot and jalapeño and sauté until the shallot is translucent, about 4 minutes. Add the clam juice, wine, thyme, bay leaf, orange zest, fennel seeds, saffron and its liquid, and 1 cup (8 fl oz/250 ml) water. Bring to a boil, reduce the heat to medium-low, cover, and simmer for 10 minutes to blend the flavors.

Remove the broth from the heat and strain through a fine-mesh sieve. Set aside. Discard the solids and rinse out the pot.

Cut off the stems and feathery leaves from the fennel bulb. Discard the outer layer of the bulb if it is tough, and cut away any discolored areas. Halve the bulb lengthwise and cut away any tough base portions. Cut each half lengthwise into 8 wedges. Remove the top, seeds, and ribs from the bell pepper. Cut the flesh into strips 1 1/2 inches (4 cm) long by 3/4 inch (2 cm) wide.

Add the remaining 2 teaspoons olive oil to the rinsed pot and place over medium-high heat. Add the fennel, bell pepper, and onion and sauté until the onion is translucent, about 4 minutes. Pour the reserved broth into the pot and stir in 1/2 teaspoon salt, or more to taste, and several grinds of pepper. Bring to a boil, reduce the heat to medium-low, and simmer, uncovered, for 10 minutes. Add the fish, pushing down on it to immerse it in the liquid. Simmer gently until the fish is opaque when tested with a fork at its thickest point, about 10 minutes. Remove from the heat.

Using a slotted spoon, place a piece of fish in the center of each warmed wide, shallow bowl. Lift the vegetables from the pot and divide evenly among the bowls. Ladle 1 cup (8 fl oz/250 ml) of the broth from the pot into a small bowl. Whisk in the sour cream until combined. Pour this mixture back into the pot, stirring gently. Ladle as much of the broth into each bowl as desired. Garnish with the mint and serve at once.

While the use of saffron, the orange stigmas of a type of crocus, elevates any dish to specialty status, this elegant stew is simple to prepare. Heavy (double) cream is typically added to similar fish stews, but here nonfat sour cream delivers the desired richness. Fennel seeds fortify the anise flavor, creating a taste more like that imparted by the wild fennel often used in Mediterranean cooking.

Italian Shellfish Stew

Italian Americans make lavish seafood stews similar to this one for Christmas Eve dinner, just as their ancestors did in Italy. This particular recipe is adapted from *cacciucco*, a combination of seafood cooked with tomatoes and wine popular along the Tuscan coast, especially in the port city of Livorno. Although the list of ingredients looks relatively long, the dish can be assembled and cooked within an hour. Mussels, well scrubbed and debearded, may be substituted for the clams, and cod fillet for the monkfish. Because generous amounts of fish and shellfish are used, a bowl of this stew provides enough protein for the whole day.

In a large Dutch oven or other deep, heavy pot over medium-high heat, warm the olive oil. Add the onion and garlic and sauté until the onion is soft, about 4 minutes. Add the tomatoes and red pepper flakes and sauté until the tomatoes soften, about 5 minutes. Pour in the tomato sauce and wine, bring to a boil, reduce the heat to medium, cover, and cook for 10 minutes.

Add the squid, re-cover, and simmer for 10 minutes. Add the monkfish, scallops, and shrimp, re-cover, and cook until the shrimp and scallops are opaque throughout but still tender, about 10 minutes. Add the clams, discarding any that do not close to the touch, cover, and cook just until they open, 4–5 minutes. Discard any clams that failed to open.

Rub each bread slice generously on one side with a garlic clove half. Place each slice, garlic side up, in a warmed wide, shallow soup bowl. Ladle one-fourth of the stew into each bowl, dividing the fish and shellfish evenly. Garnish with the parsley and serve at once.

2 tablespoons extra-virgin olive oil

1 large yellow onion, chopped

1 clove garlic, minced

8 plum (Roma) tomatoes, halved lengthwise, seeded, and diced

$^1/_4$ teaspoon red pepper flakes

$^1/_2$ cup (4 fl oz/125 ml) tomato sauce

$^1/_2$ cup (4 fl oz/125 ml) dry red wine

$^3/_4$ lb (375 g) cleaned squid (page 284), tentacles trimmed, bodies cut in $^1/_2$-inch (12-mm) rings

$^3/_4$ lb (375 g) monkfish fillet, cut into $^3/_4$-inch (2-cm) pieces

$^1/_2$ lb (250 g) sea scallops, side muscle removed, halved horizontally

$^1/_4$ lb (125 g) shrimp (prawns), peeled and deveined (page 277)

12 littleneck clams, well scrubbed

4 slices coarse county bread, each about 1 inch (2.5 cm) thick, toasted

2 cloves garlic, halved lengthwise

Chopped fresh flat-leaf (Italian) parsley

MAKES 4 SERVINGS

Salads

About Salads

Salads made from fresh greens and other vegetables, grains, or lean protein play an important role in a healthful diet. Low-fat vinaigrettes or buttermilk-based creamy dressings and garnishes of strong-flavored cheese or crunchy nuts deliver extra flavor, texture, and nutrients.

With their bounty of fresh ingredients, salads would seem destined to have a big part in any sound eating plan. But these mealtime mainstays can quickly become unhealthful as more and more ingredients are tossed into the bowl. Whether serving a simple green salad as an appetizer, a vegetable salad as a side dish, or a protein-rich chicken or beef salad as a light meal, careful ingredient selection and preparation are critical to making any salad healthful.

Fresh vegetable salads, such as Green Bean and Yellow Tomato Salad with Mint (page 75), are a wonderful way to show off the season's harvest. Grains and pasta, such as the couscous combined with vegetables on page 80, can form the base for healthful salads as well. Consider, too, beans and other legumes for salads rich in fiber and protein. The colorful mix of *edamame* (fresh soybeans) and orange segments on page 82 also provides valuable calcium, iron, vitamin C, and folate. Cooked dried beans form a satisfying foundation for a main-dish salad when combined with lean protein, as in Cannellini Bean, Fennel, and Shrimp Salad (page 87).

THE FUNDAMENTALS: GREENS AND DRESSINGS

Salads frequently feature one or more types of greens. Greens of different flavors, colors, and textures make a particularly appealing mix. To maximize the amount of beneficial phytochemicals, try to use some dark-colored greens, such as the spinach in Spinach, Tomato, and Corn Salad (page 84). "Greens" include red and purple leaves and lettuces that add phytochemicals different from those found in greens that are green in color.

Proper storage and preparation help preserve the nutrition and flavor of fresh greens. When you bring greens home from the market, store them, loosely enclosed in a plastic bag, in the coldest area of your refrigerator. Just before serving the greens, wash them well and dry them thoroughly, as excess moisture will cause them to wilt and will also dilute the dressing. A salad spinner is ideal for drying greens, but shaking them gently in a clean kitchen towel works, too.

Selecting a suitable dressing is the next step. Mayonnaise- and/or cheese-based dressings are popular, but they often contain saturated fat and are quite high in calories (kilojoules). In addition, their thick consistencies and strong flavors can mask the natural virtues of seasonal produce. Labels on commercial products provide nutrient levels based on a 2 tablespoon serving of salad dressing, but most people use more of thick, creamy dressings because it takes more to coat salad greens. The salads in this chapter are all dressed with low-fat vinaigrettes, simple mixtures of vinegar (or citrus juice), oil, and seasonings. As the recipes show, vinaigrettes are quick to make, coat greens gently, and are easy to customize:

■ In the French-Style Potato Salad (page 83), a touch of mustard is whisked into the vinaigrette for pungency and body. Mustard is high in flavor and fat free and also acts as an emulsifier, binding all the ingredients together.

■ Chopped leafy fresh herbs, grated citrus zest, or other bold seasonings can heighten the flavor of a vinaigrette. Toasted cumin and minced fresh chile perk up the lime dressing for Carrot and Jicama Salad (page 78), while sun-dried tomatoes, garlic, herbs, and orange zest brighten the vinaigrette for Salmon, Red Potato, and Asparagus Salad (page 89).

■ Traditional vinaigrettes are made from about three parts oil to one part vinegar. However, if you choose a mild vinegar or mellow citrus juice, you can create a satisfying dressing with considerably less or no oil, such as the dressing for Thai Beef Salad (page 93), which marries lime juice and Asian fish sauce. Additional vinaigrettes are on pages 273–74.

GARNISHES USED SPARINGLY

Wisely chosen salad garnishes also help create a healthful profile. Cheese is a common salad ingredient, but too much can add considerable saturated fat and cholesterol. Instead, use a strong-flavored cheese and add it sparingly. The pungent Stilton that tops the beet salad on page 76 is a good example. Nuts also make a flavorful topping, but they are rich in fat, so they should be used judiciously. To intensify their flavors, toast them in a dry frying pan over medium heat until they are fragrant and take on color. Lastly, Herb and Cheese Croutons (page 274), made from whole-wheat (wholemeal) bread, herbs, and Parmigiano-Reggiano cheese, are wonderfully crunchy additions to a variety of salads.

Sprinkling shredded or crumbled cheese or toasted nuts atop a salad, rather than mixing them within it, enables you to use less while maximizing visual impact and taste. For other ideas see Top It Off on page 11.

With these tips in mind, it is easy to create your own healthful salads.

Belgian Endive, Apple, and Walnut Salad

2 or 3 heads Belgian endive (chicory/witloof), $^{1}/_{2}$–$^{3}/_{4}$ lb (250–375 g) total weight

2 tablespoons canola oil

2 tablespoons fresh lemon juice

2 teaspoons walnut oil

1 teaspoon grated lemon zest

Kosher salt

$^{1}/_{2}$ cup (2 oz/60 g) coarsely chopped walnuts

1 *each* small Granny Smith apple, Braeburn apple, and Golden Delicious apple

2 tablespoons chopped fresh dill

MAKES 4 SERVINGS

In a bowl, combine the Belgian endives with ice water to cover and let stand for 20 minutes to crisp. Drain and pat dry. Pull the leaves from the heads, trimming the bases as needed to release them. Set aside.

In a large bowl, whisk together the canola oil, lemon juice, walnut oil, lemon zest, and $^{1}/_{2}$ teaspoon salt until blended.

In a small, dry frying pan over low heat, toast the walnuts, stirring occasionally, until warmed and fragrant, about 5 minutes. Remove from the heat and transfer to a plate.

Quarter each apple, trim away the core, and then cut into very thin wedges. Add the apple wedges, endive leaves, and dill to the dressing and toss to mix.

Divide the salad among individual bowls or plates. Sprinkle with the walnuts, dividing evenly. Serve at once.

Rich-tasting walnut oil adds a distinctive flavor to the dressing for this autumn salad, and it also reinforces the natural character of the walnut meats. Nut oils contain heart-healthy fats, but should be consumed in modest amounts. Use them in favorite salad dressings, on cooked vegetables, or on baked potatoes. Nut oils easily become rancid, so make sure the oil you purchase is fresh. If you are unable to find red-leaved Belgian endive, use the yellow variety only.

Green Bean and Yellow Tomato Salad with Mint

For the green beans to absorb the flavor of the mint fully, toss them together while the beans are steaming hot. Yellow tomatoes have a sweeter, less acidic flavor than red tomatoes, but red ones can be substituted for the yellow, or use equal amounts of each. If using red tomatoes, you will need to reduce the amount of red wine vinegar to taste.

Bring a large pot three-fourths full of water to a boil. Trim the ends of the green beans. Add the beans to the boiling water and cook until tender, 5–7 minutes; the timing will depend on their size. Drain.

In a large serving bowl, combine the hot beans, mint, olive oil, and ¹/₂ teaspoon salt and toss to mix. Set aside to cool to room temperature, about 20 minutes.

Cut the tomatoes into wedges about ¹/₂ inch (12 mm) thick. Just before serving, add the tomatoes, onion, 2 teaspoons vinegar, and a grind of pepper to the bean mixture and toss to mix. Taste and add more vinegar, if necessary. Serve the salad at room temperature.

1 lb (500 g) long, slender green beans such as Blue Lake or Kentucky Wonder

¹/₂ cup (³/₄ oz/20 g) chopped fresh mint

2 tablespoons extra-virgin olive oil

Kosher salt

1 or 2 yellow tomatoes

¹/₂ cup (2 oz/60 g) thin red onion wedges

2 teaspoons red wine vinegar, or to taste

Freshly ground pepper

MAKES 4 SERVINGS

Beet and Stilton Salad
with Orange Vinaigrette

4 beets, about 1¹/₄ lb (625 g) total weight

For the Orange Vinaigrette

3 tablespoons fresh orange juice

2 tablespoons extra-virgin olive oil

1 tablespoon red wine vinegar

1 tablespoon minced fresh dill

1 teaspoon grated orange zest

¹/₄ teaspoon minced garlic

Kosher salt and freshly ground pepper

3 green (spring) onions, including tender green tops, thinly sliced on the diagonal

1 tablespoon finely slivered orange zest

10 oz (315 g) mixed salad greens (about 8 cups loosely packed)

¹/₂ cup (2¹/₂ oz/75 g) thinly sliced English (hothouse) cucumber

3 oz (90 g) cold Stilton cheese, crumbled (about ¹/₂ cup)

Fresh dill sprigs

MAKES 4 SERVINGS

Baked beets have a deeper, richer taste than boiled beets. If you like, you can cook them a day or two ahead and refrigerate, still wrapped in foil, until you are ready to peel and slice them for this salad. Beets are high in folate, a B vitamin needed for building cells, especially red blood cells. Folate also protects against birth defects, certain cancers, and heart disease. Some research suggests that folate prevents fatigue and depression. Stilton, a sharply flavored English blue cheese, balances the natural sweetness of the beets, but other blue-veined cheeses, such as Gorgonzola, Roquefort, or Saga blue, can be substituted.

Preheat the oven to 400°F (200°C). Trim off the leafy green tops from the beets and reserve for another use. Wrap the beets individually in squares of aluminum foil, tightly securing the foil. Place on a baking sheet.

Bake the beets until tender when pierced with a skewer, about 1 hour. Remove from the oven and let cool in the foil. Unwrap and peel off the loosened skins. Cut each beet crosswise into 4 or 5 slices. Place in a bowl.

To make the orange vinaigrette, in a small bowl, whisk together the orange juice, olive oil, vinegar, minced dill, grated orange zest, garlic, ¹/₂ teaspoon salt, and a grind of pepper until blended.

Pour all but 2 tablespoons of the vinaigrette over the beets. Add half of the green onions and half of the slivered orange zest; stir gently just to blend. In a separate bowl, combine the salad greens and the reserved 2 tablespoons vinaigrette and toss to coat the greens.

Arrange the salad greens evenly on a platter or divide among individual plates. Using a slotted spoon, remove the beets from the bowl and place on the greens, dividing them evenly if using individual plates. Tuck the cucumber slices in among the beets. Drizzle any vinaigrette remaining in the bowl over the beets. Sprinkle the salad(s) evenly with the remaining green onions and slivered orange zest. Top the salad(s) with the cheese, dividing evenly if using individual plates. Garnish with the dill sprigs and serve.

Carrot and Jicama Salad with Lime Vinaigrette

2 teaspoons ground cumin

3 tablespoons fresh lime juice

2 tablespoons canola oil

1 tablespoon minced, seeded jalapeño chile

1 teaspoon minced garlic

Kosher salt

1 large or 2 medium jicamas, about 3/4 lb (375 g)

3 carrots, about 10 oz (315 g), peeled

1/4 cup (1/3 oz/10 g) finely chopped fresh cilantro (fresh coriander)

MAKES 4–6 SERVINGS

In a small, dry frying pan over medium-low heat, warm the cumin just until fragrant, about 20 seconds. Transfer to a small bowl. Add the lime juice, canola oil, jalapeño, garlic, and 1/2 teapoon salt and whisk until blended. Set the lime vinaigrette aside.

Using a sharp knife, trim the stem and root ends from the jicama(s), then cut into 4 or 6 manageable wedges. Cut and lift up a small piece of the brown skin near the stem end and pull down to remove. Use a vegetable peeler to remove any tenacious pieces of skin and the tough layer underneath.

Using a food processor fitted with the shredding disk or the largest holes of a box grater-shredder, shred the carrots and jicama(s). In a large bowl, combine the carrots, jicama(s), and cilantro. Pour the vinaigrette over the vegetables and toss gently to mix.

Divide the salad evenly among small plates or bowls. Serve at once.

Carrots and jicama, both of them crunchy and sweet, are a winning combination in this tangy salad. Jicama is a large, bulbous root with thin, brown skin and a nutty taste. Serve this salad as an accompaniment to a smoked turkey sandwich or grilled chicken, shrimp, or fish. It has only about 100 calories per serving and lots of dietary fiber.

Tomato and Cucumber Salad

This salad is reminiscent of the deli-style Greek versions made with iceberg lettuce, but instead of lettuce, it uses lots of juicy ripe tomatoes and crunchy cucumbers. A medium tomato has only 35 calories but is high in vitamins C and A, lycopene, and flavonoids that fight cancer and some types of heart disease. Very red tomatoes are richest in lycopene.

Cut the tomatoes into $1/2$-inch (12-mm) cubes. In a large bowl, combine the tomatoes, basil, olive oil, garlic, and $1/4$ teaspoon salt and toss gently to mix. Let stand for 5 minutes.

Cut the cucumber in half lengthwise and remove and discard the seeds, then cut into $1/2$-inch (12-mm) cubes. Cut the onion into $1/4$-inch (6-mm) cubes.

Add the cucumber, onion, cheese, and olives to the tomato mixture, then sprinkle with the vinegar and toss to mix. Season with pepper and stir to blend. Serve the salad at room temperature.

$1^{1/2}$ lb (750 g) ripe tomatoes

$1/2$ cup ($3/4$ oz/20 g) torn fresh basil leaves

2 tablespoons olive oil

$1/2$ teaspoon minced garlic

Kosher salt

6-inch (15-cm) piece English (hothouse) cucumber

$1/2$ sweet onion (page 285)

$1/2$ cup ($2^{1/2}$ oz/75 g) crumbled ricotta salata cheese

2 tablespoons sliced, pitted Kalamata olives

1 teaspoon red wine vinegar

Freshly ground pepper

MAKES 4–6 SERVINGS

Couscous Vegetable Salad

1 cup (6 oz/185 g) couscous

Kosher salt

1¹/₂ cups (12 fl oz/375 ml) boiling water

3 tablespoons extra-virgin olive oil

3 tablespoons fresh lemon juice

¹/₂ teaspoon minced garlic

Freshly ground pepper

¹/₂ cup (2¹/₂ oz/75 g) thawed, frozen petite peas or blanched fresh petite peas

¹/₂ cup (1¹/₂ oz/45 g) thin sliced green (spring) onion

¹/₂ cup (2¹/₂ oz/75 g) minced red bell pepper (capsicum)

¹/₂ cup (2¹/₂ oz/75 g) finely diced English (hothouse) cucumber

¹/₄ cup (¹/₃ oz/10 g) finely chopped fresh flat-leaf (Italian) parsley

1 cup (2 oz/60 g) firmly packed, chiffonade-cut romaine (cos) lettuce leaves (page 279)

MAKES 6 SERVINGS

Couscous, a semolina pasta of tiny, round pellets that is a staple of North African cuisine, makes an excellent salad when tossed with a mixture of finely chopped, brightly colored vegetables. Other vegetables in season may be used; select them with contrasting flavors, textures, and colors in mind. Generally, the deeper the color of the vegetable (green, red, or orange), the higher the nutrient level. Even relatively small amounts of several vegetables add up.

In a heatproof bowl, combine the couscous, ¹/₂ teaspoon salt, and the boiling water. Stir to blend. Cover tightly and let stand until all the liquid has been absorbed, about 20 minutes. Uncover the couscous and let cool to room temperature, about 15 minutes.

In a small bowl, whisk together the olive oil, lemon juice, garlic, ¹/₄ teaspoon salt, 1 tablespoon water, and a grind of pepper until blended.

Add the peas, green onion, bell pepper, cucumber, parsley, and all but 1 tablespoon of the dressing to the couscous. Toss to mix.

Place the romaine in a separate bowl. Add the remaining 1 tablespoon dressing and toss to coat.

To serve, divide the couscous mixture evenly among individual bowls or plates. Top each serving with an equal amount of the romaine lettuce. Serve at once.

Edamame and Orange Salad

1 package (10 or 12 oz/ 310 or 375 g) frozen shelled *edamame*

2 navel oranges

¹/₂ cup (2 oz/60 g) diced red onion (¹/₄-inch/6-mm dice)

¹/₄ cup (2¹/₂ oz/75 g) minced red bell pepper (capsicum)

3 tablespoons rice vinegar

2 tablespoons canola oil

1 teaspoon reduced-sodium soy sauce

¹/₂ teaspoon *each* grated orange zest and peeled and grated fresh ginger

¹/₄ cup (¹/₃ oz/10 g) torn fresh cilantro (fresh coriander) leaves

MAKES 4 SERVINGS

Bring a saucepan three-fourths full of water to a boil. Add the *edamame* and cook according to the package directions. Drain well. Set aside.

Cut a thick slice off the top and bottom of each orange to reveal the flesh. Stand the orange upright on a cutting board. Following the contour of the fruit and rotating it with each cut, slice downward to remove the peel, pith, and membrane. Holding the fruit over a bowl, cut along each side of the membrane between the sections, letting each freed section drop into the bowl. Cut each orange section crosswise into 3 or 4 pieces.

In a salad bowl, combine the oranges, *edamame*, onion, and bell pepper.

In a small bowl, whisk together the rice vinegar, canola oil, soy sauce, orange zest, and ginger until blended.

Pour the dressing over the vegetables and stir gently to mix. Transfer to a serving bowl, garnish with the cilantro, and serve.

Edamame are soybeans sold in their fuzzy pods fresh, cooked and refrigerated, or cooked and frozen. For added convenience, they are also available frozen without their pods. The beans are not only low in fat. They are an excellent source of protein, calcium, iron, and many B vitamins.

French-Style Potato Salad

Avoiding the richness of the typical mayonnaise-dressed potato salad, this version is dressed French style, with a red wine vinaigrette seasoned with Dijon mustard. The flavors are tangy and robust without the excessive fat and calories of mayonnaise. Small red-skinned potatoes are ideal for this simple salad: they are pretty, cook quickly, and do not need to be peeled. Use only the tender, light-colored stalks at the heart of a head of celery for slicing and mixing with the cooked potatoes.

Place the potatoes in a large saucepan with water to cover. Bring to a boil over high heat, reduce the heat to medium-low, cover, and simmer until the potatoes are tender when pierced with a knife, about 15 minutes.

Meanwhile, in a large bowl, whisk together the olive oil, vinegar, mustard, $^1/_2$ teaspoon salt, and pepper to taste until blended.

When the potatoes are ready, drain them. As soon as they are cool enough to handle, quarter them and add them to the dressing. Add the celery and chervil, folding gently to distribute the ingredients evenly. Serve the salad warm or at room temperature.

2 lb (1 kg) small, round red-skinned potatoes, each about 1$^1/_2$ inches (4 cm) in diameter

3 tablespoons extra-virgin olive oil

2 tablespoons red wine vinegar

1 tablespoon Dijon mustard

Kosher salt and freshly ground pepper

$^1/_2$ cup (2 oz/60 g) thinly sliced celery heart (see note)

$^1/_4$ cup ($^1/_4$ oz/7 g) fresh chervil leaves, coarsely chopped

MAKES 6 SERVINGS

Spinach, Tomato, and Corn Salad

2 ears corn (see note)

1 large tomato, diced

¹/₂ cup (2¹/₂ oz/75 g) diced English (hothouse) cucumber

¹/₂ cup (2 oz/60 g) diced sweet onion (page 285)

2 tablespoons *each* chopped fresh basil, mint, flat-leaf (Italian) parsley, and dill

1 teaspoon chopped garlic

1 teaspoon ground cumin

¹/₄ cup (2 fl oz/60 ml) extra-virgin olive oil

2 tablespoons red wine vinegar

Kosher salt and freshly ground pepper

5 oz (155 g) baby spinach leaves

MAKES 4 SERVINGS

Husk the corn ears and carefully remove all the silk. Hold 1 ear upright, stem end down, in the center of a wide, shallow bowl. Using a sharp knife, slice straight down between the kernels and the cob, rotating the ear a quarter turn after each cut. Repeat with the second ear. You will have about 1 cup (6 oz/185 g) kernels.

In a large salad bowl, combine the corn, tomato, cucumber, and onion. Combine the basil, mint, parsley, dill, and garlic on a cutting board and finely chop. Add to the vegetables.

In a small, dry frying pan over medium-low heat, warm the cumin just until fragrant, about 20 seconds. Transfer to a small bowl. Add the olive oil, vinegar, ¹/₂ teaspoon salt, and a grind of pepper and whisk until blended.

Carefully rinse the spinach in 2 or 3 changes of water. Drain briefly in a colander and pat dry. Add the spinach and the dressing to the corn-tomato mixture. Toss to mix and coat with the dressing. Serve at once.

Chopped basil, mint, parsley, and dill give depth to this spinach salad. A small amount of ground cumin is stirred into the dressing after being heated in a dry frying pan to release its earthy aroma and intensify its flavor. Spinach, tomatoes, and corn provide carotenoids and a variety of protective phyto-chemicals. Spinach is rich in lutein, which is associated with reducing the risk of the leading cause of blindness in people over age sixty-five. Because the corn is used raw, look for the freshest young corn you can find.

Cannellini Bean, Fennel, and Shrimp Salad

The combination of beans and fennel makes this salad a superior source of fiber. Canned cannellini beans may be substituted. Use 2 cans (15 oz/470 g each); drain the beans well, rinse, then drain well again before combining with the other ingredients. Garnish each salad, if desired, with a lemon wedge.

Soak and drain the beans as directed on page 278. Place the soaked, drained beans in a saucepan and add water to cover generously. Bring to a boil over high heat, reduce the heat to low, cover partially, and simmer gently until tender, 1–1 1/2 hours. Drain well, measure out 3 cups (21 oz/655 g), and set aside; reserve any remaining beans for another use.

Cut off the stems and feathery leaves from the fennel bulb; set the leaves aside. Discard the outer layer of the bulb if it is tough, and cut away any discolored areas. Quarter the bulb lengthwise and cut away any tough base portions. In a large bowl, combine the fennel with ice water to cover and let soak for 30 minutes. Drain well and cut into 1/4-inch (6-mm) dice. You will have about 2 cups (10 oz/ 315 g). Finely chop 1/2 cup (3/4 oz/20 g) of the reserved fennel leaves.

Peel the shrimp as directed on page 277, then cut into pieces slightly larger than the beans. In a mortar, using a pestle, coarsely crush the fennel seeds. In a large bowl, whisk together the olive oil, vinegar, fennel seeds, garlic, 1/2 teaspoon salt, and pepper to taste until blended. Add the chopped fennel leaves, beans, shrimp, and onion. Fold gently until all the ingredients are evenly distributed.

Place a lettuce leaf on each plate. Top with the salad, dividing it evenly, and serve at once.

1 1/2 cups (10 1/2 oz/330 g) dried cannellini beans

1 fennel bulb, about 1 lb (500 g)

1 lb (500 g) cooked medium shrimp (prawns)

1/2 teaspoon fennel seeds

1/4 cup (2 fl oz/60 ml) extra-virgin olive oil

3 tablespoons red wine vinegar

1/2 teaspoon minced garlic

Kosher salt and freshly ground pepper

1/2 cup (2 oz/60 g) diced red onion

6 large butter (Boston) lettuce leaves

MAKES 6 SERVINGS

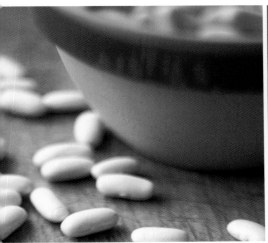

Salmon, Red Potato, and Asparagus Salad

Perfect for a light supper or a special luncheon, the salad can be prepared quickly just before serving, or the salmon, potatoes, and asparagus can be prepared up to 1 day ahead, then combined with the dressing just before serving. This is one of the most heart-healthy salads you will ever eat.

Prepare a CHARCOAL or GAS GRILL for direct-heat grilling over high heat, or preheat the oven to 400°F (200°C). Oil the grill rack. Season the salmon evenly with salt and pepper.

BY GRILL: Using tongs, place the salmon fillet over the hottest part of the fire or directly over the heat elements, and grill, turning once, until opaque throughout when tested with a fork, about 4 minutes per side.

BY OVEN: Place the salmon fillet in a baking pan. Place the pan in the oven and roast the salmon until opaque throughout when tested with a fork, 10–12 minutes.

Transfer the salmon to a plate and let cool to room temperature. Meanwhile, place the potatoes in a large saucepan with water to cover. Bring to a boil over high heat, reduce the heat to medium-low, cover, and simmer until the potatoes are tender when pierced with a knife, about 15 minutes. Drain and, when cool enough to handle, peel and cut into slices $1/2$ inch (12 mm) thick. Set aside on a large plate to cool completely.

If the asparagus spears are thick, use a vegetable peeler to pare away the tough outer skin of each spear to within about 2 inches (5 cm) of the tip. Cut the spears on the diagonal into 1-inch (2.5-cm) lengths. Place in a steamer rack over boiling water, cover the steamer, and cook until tender-crisp, about 3 minutes. Remove the rack from the pan and rinse the asparagus under running cold water until cool. Pat dry and arrange next to the potatoes on the plate.

When the salmon is cool, cut it into 1-inch (2.5-cm) chunks and place the chunks alongside the potatoes and asparagus.

To make the vinaigrette, place the sun-dried tomatoes in a heatproof bowl, pour in boiling water to cover, let stand for 5 minutes, and then drain and cut into $1/4$-inch (6-mm) dice. In a small bowl, whisk together the olive oil, lemon juice, tomatoes, parsley, dill, orange zest, garlic, 2 tablespoons water, $1/2$ teaspoon salt, and a grind of pepper until blended.

In a large bowl, toss the salad greens with 2 tablespoons of the vinaigrette. Spoon the remaining vinaigrette over the asparagus, potatoes, and salmon. Using a large, flat spoon or spatula, gently coat the ingredients evenly with the dressing. Arrange the greens on a large platter. Top with the asparagus, potatoes, and salmon, sprinkle with the green onions, and serve at room temperature.

1 lb (500 g) salmon fillet, skin removed (page 276)

Kosher salt and freshly ground pepper

1 lb (500 g) small, round red-skinned potatoes, each about $1^1/2$ inches (4 cm) in diameter

$3/4$ lb (375 g) asparagus, tough ends removed

For the Vinaigrette

4 dry-packed sun-dried tomato halves

Boiling water

$1/4$ cup (2 fl oz/60 ml) extra-virgin olive oil

3 tablespoons fresh lemon juice

1 tablespoon finely chopped fresh flat-leaf (Italian) parsley

1 tablespoon finely chopped fresh dill

1 teaspoon grated orange zest

$1/2$ teaspoon minced garlic

Kosher salt and freshly ground pepper

10 oz (315 g) mixed baby greens (about 8 cups loosely packed)

3 green (spring) onions, including tender green tops, thinly sliced

MAKES 4 SERVINGS

Chicken, Roasted Red Pepper, and Green Bean Salad

2 large red bell peppers (capsicums), about 1 lb (500 g) total weight

1 teaspoon olive oil

Kosher salt and freshly ground pepper

¹/₂ lb (250 g) green beans such as Blue Lake, trimmed

Ice water

For the Sherry-Thyme Vinaigrette

¹/₄ cup (2 fl oz/60 ml) extra-virgin olive oil

3 tablespoons sherry vinegar

1 tablespoon chopped fresh thyme

¹/₂ teaspoon minced garlic

Kosher salt and freshly ground pepper

1 teaspoon olive oil

³/₄ lb (375 g) skinless, boneless chicken breasts, cut lengthwise into strips 1 inch (2.5 cm) wide

1 small red onion

2 celery stalks

10 oz (315 g) mixed baby salad greens (about 8 cups loosely packed)

MAKES 4 MAIN-COURSE SERVINGS

Sherry vinegar has a sweet floral essence that makes a delicious salad dressing. The dressing is also used to glaze the strips of boneless chicken breasts as they quickly cook in a hot frying pan. High in protein and low in saturated fat, this main-course salad is as satisfying as it is healthful.

Preheat the oven to 400°F (200°C). Cut the bell peppers lengthwise into strips about 1 inch (2.5 cm) wide. Remove the seeds and ribs. Arrange the peppers in a roasting pan. Drizzle with the olive oil and season lightly with the salt and a grind of pepper. Roast, turning once, until the edges are charred and the skins are blistered, about 45 minutes. Remove from the oven and let cool, then peel away any loosened skins. Set aside.

Bring a saucepan three-fourths full of water to a boil, add the green beans, and boil until tender, 5–7 minutes; the timing will depend on their size. Drain and immerse in a bowl of ice water. Drain and set aside.

To make the sherry-thyme vinaigrette, in a small bowl, whisk together the olive oil, vinegar, thyme, garlic, ¹/₂ teaspoon salt, and a grind of pepper until blended.

Brush a large, nonstick frying pan with the olive oil. Place over medium heat and heat until hot enough for a drop of water to sizzle and then immediately evaporate. Add the chicken, a few pieces at a time, and cook for 2 minutes. Turn the chicken pieces, whisk the vinaigrette to combine, and drizzle 2 tablespoons of the vinaigrette on the chicken. Continue to cook for 2 minutes; the chicken should be opaque throughout. Turn the chicken to coat it well with the vinaigrette and remove the pan from the heat. Let the chicken stand in the pan.

Cut the onion in half through the stem end. Place cut side down and thinly slice lengthwise until you have about ¹/₂ cup (1³/₄ oz/50 g). Reserve the remainder for another use. Cut the celery stalks on the diagonal into ¹/₄-inch (6-mm) slices.

In a large bowl, combine the salad greens and 1 tablespoon of the vinaigrette. Toss to coat the greens. Spread the greens in a layer on a large platter. In the same bowl, combine the roasted bell peppers, green beans, cooked chicken and any pan juices, onion, celery, and remaining vinaigrette. Toss to mix. Spoon on top of the greens and serve.

Thai Beef Salad

This salad, popular on Thai-restaurant menus, is easy to prepare at home. The fish sauce, traditionally made by salting small fish, leaving them to ferment in the sun, and then pressing them to extract a clear amber or darker liquid with a pungent aroma, is essential to creating a salad with authentic flavors. This salad contains an abundance of three fresh herbs that are high in beta-carotene and protective phytochemicals. The low-fat vinaigrette and lean meat make this salad recipe a healthful main-course salad.

To make the Thai vinaigrette, in a large bowl, stir together the fish sauce, lime juice, sugar, and chiles until blended. Set aside.

Preheat a BROILER (GRILL), or prepare a CHARCOAL or GAS GRILL for direct-heat grilling over high heat. Oil the grill rack. Sprinkle the flank steak evenly with salt and pepper; rub the seasonings into the meat. Brush lightly on both sides with the canola oil.

BY GRILL: Using tongs, place the flank steak over the hottest part of the fire or directly over the heat elements, and grill, turning once, until seared on the outside and cooked rare to medium-rare in the center, about 4 minutes per side.

BY BROILER: Place the flank steak on a broiler pan and slip it under the broiler about 2 inches (5 cm) from the heat source. Broil (grill), turning once, until the meat is seared on the outside and cooked rare to medium-rare in the center, about 4 minutes per side.

Transfer the steak to a cutting board and let rest for 20 minutes. Cut across the grain and on the diagonal into very thin slices.

Add the slices of meat to the dressing and toss to coat. Add the lettuce, cucumber, onion, bell pepper, mint, cilantro, and Thai basil (if using) and toss to coat. Serve at once.

For the Thai Vinaigrette

3 tablespoons Thai fish sauce

3 tablespoons fresh lime juice

2 teaspoons sugar

1–2 teaspoons minced fresh hot chiles with seeds

1 flank steak, $^3/_4$–1 lb (375–500 g)

Kosher salt and freshly ground pepper

2 teaspoons canola oil

1 large head butter (Boston) or other soft-textured leaf lettuce, torn into bite-sized pieces (about 8 cups/10 oz/ 315 g loosely packed)

1 cup (5 oz/155 g) thinly sliced English (hothouse) cucumber

$^1/_2$ cup ($1^3/_4$ oz/50 g) thinly sliced sweet onion (page 285) or red onion

$^1/_2$ cup ($2^1/_2$ oz/75 g) red bell pepper (capsicum) strips (2 inches/5 cm long by $^1/_4$ inch/6 mm wide)

$^1/_2$ cup ($^3/_4$ oz/20 g) lightly packed torn fresh mint leaves

$^1/_2$ cup ($^3/_4$ oz/20 g) lightly packed torn fresh cilantro (fresh coriander) leaves

$^1/_4$ cup ($^1/_3$ oz/10 g) lightly packed torn fresh Thai basil leaves (optional)

MAKES 4 SERVINGS

Main Dishes

About Main Dishes

Healthful main dishes featuring fish and poultry are particularly high in protein and low in fat, while whole-wheat (wholemeal) pastas and whole grains allow vegetarians and meat eaters alike to boost their intake of valuable complex carbohydrates, fiber, vitamins, and minerals.

The cook in search of a well-balanced repertory of healthful main courses will discover plentiful options in this chapter. Recipes built on fresh vegetables, legumes, grains, pastas, meats, poultry, and seafood are all here, each of them developed with sound nutrition, good taste, and an appealing presentation in mind.

Grains, legumes, and pasta are ideal bases for vegetarian main dishes. Pasta, which is high in complex carbohydrates and low in fat, can be combined with colorful vegetables and a simple sauce to make a quick, tasty main course that will satisfy meat eaters, too. For extra nutrients and fiber, choose whole-wheat or vegetable pasta, which is increasingly available in many shapes and sizes.

COOKING WITH LEAN PROTEIN

Nearly a score of fish and shellfish, poultry, and meat dishes are in these pages, all of them top-notch examples of how to use lean protein in a healthful eating plan. Fish and shellfish provide the bonus of heart-healthy fats. Light-meat chicken and turkey are good for you as well, with a 4-ounce (125-gram) serving of cooked, skinless light meat containing about 200 calories (840 kilojoules), about 5 grams of fat (about 1 gram of which is saturated), and about 90 milligrams of cholesterol.

Although most cuts of beef, pork, and lamb have higher figures in all of these nutrient categories, other attributes make them smart choices. Pork, for example, is a particularly good source of thiamin, niacin, and potassium. Beef and lamb are rich in B vitamins, iron, and zinc. When these meats are paired with vegetables, as in Pork Tenderloin with Fennel and Bell Peppers (page 132), or with legumes, as in Bread Crumb–Crusted Rack of Lamb with White Beans (page 141), they become satisfying components of a nutritious meal. To be sure a dish remains within the guidelines of sensible eating, keep poultry, meat, or seafood at 3 to 4 ounces (90 to 125 g) per serving, not counting the weight of bones.

If you enjoy beef or lamb, you might also like venison, which is a surprisingly good choice for a healthful main dish. Although its color and texture will remind you of beef, venison is lower in fat, especially saturated fat. It is also easier to find than it once was, with many specialty-food stores and good-quality butcher shops either carrying it regularly or willing to special-order it.

The addition of fruits and vegetables to some of these protein-packed main courses increases their healthful profile. Consider the turkey meat loaf (page 128), which boasts a flavorful spinach and onion stuffing and a spicy tomato sauce, making it a good source of fiber and rich in antioxidants, as well as high in protein. Salsas made from vegetables or fruits, such as the mango salsa for the grilled halibut on page 111, increase the nutrient value of a dish and eliminate the need for sauces with butter or cream. See page 34 for tips on creating your own salsas.

Sauces provide flavor and moisture along with nutrients. Reduction sauces are prepared by adding liquid to the pan in which sautéed or roasted fish, poultry, or meats were cooked and then simmering the liquid until it reduces and thickens (page 21). These sauces use the flavor and nutrients of the recipe ingredients and eliminate the need for a fat-rich thickener. Reductions are often delicious just as they are, but if you desire a richer finish, you can swirl in a bit of unsalted butter or heart-healthy olive oil at the end of cooking, as in the red wine sauce on page 137. The amount of added fat is so small that it contributes body and sheen to the sauce without sabotaging the healthfulness of the dish.

CLASSICS IN DISGUISE

Many recipes in this chapter will be familiar, but a closer look reveals that they are classics modified to fit within healthful guidelines. Spinach and Roasted Red Pepper Lasagna (page 100) is layered with vegetables instead of meat and substitutes crumbled tofu for some of usual ricotta cheese, providing the benefits of soy and making this dish higher in antioxidants and lower in fat than the classic.

Oven-Crisped Chicken (page 119) calls for coating lean breast strips with flaky Japanese bread crumbs (panko), then lightly spraying them with a heart-healthy oil to make a wholesome alternative to battered and fried chicken legs. Eggplant Cannelloni (page 125) uses ground (minced) turkey instead of beef in the filling; eggplant (aubergine) slices instead of pasta sheets for wrapping; and a low-fat version of béchamel, or white sauce.

Finally, select companion dishes that will complement your main course and balance your nutrient intake. If your main dish is high in protein, consider a fiber-rich grain side dish, vitamin-packed vegetable accompaniment, or antioxidant-rich salad. Look to other chapters in this book for inspiration.

Roasted Vegetables with Warm Lemon Dressing

The giant beans Greeks call *gigantes* are ideal for this dish, but dried limas of any size, or even cannellini beans, are delicious, too. The low-fat dressing uses fat-free broth and a minimum of olive oil, and is thickened with cornstarch. For the best result, pour the warm dressing over the vegetables and beans while they are still warm.

If using dried beans, soak and drain as directed on page 278. Place the soaked, drained beans in a saucepan and add water to cover generously. Bring to a boil over high heat, reduce the heat to low, cover partially, and simmer gently until tender, 1–1 1/2 hours. Drain well and set aside. If using canned beans, drain well, rinse under running cold water, drain well again, and set aside.

Position racks in the upper and lower third of the oven; preheat to 450°F (230°C).

Halve the zucchini lengthwise and then cut crosswise into 1-inch (2.5-cm) pieces. Trim the fennel and cut lengthwise into 1/2-inch (12-mm) wedges. Cut each bell pepper lengthwise into quarters and remove the seeds and ribs. Brush the zucchini, fennel, bell pepper, green beans, and tomatoes evenly with 3 teaspoons of the olive oil. Brush 2 nonstick baking sheets with 2 teaspoons of the oil, or line the sheets with aluminum foil and brush with the oil. Keeping each type of vegetable together, place the zucchini, fennel, green beans, tomatoes, and bell peppers, the last two skin side down, on the baking sheets. Sprinkle with 1/4 teaspoon salt, or more to taste, and season generously with pepper.

Roast the vegetables until they are tender when pierced with a knife but still hold their shape, about 20 minutes. Remove from the oven and transfer the vegetables to a platter. Using tongs, lift the skins off the tomatoes and discard.

In a small saucepan, whisk together the broth, lemon juice, and cornstarch until blended. Whisk in the oregano, the garlic (if using), the remaining 1 teaspoon oil, 1/2 teaspoon salt, and pepper to taste. Place over medium heat and bring to a boil, stirring constantly. When the dressing has thickened and turned clear, after about 3 minutes, remove from the heat.

Arrange one-fourth of the lima beans on each individual plate, forming a bed. Top each bed of beans with one-fourth of each of the roasted vegetables. Pour one-fourth of the warm dressing over each serving and top with one-fourth of the crumbled feta, if using. Serve at once.

2 cups (14 oz/440 g) dried giant lima beans or cannellini beans or 2 cans (15 oz/470 g each) cannellini beans

1 zucchini (courgette)

1/2 fennel bulb

1 green bell pepper (capsicum)

1 red bell pepper (capsicum)

1/4 lb (125 g) green beans, trimmed

4 plum (Roma) tomatoes, halved lengthwise

6 teaspoons extra-virgin olive oil

Kosher salt and freshly ground pepper

1/4 cup (2 fl oz/60 ml) reduced-sodium, fat-free chicken or vegetable broth

3 tablespoons fresh lemon juice

1 teaspoon cornstarch (cornflour)

1 teaspoon dried oregano

1 small clove garlic, minced (optional)

1/4 cup (1 oz/30 g) reduced-fat feta cheese, crumbled (optional)

MAKES 4 SERVINGS

Spinach and Roasted Red Pepper Lasagna

4 lb (2 kg) fresh spinach or 2 lb (1 kg) frozen chopped spinach

1 lb (500 g) soft tofu

2 cups (1 lb/500 g) part-skim ricotta cheese

2 large egg whites

$1/2$ cup (2 oz/60 g) grated Parmigiano-Reggiano cheese

1 cup (4 oz/120 g) shredded part-skim mozzarella cheese

Kosher salt and freshly ground pepper

8 cups (64 fl oz/2 l) Spicy Tomato Sauce (page 271)

9 dried lasagna noodles

3 large red bell peppers (capsicums), roasted and seeded (page 277)

2 large cloves garlic, minced

MAKES 8–10 SERVINGS

If using fresh spinach, rinse it carefully in 2 or 3 changes of water, discarding the tough stems and any damaged leaves. Drain briefly in a colander and then, working in batches if necessary, transfer to a large saucepan with only the water that clings to the leaves. Place over medium-high heat, cover, and cook, turning the leaves a couple of times, until wilted and still slightly firm to the bite, 5–6 minutes. Drain well and chop finely. Squeeze the spinach with your hands to remove most of the moisture. If using frozen spinach, cook according to the package directions, let cool, and squeeze out.

Cut the tofu into about 16 pieces. Hold each piece in your hand over the sink or a bowl and gently squeeze to remove some of the water. Crumble the tofu into a large bowl; it should resemble cottage cheese. Add the ricotta and egg whites and stir until well combined. Stir in the Parmigiano-Reggiano and $1/2$ cup (2 oz/60 g) of the mozzarella cheese. Stir in 1 teaspoon salt and $1/4$ teaspoon pepper.

Preheat the oven to 350°F (180°C).

To assemble the lasagna, cover the bottom of a 9-by-13-by-3-inch (23-by-33-by-7.5 cm) baking dish with 4 cups (32 fl oz/1 l) of the tomato sauce. Arrange 3 of the noodles on top of the sauce. Cover the noodles with half of the bell peppers, cutting them as needed to lay flat. There will be spaces. Cover the peppers with half of the spinach, using your fingers to pull any clumps apart. Sprinkle half of the garlic evenly over the spinach. Using a large spoon, dollop half of the cheese mixture on top of the spinach. With the back of the spoon, gently spread the cheese as much as possible without pulling up the spinach. There will be some spaces. Top with another layer of the pasta, and then the remaining peppers, spinach, garlic, and cheese mixture. Cover with the remaining 3 noodles. Spread the remaining 4 cups tomato sauce over the top. Cover the baking dish with aluminum foil.

Bake until the pasta is almost soft when tested with a knife, about $1 1/4$ hours. Uncover the lasagna. Sprinkle the remaining $1/2$ cup mozzarella evenly over the top. Replace the foil. Continue to bake until the pasta is soft and the cheese on top of the lasagna is melted, about 15 minutes longer. Uncover and let the lasagna rest for 20 minutes before cutting into 8–10 rectangles and serving.

Homemade lasagna always draws raves, particularly this layering of garlic-infused spinach, sweet roasted bell peppers, and creamy cheeses. While vegetarians feast, meat eaters will barely notice this dish is meatless. No one will realize that tofu has been added, an easy way of reducing calories, fat, and cholesterol. This recipe lets you skip boiling the lasagna noodles, while letting you use the real thing, rather than the thin, precooked kind. The secret is using lots of moist sauce that cooks the noodles while the lasagna bakes. Serve White Wine–Poached Pears (page 244) for dessert.

Wild Mushroom Risotto

It takes only a small amount of dried porcini to make this intensely flavored risotto. Carnaroli rice, a short-grain variety grown in Italy, has the perfect texture for this dish, although Italian Arborio rice is an excellent second choice. Traditionally made with chicken broth, this risotto is so rich that vegetarians can use water instead. (Water is preferable to vegetable broth because most of the prepared versions have flavors that do not combine well with wild mushrooms.) This creamy risotto also makes a good first course served in smaller portions for six diners.

Place the mushrooms in a bowl with 1$\frac{1}{2}$ cups (12 fl oz/375 ml) lukewarm water and let soak until the mushrooms are soft, 20–30 minutes. Lift out the mushrooms, reserving the soaking liquid. Squeeze the mushrooms dry and chop them. Strain the soaking liquid through a fine-mesh sieve lined with cheesecloth (muslin). Reserve $\frac{1}{2}$ cup (4 fl oz/125 ml) for the risotto. Save the remaining liquid for another use.

In a saucepan over medium heat, warm the broth until bubbles appear around the edges of the pan. Adjust the heat to maintain a gentle simmer.

In a small Dutch oven or deep, heavy saucepan over medium-high heat, warm 1 tablespoon of the olive oil. Add the shallot and sauté until translucent, about 2 minutes. Add the remaining 1 tablespoon oil and stir in the rice. Reduce the heat to medium, and cook, stirring, until the rice is evenly coated with the oil and the grains turn translucent at the edges, about 1 minute. Pour in the wine and stir until it is absorbed, 2–3 minutes.

Add $\frac{1}{2}$ cup (4 fl oz/125 ml) of the hot broth and cook, stirring occasionally, until most of the liquid has been absorbed and the rice is just moist, about 3 minutes. Continue adding broth, $\frac{1}{2}$ cup at a time, always waiting until the rice is just moist before adding more. After 2 cups (16 fl oz/500 ml) broth have been used, add the $\frac{1}{2}$ cup mushroom soaking liquid and the chopped mushrooms. When the liquid is almost fully absorbed, resume adding the broth.

The risotto is ready when it is creamy and slightly soupy and the kernels are tender but still slightly firm at the center, about 35 minutes after the first addition of broth. Remove from the heat.

Stir in the cheese and $\frac{1}{4}$ teaspoon salt, or more to taste, and season with pepper. Divide evenly among warmed wide, shallow bowls or among warmed plates and serve at once.

$\frac{2}{3}$ cup ($\frac{2}{3}$ oz/20 g) dried porcino mushrooms

4 cups (32 fl oz/1l) reduced-sodium, fat-free chicken broth or water

2 tablespoons olive oil

2 tablespoons finely chopped shallot

1$\frac{1}{2}$ cups (10$\frac{1}{2}$ oz/330 g) Carnaroli or Arborio rice

$\frac{1}{2}$ cup (4 fl oz/125 ml) dry white wine such as Pinot Grigio

$\frac{1}{4}$ cup (1 oz/30 g) grated Parmigiano-Reggiano cheese

Kosher salt and freshly ground pepper

MAKES 4 SERVINGS

Whole-Wheat Pasta with Broccoli Rabe

1 large bunch broccoli rabe, about 1¹/₂ lb (750 g)

Kosher salt

³/₄ lb (375 g) *farro* linguine (see note)

2 tablespoons extra-virgin olive oil

1 cup (4 oz/125 g) chopped red onion

2 cups (16 fl oz/500 ml) reduced-sodium, fat-free chicken broth or water

3 roasted garlic cloves (page 271)

Freshly ground pepper

MAKES 4 SERVINGS

Trim off and discard the tough stem ends from the broccoli rabe. Cut off the florets and set them aside. Coarsely chop the leaves and tender stems and set aside.

Bring a large pot three-fourths full of water to a boil. Add 2 tablespoons salt and the pasta and cook according to the package directions until al dente.

While the water is heating, in a large frying pan over medium-high heat, warm the olive oil. Add the onion and sauté until soft, about 4 minutes. Stir in half of the greens, including the florets, coating them with the oil. Cook until the greens collapse, 2–3 minutes. Stir in the remaining greens and cook, stirring occasionally, until the greens start to soften, about 5 minutes. Pour in the broth and mix in the garlic, breaking it up with the back of the spoon until it dissolves. Reduce the heat to medium and simmer until the broccoli rabe is tender, 10–12 minutes. Stir in ¹/₄ teaspoon salt, or more to taste, and season with pepper.

When the pasta is ready, drain, reserving about ¹/₂ cup (4 fl oz/125 ml) of the cooking water. Place the pasta in a serving bowl and top with the greens. If the greens are dry, add some of the reserved cooking water. Serve at once.

Pasta made from *farro*, an ancient variety of wheat, has a nutty flavor that goes perfectly with the broccoli rabe in this hearty dish. You can also use whole-wheat (wholemeal) linguine. If you prefer more pungent greens, add ¹/₈ teaspoon red pepper flakes with the garlic. This pasta dish is very heart-healthy and contains several ingredients that reduce the risk of cancer.

Pasta with Tomatoes, Arugula, and Goat Cheese

Arugula wilted by the heat of the pasta and tomatoes sautéed just until their skins pop make this pasta colorful and fresh tasting. The goat cheese melts into the pasta, creating a creamy sauce. Use Montrachet or another fresh goat cheese sold in a log, or a light goat cheese, such as Chavrié, if you want to cut a few grams of fat. Any pasta shape that traps and holds the sauce and greens is good, including curled cavatappi, spiral fusilli, or tubular, hollow ziti.

Bring a large pot three-fourths full of water to a boil. Add 2 tablespoons salt and the pasta and cook according to package directions until al dente. Drain the pasta, reserving about 1/4 cup (2 fl oz/60 ml) of the cooking water, and place the pasta in a warmed serving bowl. Mix in the arugula and keep warm.

Just before the pasta is ready, in a large frying pan over medium-high heat, warm the olive oil. Add the tomatoes and, holding the pan handle, roll the tomatoes around by jerking the pan toward you, then pushing it away. While the tomatoes cook, sprinkle on the garlic. Keep the tomatoes moving until their skins crack, 1–3 minutes. Remove from the heat and season with 1/2 teaspoon salt. Spoon the tomatoes over the pasta.

Dollop the goat cheese, 1 tablespoon at a time, on top of the tomatoes. Using a large fork and spoon, toss to combine, adding 1 or 2 tablespoons, or more, of the cooking water if the pasta seems dry. Season with pepper and serve.

Kosher salt

3/4 lb (375 g) cavatappi, fusilli, or ziti

2 cups (2 oz/60 g) loosely packed arugula (rocket) leaves (about 1/2 bunch)

1 tablespoon extra-virgin olive oil

2 cups (12 oz/375 g) grape or cherry tomatoes, stems removed

1 clove garlic, minced

1/4 cup (1 oz/30 g) crumbled fresh goat cheese (see note)

Freshly ground pepper

MAKES 4 SERVINGS

Spicy Scallops with Vegetable-Rice Pilaf

Kosher salt

1 cup (7 oz/220 g) long-grain white rice

3/4 cup (4 oz/125 g) shelled fresh or frozen English peas

1 slice preservative-free bacon

1/4 cup (1 1/2 oz/45 g) finely chopped red onion

1/4 cup (3/4 oz/20 g) finely chopped green (spring) onion, white part only

For the Spice Mixture

1 teaspoon sweet paprika

1/2 teaspoon garlic powder

1/2 teaspoon onion powder

1/2 teaspoon ground or finely crushed dried thyme

1/4 teaspoon ground cayenne pepper

1/4 teaspoon freshly ground white pepper

Kosher salt and freshly ground black pepper

3/4 lb (375 g) sea scallops

2 teaspoons canola oil

Lemon wedges (optional)

MAKES 4 SERVINGS

In a heavy saucepan, bring 2 cups (16 fl oz/500 ml) water and 1/2 teaspoon salt to a boil. Slowly add the rice, reduce the heat to low, cover, and cook for 20 minutes. Uncover and check to see if the rice is tender and all the water has been absorbed. If not, re-cover and continue to cook for a few minutes longer.

If using fresh peas, while the rice is cooking, bring a small saucepan three-fourths full of water to a boil. Add the peas and boil until tender, about 5 minutes. Drain and set aside. If using frozen peas, set them aside.

Just before the rice is ready, in a frying pan over medium-high heat, fry the bacon until it starts to brown at the edges, 3–4 minutes. Transfer to a paper towel to drain, then chop into 1/4-inch (6-mm) pieces. Return the pan to medium-high heat, add the red onion and green onion to the bacon fat remaining in the pan, and sauté until translucent, 3–4 minutes, reducing the heat as needed. Stir in the cooked fresh or frozen peas. Transfer the rice to a large bowl. Add the vegetables and bacon and, using a fork, combine them, taking care not to mash the rice. Cover the bowl with plastic wrap to keep the rice warm and set aside.

To make the spice mixture, in a small bowl, stir together the paprika, garlic and onion powders, thyme, cayenne, white pepper, 1/2 teaspoon salt, and 1/4 teaspoon black pepper. Measure out 1 1/2 teaspoons to use on the scallops. Store the remaining spice mixture in a tightly covered container at room temperature for up to 4 weeks.

Remove the small muscle from the side of each scallop, if necessary. Halve the scallops horizontally. Sprinkle the 1 1/2 teaspoons spice mixture over the scallop pieces, turning to coat evenly on both sides.

In a large, nonstick frying pan over medium-high heat, warm the canola oil. Add the scallops in a single layer. Cook until seared and slightly blackened around the edges, 2–3 minutes. Using tongs, turn the scallops and sear on the other side, about 2 minutes.

Mound one-fourth of the rice in the center of each warmed individual plate. Arrange one-fourth of the scallops around each mound of rice. Accompany with lemon wedges, if desired, and serve.

The spice and smoke usually associated with Cajun dishes and barbecue give this unexpected combination of sea scallops and long-grain rice a big flavor. There are a number of Cajun spice mixtures on the market, but making your own lets you control its heat. As a first course, serve Roasted Asparagus with Toasted Bread Crumbs (page 176) or Edamame and Orange Salad (page 82).

Stir-Fried Shrimp with Snow Peas and Mushrooms

2 teaspoons cornstarch (cornflour)

1 teaspoon dry sherry

4 teaspoons peanut oil

1 lb (500 g) shrimp (prawns), peeled and deveined (page 277)

1 tablespoon peeled and minced fresh ginger

1 small clove garlic, minced

16 snow peas (mangetouts), trimmed and strings removed

¹/₂ lb (250 g) fresh shiitake mushrooms, brushed clean, stems removed, and caps cut into 1-inch (2.5-cm) pieces

¹/₄ cup (2 fl oz/60 ml) reduced-sodium, fat-free chicken broth

¹/₄ teaspoon Asian sesame oil

Kosher salt and freshly ground pepper

MAKES 4 SERVINGS

In a small bowl, stir together the cornstarch, dry sherry, and 2 teaspoons water. Set aside.

Preheat a wok or deep, heavy frying pan over high heat. Add 2 teaspoons of the peanut oil and carefully tilt and rotate the pan to distribute the oil. When the oil is hot, add the shrimp and stir-fry until they are bright pink but not yet cooked through, about 3 minutes. Do not overcook them. Transfer to a plate.

Return the pan to high heat. Drizzle in the remaining 2 teaspoons peanut oil, tilting the pan to coat the bottom and sides with the oil. Add the ginger and garlic and stir-fry until fragrant, about 30 seconds. Add the snow peas and mushrooms and return the shrimp to the pan. Stir-fry until the snow peas are bright green, 30–60 seconds. Pour in the broth and cook until the shrimp are opaque throughout, 2–3 minutes longer.

Briefly stir the cornstarch mixture to recombine, then pour it into the pan. Stir-fry until the sauce thickens and turns clear, about 2 minutes. Add the sesame oil and ¹/₄ teaspoon salt, or more to taste, and season with pepper. Transfer to a warmed serving dish and serve at once.

Fresh shiitake mushrooms bring a rich taste to this hearty stir-fry. They also have better texture than the canned straw mushrooms usually found in similar dishes. Peanut oil is typically used in Chinese cooking. If possible, purchase one of the brands sold in Asian markets, which have a particularly nutty aroma. Without the shrimp, this stir-fry makes a good vegetarian dish. Serve over brown rice and accompany with Stir-Fried Baby Greens with Ginger and Garlic (page 188).

Grilled Halibut with Mango Salsa

Grilled fish with boldly flavored salsa is an ideal meal—delicious, easy to make, and healthful. You can enjoy this colorful salsa whenever mangoes are in the market, as it is good even when the fruit is underripe. Halibut steaks are large, so dividing two of them serves four people comfortably. Mangoes are a nutritional powerhouse. Their yellow-orange flesh is rich in beta-carotene and vitamin C, plus some fiber and vitamin E. Accompany the halibut with steamed baby bok choy.

To make the mango salsa, stand the mango on one of its narrow sides, with the stem end facing you. Using a sharp knife, and positioning it about 1 inch (2.5 cm) from the stem, cut down the length of the fruit, just brushing the large, length-wise pit (page 279). Repeat the cut on the other side of the pit. Remove the peel from each half, then finely chop the flesh. Measure out 1 1/2 cups (9 oz/280 g). Reserve the remainder for another use.

To peel the pineapple, stand it on its base and, using a large, sharp knife, cut down the length of it, cutting deeply enough to remove all the prickly "eyes." Halve it lengthwise and cut out and discard the fibrous core from each piece. Finely chop 3/4 cup (4 1/2 oz/140 g). Reserve the remainder for another use.

In a bowl, combine the mango, pineapple, onion, serrano, and orange and lime juices. Mix in the cilantro and 1/4 teaspoon salt, or more to taste. Season with pepper. Set aside for 20 minutes to allow the flavors to meld.

Prepare a CHARCOAL or GAS GRILL for direct-heat grilling over high heat. Oil the grill rack. Season the fish on both sides with salt and pepper.

BY CHARCOAL GRILL: Using tongs, place the fish over the hottest part of the fire and grill, turning once, until the fish is opaque in the center at its thickest part, 5–7 minutes per side.

BY GAS GRILL: Using tongs, place the fish directly over the heat elements and grill, turning once, until the fish is opaque in the center at its thickest part, 5–7 minutes per side.

Remove the skin from the fish, divide each steak in half, and transfer to warmed individual plates. Spoon one-fourth of the salsa on each piece of fish and serve.

For the Mango Salsa

1 mango

1/2 small pineapple, about 1 lb (500 g)

3 tablespoons finely chopped red onion

1 serrano chile, seeded and minced

1/4 cup (2 fl oz/60 ml) fresh orange juice

1 tablespoon fresh lime juice

1/4 cup (1/3 oz/10 g) chopped fresh cilantro (fresh coriander) or mint

Kosher salt and freshly ground pepper

2 halibut steaks, each 1 inch (2.5 cm) thick, about 1 lb (500 g) total weight

Kosher salt and freshly ground pepper

MAKES 4 SERVINGS

Salmon with Ginger and Lime

2 tablespoons unsalted butter

3 limes

1 salmon fillet, 1¼ lb (625 g)

1 teaspoon canola oil, if needed

Kosher salt and freshly ground pepper

4 teaspoons peeled and minced fresh ginger

1 large shallot, finely minced

¼ cup (2 fl oz/60 ml) fresh lime juice

2 tablespoons sake

1 tablespoon Worcestershire sauce

MAKES 4 SERVINGS

Cut the butter into 8 equal pieces and return to the refrigerator until firm.

Using a vegetable peeler or very sharp knife, peel 4 strips of zest, each 2 inches (5 cm) long by ½ inch (12 mm) wide, from 1 lime. Cut the zest lengthwise into the narrowest possible julienne. Set aside. Squeeze the juice from the lime and set it aside. Cut the second lime into 8 thin slices. Cut the third lime lengthwise into 8 wedges.

Preheat the oven to 400°F (200°C).

Remove the skin from the salmon fillet (page 276) and cut the fish into 4 equal pieces. Measure the fish pieces at their thickest point. Cut 4 large rectangles of parchment (baking) paper. If the paper lacks a nonstick coating, lightly brush the top side of each rectangle with about ¼ teaspoon canola oil.

Arrange the rectangles on a work surface and lay a piece of salmon in the center of each rectangle. Sprinkle each piece of fish with ½ teaspoon salt and pepper to taste, then with 1 teaspoon of the ginger. Divide the julienned lime zest among the fish pieces. Place 2 lime slices on top of each fish piece.

Wrap each piece of fish in the paper by bringing together the long edges and folding them over to seal well, then folding in the sides and sealing them. Using a wide spatula, place the packets on a baking sheet.

Bake the fish until it is barely translucent at the thickest part; plan on slightly less than 10 minutes for each inch (2.5 cm) of thickness. Remove the baking sheet from the oven and let rest for a few minutes. (The fish will continue to cook out of the oven until it is opaque.)

While the fish cooks, in a small saucepan over medium-high heat, combine the shallot, lime juice, sake, and Worcestershire sauce. Bring to a boil and boil until the liquid is reduced by one-third, about 5 minutes. Remove from the heat. Whisk in the butter 1 piece at a time, waiting until each piece is fully absorbed into the sauce before adding the next piece. Pour the sauce into a warmed small pitcher.

As soon as the sauce is done, place a packet of the fish on each individual plate and garnish with 2 lime wedges. Diners slit open the packets, remove the cooked lime slices, and spoon some of the sauce over the fish.

Opening this salmon steamed *en papillotte* (page 26) at the table releases a cloud of wonderful aromas. The tangy sauce, a blending of sake, lime juice, and a touch of butter, complements the moist, rich fish. Serve with steamed leafy greens and steamed rice. To finish the meal, offer Chocolate Sorbet (page 240) garnished with raspberries.

Salmon with Green Lentil Ragout

Le Puy lentils, the tiny, round, dark green legumes once imported from France and now also grown in the United States, are wonderful with salmon. A full-flavored chicken stock takes the place of wine as the base that ties together the ingredients in this refined, yet easy, dish. The lentils can be made ahead and reheated. They are also good served at room temperature as a salad with other foods. Next to soybeans, lentils have the highest protein count of all vegetables.

Pick over the lentils, discarding any misshapen lentils or grit. Rinse the lentils, place them in a saucepan, and add 3 cups (24 fl oz/750 ml) water. Bring to a boil over medium-high heat, reduce the heat to medium-low, cover, and cook until the lentils are tender but not soft, 45–50 minutes. Drain and set aside.

In a saucepan over high heat, bring the stock to a boil. Continue to boil until it is reduced to 1 1/2 cups (12 fl oz/375 ml). If you are using another homemade stock, reduce it to 1 cup (8 fl oz/250 ml) to be sure it is sufficiently rich tasting. If you are using canned broth, reduce it to 1 1/3 cups (11 fl oz/345 ml). Remove from the heat.

In a nonstick frying pan over medium-high heat, warm 1/2 cup (4 fl oz/125 ml) of the concentrated stock until it bubbles, 1–2 minutes. Mix in the shallot, carrot, and potato and cook, stirring occasionally, until the liquid has almost evaporated, 3–4 minutes. Pour in the remaining stock and add the cooked lentils. Simmer over medium heat until the potato is tender, but not soft, 8–10 minutes. Stir in 1/2 teaspoon salt and pepper to taste. Remove from the heat; keep hot.

In another frying pan over medium-high heat, warm the canola oil. Season the salmon pieces on both sides with salt and a few grinds of pepper. Place them in the pan and cook until crisp and well browned on the bottom, about 8 minutes. Using a wide spatula, turn the fish and cook until slightly translucent in the very center at the thickest part, 4–5 minutes. Remove from the heat. (The fish will continue to cook off the heat until it is opaque.)

Divide the lentil mixture, with some of the liquid in the pan, among warmed wide, shallow bowls or dinner plates with a deep center. Place a piece of the salmon on top of each mound of lentils. Serve at once.

1 cup (7 oz/220 g) French lentils (see note)

2 cups (16 fl oz/500 ml) Rich Chicken Stock (page 270) or reduced-sodium, fat-free chicken broth

1/4 cup (1 1/2 oz/45 g) finely chopped shallot

1 small carrot, peeled and finely chopped

1 boiling potato, peeled and cut into scant 1/2-inch (12-mm) cubes

Kosher salt and freshly ground pepper

1 teaspoon canola oil

1 salmon fillet, 1–1 1/4 lb (500–625 g), skin removed and cut into 4 equal pieces (page 276)

MAKES 4 SERVINGS

Sicilian-Style Swordfish and Spaghetti

VARIATION
Sicilian-Style Tuna
and Spaghetti
Substitute tuna fillet, skin removed
and cut into 1/2-inch (12-mm)
cubes, for the swordfish.

Capers and olives give this hearty pasta dish a robust, southern Italian flavor. Salt-packed capers, most of which come from Sicily, are ideal for this dish, and they can now be found at many fine food stores and some supermarkets. If possible, use the imported bottled tomato sauce that Italians call *passato di pomodoro*. Any mild-flavored black or green olive will work here, although the small Niçoise olives imported from France are the best type to use. If you must restrict your sodium intake, this dish is not a good choice. Capers and olives, both high in sodium, are essential for flavor.

Bring a large pot three-fourths full of water to a boil. While the water is heating, in a frying pan over medium-high heat, warm the olive oil. Add the onion and sauté until soft, about 4 minutes. Stir in the garlic and sauté until it is fragrant, about 30 seconds.

Add the swordfish to the pan and, using tongs, turn the pieces until they lose their raw color and are seared on all sides, 4–5 minutes. Pour in the tomato sauce and mix in the oregano and capers. Reduce the heat to medium and simmer until the fish is cooked through, 10–12 minutes. Stir in the olives and heat through.

While the sauce is cooking, add 2 tablespoons salt and the pasta to the boiling water and cook according to package directions until al dente. Drain the pasta.

Season the sauce with 1/4 teaspoon salt and pepper to taste. Divide the pasta among warmed pasta bowls. Top each serving with one-fourth of the swordfish and sauce, sprinkle with 1 tablespoon of the parsley, and serve at once.

1 tablespoon extra-virgin olive oil

1 small red onion, finely chopped

1 small clove garlic, minced

1 lb (500 g) swordfish fillet, skin removed and cut into 3/4-inch (2-cm) cubes

2 cups (16 fl oz/500 ml) tomato sauce (see note)

2 tablespoons chopped fresh oregano or 1 1/2 teaspoons dried oregano

1 tablespoon capers, preferably salt packed (see note), rinsed and drained

1/4 cup (1 1/2 oz/45 g) European-style mild black or green olives (see note), pitted

Kosher salt

3/4 lb (375 g) spaghetti

Freshly ground pepper

4 tablespoons (1/3 oz/10 g) chopped fresh flat-leaf (Italian) parsley

MAKES 4 SERVINGS

Spice-Crusted Tuna

4 teaspoons fennel seeds

1 teaspoon cumin seeds

$1/4$ teaspoon peppercorns

4 sushi-grade ahi tuna steaks, each 5 oz (155 g) and 1 inch (2.5 cm) thick

2 teaspoons canola oil

MAKES 4 SERVINGS

In a small, dry frying pan over medium heat, toast the fennel and cumin seeds, stirring constantly to prevent burning, until the fennel turns yellow-beige, about 2 minutes. Transfer the seeds to a plate and let cool to room temperature.

In a mortar, combine the fennel seeds, cumin, and peppercorns and crush with the pestle. Spread the spice mixture on a plate. One at a time, coat the tuna steaks on both sides with the mixture, pressing with your fingers to help the spices adhere to the fish.

In a cast-iron or other heavy frying pan over medium-high heat, warm the canola oil until it is hot. Add the tuna and cook until lightly browned on the bottom, 4–5 minutes. Turn and cook until browned on the second side, 4–6 minutes. Remove from the heat, transfer the fish to a plate, and let rest for 10 minutes.

Transfer the fish to warmed individual plates and serve at once.

Toasted and ground cumin and fennel, with their smoky flavors, complement tuna steaks. This dish calls for impeccably fresh, sushi-grade tuna. Serve the steaks on a bed of arugula (rocket) or accompanied with grilled vegetables. The seared fish is raw in the center; for advice about consuming raw seafood, see page 9.

Oven-Crisped Chicken

Panko, coarse Japanese bread crumbs, give foods an extra-crunchy coating. They are bland, so sesame seeds and other seasonings provide a nice flavor boost here. Using aluminum foil placed directly on the oven rack, instead of a pan, helps the chicken brown better and cook through at the same time. This is one dish where the fine mist of cooking spray lets you make a great low-fat version of a fried favorite. Serve with Stir-Fried Spinach with Garlic and Lemon Zest (page 187).

Remove the center rack from the oven and cover it with a sheet of aluminum foil, leaving 1 inch (2.5 cm) uncovered on all sides so that heat can freely circulate once the rack is returned to the oven. Brush the foil lightly with the canola oil and set the prepared rack aside. Preheat the oven to 450°F (230°C).

In a wide, shallow dish, stir together the *panko,* sesame seeds, paprika, onion powder, $^1/_2$ teaspoon salt, and $^1/_8$ teaspoon pepper. In another dish, beat the egg white until foamy. Roll 1 piece of the chicken in the egg white; shake it lightly to release the excess. Then roll it in the seasoned *panko,* coating evenly and pressing with your fingers to help the mixture adhere. Place the chicken on a plate and repeat until all the chicken is coated.

One by one, coat the chicken pieces on all sides with cooking spray and place them in a single layer on the prepared oven rack. Slide the rack into the center of the oven. Bake the chicken pieces until the coating on the bottom is light golden brown, about 10 minutes. Using tongs, turn the chicken pieces and continue to bake until the pieces are golden brown all over and the meat is opaque in the center, 10–12 minutes longer. Transfer the chicken pieces to a serving plate and let rest for 10–15 minutes. The coating becomes crisper as it sits. Serve warm.

1 teaspoon canola oil

1 cup (1$^1/_4$ oz/40 g) *panko*

2 teaspoons sesame seeds

$^1/_2$ teaspoon sweet paprika

$^1/_4$ teaspoon onion powder

Kosher salt and freshly ground white or black pepper

1 large egg white

1–1$^1/_4$ lb (500–625 g) skinless, boneless chicken breasts, cut with the grain into strips $^3/_4$ inch (2 cm) wide

Canola-oil cooking spray

MAKES 4 SERVINGS

Chicken Breasts Stuffed with Prosciutto and Jarlsberg Cheese

4 skinless, boneless chicken breast halves, about 1 lb (500 g) total weight

2 slices reduced-fat Jarlsberg cheese, about 2 oz (60 g) total weight

4 slices prosciutto, about 1 oz (30 g) total weight, trimmed of all visible fat

$1/4$ cup ($1^1/2$ oz/45 g) all-purpose (plain) flour

$3/4$ cup (3 oz/90 g) Italian-seasoned fine dried bread crumbs

1 large egg white

1 tablespoon 2-percent-fat milk

3 teaspoons extra-virgin olive oil

MAKES 4 SERVINGS

Cut each chicken breast in half crosswise so you have a total of 8 pieces. Working with 1 piece of chicken at a time, place it between 2 sheets of waxed paper or plastic wrap and, using a meat pounder, pound to flatten to an even thickness of $1/2$ inch (12 mm).

Preheat the oven to 350°F (180°C).

Cut each slice of cheese in half, so you have a total of 4 pieces. Place 1 piece of cheese on 1 piece of chicken. Trim the cheese to fit. Place 1 prosciutto slice on top of the cheese, folding it so it fits neatly. Top with another piece of chicken. Repeat to make 4 "stuffed breasts" in all.

Place the flour on a wide, shallow plate and the bread crumbs on another plate. In a wide, shallow bowl, beat the egg white with the milk until blended.

Dredge a stuffed breast in the flour, coating it evenly and lightly shaking off the excess. Turn it in the egg white mixture and then dredge it in the bread crumbs, coating it evenly and using your fingers to help it adhere. Set the breaded stuffed breast on a plate. Repeat with the remaining 3 stuffed breasts.

In an ovenproof, nonstick frying pan over medium-high heat, warm $1^1/2$ teaspoons of the olive oil. Add the stuffed breasts and cook until browned on the bottom, 3–4 minutes. Drizzle the remaining oil in the pan around the chicken, carefully turn the breasts, and brown on the second side, 3–4 minutes longer. Place the pan in the oven, or transfer the chicken to a baking sheet and place in the oven, and bake the chicken until it is opaque throughout when cut into with a knife, about 15 minutes.

Remove from the oven and transfer the chicken to warmed individual plates. Serve at once.

Sometimes called chicken Cordon Bleu, these thinly pounded, stuffed breasts show how favorite, familiar dishes can have a place in a healthful diet. This recipe uses reduced-fat cheese, and egg whites in place of whole eggs. Broccoli or green peas are good accompaniments, as is Belgian Endive, Apple, and Walnut Salad (page 74).

Coq au Vin

16 pearl onions, about
¹/₂ lb (250 g)

¹/₂ lemon

6 baby artichokes

2 slices preservative-free
bacon

4 skinless chicken breast
halves, about 5 oz (155 g)
each

1 large shallot, finely chopped

¹/₂ lb (250 g) cremini mushrooms, brushed clean, stems
removed, and caps cut into
slices ¹/₂ inch (12 mm) thick

1 tablespoon all-purpose
(plain) flour

1¹/₂ cups (12 fl oz/375 ml)
fruity dry white wine such as
Pinot Gris or White Burgundy

1¹/₂ cups (12 fl oz/375 ml)
reduced-sodium, fat-free
chicken broth

Kosher salt and freshly
ground pepper

Chopped fresh flat-leaf
(Italian) parsley

MAKES 4 SERVINGS

Bring a saucepan three-fourths full of water to a boil. Add the onions, return to a boil, and boil for about 2 minutes. Drain, plunge into cold water to cool, then cut off the root ends, and the stem ends, if you like. Slip off the skins and cut a shallow cross in the root end (this prevents the onions from "telescoping" during cooking). Set the onions aside.

Squeeze the juice from the lemon half into a saucepan three-fourths full of water. Working with 1 artichoke at a time, and using a sharp knife, slice off the top half or so of the leaves (page 278). Starting at the base, pull off and discard the tough outer leaves. Then pull off the outside leaves until you reach the pale green inner leaves. Remove the tough outside flesh from the stem and drop the artichoke into the saucepan.

When all of the artichokes are trimmed, bring the pan of artichokes to a boil over high heat, then reduce the heat to medium. Cook gently, uncovered, until tender, about 15 minutes. Drain well. When the artichokes are cool enough to handle, use a small sharp knife to cut off all the leaves, reserving them for another use. With a spoon, scoop out any prickly choke to expose the heart. Cut the hearts in half lengthwise and set aside.

In a large Dutch oven or other deep, heavy pot over medium heat, fry the bacon until it is crisp, about 5 minutes. Transfer the bacon to paper towels to drain and reserve for another use. Reserve 1 tablespoon of the rendered fat in the pan, discarding the rest.

Return the pot to medium heat, add the chicken breasts, and sear on all sides until lightly browned, 6–8 minutes. Transfer the chicken to a plate.

Raise the heat to medium-high, add the shallot, pearl onions, and mushrooms and sauté until the mushrooms release their liquid and the onions have softened, about 5 minutes. Add the flour and stir for 1 minute. Stir in ¹/₂ cup (4 fl oz/ 125 ml) of the wine, reduce the heat to medium, and, using a wooden spoon, scrape up all the browned bits from the pot bottom.

Return the chicken to the pot and pour in the remaining 1 cup (8 fl oz/250 ml) wine and the broth. Cover, reduce the heat to medium-low, and simmer until the chicken is very tender, 1–1¹/₄ hours. Add the artichokes to the pot and cook until heated through, about 5 minutes. Add ¹/₄ teaspoon salt, or more to taste, and season with pepper. Remove from the heat, garnish with parsley, and serve.

Classic recipes for coq au vin call for *lardons* (diced, fatty bacon), red wine, and a stewing chicken that cooks all day. Using only a little rendered bacon fat, a fruity white wine, and skinless chicken breasts, this version is ready in just a couple hours and is much lower in fat. The addition of a bit of flour, a traditional French technique, gives the sauce the right body. Accompany the dish with a crusty baguette for soaking up the sauce. For an elegant dinner, Beet and Stilton Salad with Orange Vinaigrette (page 76) and Goat Cheese and Potato Gratin (page 200) are perfect accompaniments. Serve Very Chocolate Mousse (page 246) for dessert.

Eggplant Cannelloni

Cannelloni is a showpiece of northern Italian cooking, with pasta enveloping a filling of veal, ham, and cheese, baked under a blanket of thick, creamy béchamel sauce. Here, the filling calls for low-fat ground turkey breast, the wrappers are eggplant slices, and the dish is bathed in a low-fat béchamel. Soft bread crumbs made from fresh bread help lighten the filling. The prosciutto should be cut in one thick piece, rather than in the usual thin slices. If you keep olive oil in a spray container (page 31), use it to coat the eggplant slices, instead of brushing them with oil. Accompany the cannelloni with a tomato salad.

Position racks in the upper third and lower third of the oven and preheat to 375°F (190°C). Brush 2 large baking sheets with 2 teaspoons of the olive oil.

Cut off the stem end of the eggplant. Standing it upright on the cut end, and using a serrated knife or very sharp, thin-bladed knife, cut the eggplant vertically into slices $1/4$ inch (6 mm) thick. Discard the 2 outer slices, which are mostly skin. You will have 12 slices. Arrange 6 eggplant slices on each baking sheet and brush with $1^1/2$ teaspoons of the oil. Turn the slices and brush with the remaining $1^1/2$ teaspoons oil. Bake the eggplant until it starts to soften, about 10 minutes. Turn the eggplant slices and return the baking sheets to the oven, putting them on opposite racks. Bake until the eggplant slices are flexible at the neck end and still hold together at the wide end, 6–10 minutes longer. Using a spatula, transfer the slices to a plate and set aside. Reduce the oven temperature to 350°F (180°C).

To make the filling, in a nonstick frying pan over medium-high heat, warm the olive oil. Add the onion and sauté until it starts to brown, about 5 minutes. Mix in the mushrooms, cook until they release their liquid, and then continue to cook, stirring occasionally, until they are dry and start to brown, 6–7 minutes total. Stir in the turkey, breaking it up with a wooden spoon. When the meat loses its pink color, after 4–5 minutes, transfer the mixture to a bowl. Mix in the ricotta and prosciutto, then stir in the bread crumbs and $1/8$ teaspoon pepper just until the ingredients are evenly distributed; be careful not to overmix the filling, or it will become gluey.

Spread 1 cup (8 fl oz/250 ml) of the béchamel sauce to cover the bottom of a shallow 1-qt (1-l) baking dish. Lay an eggplant slice, with the wide end closest to you, on a work surface. Place $1/4$ cup (2 oz/60 g) of the filling at the wide end of the eggplant. Lift the slice and roll away from you, pressing lightly so the filling spreads the whole width of the slice and enclosing the filling completely. Place in the prepared baking dish. Repeat with the remaining eggplant slices, forming 2 rows in the dish. You may not need all the filling. Pour the remaining béchamel sauce evenly over the eggplant. Sprinkle on the Parmigiano-Reggiano cheese. Cover the baking dish with aluminum foil.

Bake until the eggplant is soft and a knife inserted into the center of a roll is hot to the touch when removed, 1–$1^1/4$ hours. Remove from the oven and let rest for 15 minutes. Divide the cannelloni evenly among warmed plates and serve.

5 teaspoons extra-virgin olive oil

1 large globe eggplant (aubergine), $1^3/4$–2 lb (875 g–1 kg)

For the Mushroom-Turkey Filling

1 teaspoon extra-virgin olive oil

$3/4$ cup (4 oz/125 g) finely chopped yellow onion

6 oz (185 g) white mushrooms, brushed clean, stems removed, and caps finely chopped (about $1^1/2$ cups/$4^1/2$ oz/140 g)

$1/2$ lb (250 g) ground (minced) turkey breast

1 cup (8 oz/250 g) part-skim ricotta cheese

2 oz (60 g) prosciutto, trimmed of all visible fat and finely chopped

2 cups (4 oz/125 g) fresh bread crumbs (about 4 pieces soft white bread) (page 278)

Freshly ground white or black pepper

3 cups (24 fl oz/750 ml) Lean Béchamel Sauce (page 271)

$3/4$ cup (3 oz/90 g) grated Parmigiano-Reggiano cheese

MAKES 6 SERVINGS

Roasted Turkey Breast

1 large yellow onion, halved

2 large carrots

2 large celery stalks

1 large parsnip

1 clove garlic (optional)

1 bone-in whole turkey breast, 6–8 lb (3–4 kg)

1 tablespoon unsalted butter, at room temperature

Kosher salt and freshly ground pepper

3–4 cups (24–32 fl oz/ 750 ml–1 l) Rich Chicken Stock (page 270) or canned reduced-sodium, fat-free chicken broth

MAKES 10–12 SERVINGS

Position a rack in the lower third of the oven and preheat to 450°F (230°C).

Place the 2 onion halves next to each other in the center of a roasting pan. Line up the carrots, celery, and parsnip on either side. If using the garlic, tuck it in among the other vegetables.

Rinse the turkey breast and pat dry with paper towels. Working your hand carefully under the skin of the turkey to avoid tearing it, separate the skin from the meat on both sides of the breast, but do not detach it. Pat the meat dry with a paper towel. Rub half of the butter over the meat under the skin on each side of the breast. Season with 1 teaspoon salt and $1/8$ teaspoon pepper. Pull the skin down to cover the meat. If necessary, stick toothpicks through the skin and the ribs to secure the skin. Set the breast skin side down on top of the vegetables. Pour in 3 cups of the stock.

Roast the turkey for 30 minutes. Reduce the oven temperature to 325°F (165°C). Turn the breast to rest on one side and baste the breast with the liquid in the pan. Roast for another 30 minutes. Turn the breast to rest on the opposite side, and baste again with the pan liquid. Roast for another 30 minutes. Turn the breast skin side up in the pan and baste again. If the liquid has begun to evaporate, add the remaining 1 cup (8 fl oz/250 ml) stock to the pan. Roast for 30 minutes, baste, and then continue roasting until an instant-read thermometer inserted into the thickest part away from the bone registers 165°F (74°C), 2–2$1/2$ hours total at 20 minutes per pound (500 g). If the top of the breast begins to overbrown, tent loosely with aluminum foil.

Remove the turkey from the oven and transfer to a cutting board. Let it rest for 20 minutes. (The internal temperature of the meat will rise to 170°F/77°C during the first 10 minutes of resting, and the juices will settle.) Carve into slices and serve at once.

Turkey is very high in protein and low in both total fat and saturated fat. Roasting a turkey breast is much easier than roasting the whole bird. It also lets you cook the white meat perfectly, rather than have it dry out while waiting for the dark meat to finish cooking. The breast is easy to turn, allowing it to self-baste as it roasts. Always buy a fresh turkey breast to ensure the most succulent result. Do not think of turkey as fitting only for a Thanksgiving meal. Roasted turkey breast is versatile, perfect for hot or cold slices or for sandwiches and salads. Serve the roasted turkey with Sweet Potato and Cranberry Hash (page 206).

Spinach-Stuffed Turkey Meat Loaf

1¹/₂ teaspoons canola oil

6 slices white bread, crusts removed and bread torn into 1-inch (2.5-cm) pieces

¹/₂ cup (4 fl oz/125 ml) 1-percent-fat milk

2 lb (1 kg) ground (minced) turkey breast

2 tablespoons Dijon mustard

2 teaspoons dried oregano

Kosher salt and freshly ground pepper

1 large egg white

For the Stuffing

2 lb (1 kg) fresh spinach or 1 lb (500 g) frozen chopped spinach

1 tablespoon extra-virgin olive oil

3 green (spring) onions, tender green tops only, chopped

1 large egg white

Freshly ground pepper

¹/₃ cup (1¹/₂ oz/45 g) grated Romano cheese

4–5 cups (32–40 fl oz/ 1–1.25 l) Spicy Tomato Sauce (page 271)

1 teaspoon grated orange zest

MAKES 8–10 SERVINGS

Line a 10¹/₂-by-15¹/₂-inch (26-by-39-cm) jelly-roll pan with aluminum foil, leaving at least 1 inch (2.5 cm) hanging over the long edge on both sides. Brush the foil with ¹/₂ teaspoon of the canola oil.

In a bowl, using a fork, mash the bread with the milk until the milk is fully absorbed. Squeeze the bread to eliminate excess milk. In another bowl, using a fork, combine the turkey, mustard, oregano, 1 teaspoon salt, and ¹/₄ teaspoon pepper. Add the soaked bread and egg white and mix until creamy, 2–3 minutes. Spread in the prepared pan to make an even layer. Cover the pan with plastic wrap. Refrigerate for 1–3 hours.

Preheat the oven to 350°F (180°C).

To make the stuffing, if using fresh spinach, rinse carefully in 2 or 3 changes of water, discarding the tough stems and any damaged leaves. Drain the leaves briefly in a colander and transfer to a large saucepan with only the water that clings to them. Place over medium-high heat, cover, and cook, turning the leaves 2 or 3 times, until wilted and still slightly firm to the bite, about 4 minutes. Drain and chop finely. Squeeze the spinach with your hands to remove about half of the moisture. If using frozen spinach, cook according to the package directions, let cool, and squeeze out.

In a nonstick frying pan over medium-high heat, warm the olive oil. Add the spinach, pulling it apart to eliminate any clumps. Stir in the green onions and cook, stirring occasionally, until the onions are wilted and the spinach is dry and fluffy, 5–6 minutes. Remove from the heat and let cool to room temperature. Stir in the egg white and season generously with pepper.

Remove the plastic wrap from the meat. Spread the stuffing evenly over the meat, leaving a 1-inch (2.5-cm) uncovered border on all sides. Sprinkle the cheese evenly over the stuffing. Lifting the foil along the long side facing you, roll up the meat and stuffing like a jelly roll, pushing it forward a bit at a time and lifting the foil away, until a long log has formed. Pat the log gently to compact it. Brush with the remaining 1 teaspoon canola oil and center it on the pan.

Bake the meat loaf, uncovered, until an instant-read thermometer inserted into the center registers 160°F (71°C), about 1 hour. Let rest for 15 minutes. In a saucepan over medium heat, combine the tomato sauce and orange zest and heat until hot. Spoon ¹/₂ cup (4 fl oz/125 ml) of the sauce onto each plate. Cut the meat loaf into 8 or 10 slices. Place a slice in the center of the sauce and serve.

This rolled turkey meat loaf is a clever way of coaxing any meat-and-potatoes eater into enjoying two whole servings of vegetables, antioxidant-rich spinach and tomatoes. It makes a great dish for potlucks and buffet dinners. Accompany with Mashed Yukon Gold Potatoes (page 202).

Cider-Braised Pork Chops with Apples

Pork today is far leaner than it was even a decade ago, as breeding practices and feeds produce leaner animals. It is a richer source of the B vitamin thiamin than any other meat. Pork is also a good source of niacin, phosphorus, and potassium. This dish of lean, boneless pork loin chops rubbed with herbs and spices and then braised in cider is a contemporary version of old-fashioned smothered pork chops, which are typically panfried before simmering. This recipe even boasts a creamy sauce. Serve with Cauliflower with Orange Zest and Green Onion (page 191).

To make the spice rub, in a small bowl, stir together the oregano, five-spice powder, paprika, $1/2$ teaspoon salt, and $1/4$ teaspoon pepper.

Coat the pork chops evenly on both sides with the spice mixture. Set the meat on a plate for 10 minutes.

In a large, deep, nonstick frying pan over medium-high heat, warm 2 teaspoons of the canola oil. Add the onion and sauté until lightly browned, about 5 minutes. Transfer the onion to a plate.

Add the remaining 2 teaspoons oil to the pan and return it to medium-high heat. Add the pork chops and sear until lightly browned on the bottom, about 4 minutes. Turn and brown the meat on the other side, 3–4 minutes. Transfer the meat to the plate holding the onion.

Return the pan to medium heat and pour in the cider and vinegar. Using a wooden spoon, scrape up all the browned bits from the pan bottom. Return the meat and onion to the pan and place the apple wedges on top of the meat. Pour in the broth, cover, and simmer until the chops are opaque throughout, about 10 minutes, reducing the heat if the liquid begins to boil.

Transfer the chops, apple wedges, and onion to a warmed platter. Pour the milk into the pan, raise the heat to high, and boil until the liquid is reduced by one-third, about 5 minutes. Pour the sauce over the chops and serve at once.

For the Spice Rub

1 teaspoon dried oregano

$1/2$ teaspoon five-spice powder

$1/2$ teaspoon sweet paprika

Kosher salt and freshly ground pepper

4 thin boneless center-cut pork loin chops, about 1 lb (500 g) total weight, trimmed of all visible fat

4 teaspoons canola oil

1 yellow onion, thinly sliced

$1/3$ cup (3 fl oz/80 ml) sweet apple cider

2 tablespoons red wine vinegar

1 Fuji apple, halved, peeled, cored, and cut into 8 wedges

1 cup (8 fl oz/250 ml) reduced-sodium, fat-free chicken broth

$1/4$ cup (2 fl oz/60 ml) 2-percent-fat evaporated milk

MAKES 4 SERVINGS

Pork Tenderloin with Fennel and Bell Peppers

2 pork tenderloins, ³/₄ lb (375 g) each, trimmed of all visible fat

3 large rosemary sprigs, each 4–5 inches (10–13) cm long

Kosher salt and freshly ground pepper

1 large fennel bulb, ³/₄–1 lb (375–500 g)

1 tablespoon extra-virgin olive oil

1 large orange bell pepper (capsicum), seeded and cut lengthwise into strips a scant ¹/₂ inch (12 mm) wide

1 large red bell pepper (capsicum), seeded and cut lengthwise into strips a scant ¹/₂ inch (12 mm) wide

1 yellow onion, cut lengthwise into wedges ³/₈ inch (1 cm) wide

¹/₂ cup (4 fl oz/125 ml) dry white wine such as Sauvignon Blanc

1 cup (8 fl oz/250 ml) reduced-sodium, fat-free chicken broth

MAKES 4 SERVINGS

Preheat the oven to 350°F (180°C).

Cut a piece of kitchen string 30 inches (75 cm) long. Place 1 tenderloin on a work surface. Arrange the rosemary down the center of the meat. Set the second tenderloin on top. Slip one end of the kitchen string under the meat, 1 inch (2.5 cm) from the end. Tie the meat tightly, making a knot by tying the short end over the long one. Snip off the long piece of string. Repeat, tying the meat every 1¹/₂ inches (4 cm), and finishing 1 inch from the end. Season the meat with 1¹/₂ teaspoons salt and ¹/₄ teaspoon pepper.

Cut off the stems and feathery leaves from the fennel bulb. Discard the outer layer of the bulb if it is tough and cut away any discolored areas. Halve the bulb lengthwise and cut away any tough base portions. Cut each half into wedges a scant ¹/₂ inch (12 mm) wide.

In a large, ovenproof frying pan or other shallow, ovenproof pan over medium-high heat, warm the olive oil. Add the fennel, bell peppers, and onion and sauté until they start to soften, about 3 minutes. Transfer the vegetables to a platter.

Return the pan to the medium-high heat, add the pork, and sear, turning as needed, until lightly browned on all sides, about 6 minutes. Transfer the meat to the platter with the vegetables.

Return the pan to medium heat and pour in the wine. Using a wooden spoon, scrape up any browned bits from the pan bottom. Pour in the broth and return the vegetables to the pan. Set the meat on top of the vegetables.

Transfer to the oven and roast the pork until firm to the touch or an instant-read thermometer inserted into the thickest part of the meat registers 155°F (68°C), 30–40 minutes. Remove the pork from the oven, tent loosely with aluminum foil, and let rest for 20 minutes. (The internal temperature of the meat will rise to 160°F/71°C during the first 10 minutes of resting.)

Divide the roasted vegetables among warmed individual plates. Snip the strings around the pork and discard. Cut the meat into 8 slices. Arrange 2 slices on top of the vegetables on each plate. Spoon the pan juices over the meat, dividing evenly, and serve at once.

This rosemary-stuffed tenderloin is roasted on a bed of sweet peppers, fennel, and onions for a Mediterranean-style one-dish meal. If you are hesitant about tying the roast, ask your butcher to do it for you. Or cook the meat in two pieces, reducing the time accordingly, and tuck the rosemary in with the vegetables.

Beef Bourguignon with Noodles

For the Four-Spice Blend

1/2 teaspoon freshly grated nutmeg

1/4 teaspoon ground ginger

1/8 teaspoon ground cloves

Freshly ground white or black pepper

1 small yellow onion

1 carrot, peeled

2 large cloves garlic

4 fresh thyme sprigs

1 tablespoon coarsely chopped fresh flat-leaf (Italian) parsley, including stems

2 juniper berries, crushed

1/4 teaspoon coriander seeds, crushed

1/4 teaspoon dried sage

1 bottle (3 cups/24 fl oz/ 750 ml) Pinot Noir

2 lb (1 kg) beef fillet

2 tablespoons canola oil

1/2 cup (4 fl oz/125 ml) *glace de viande* (see note)

1/3 cup (1 1/2 oz/45 g) pitted green olives

Kosher salt

3/4 lb (375 g) medium-width fresh or dried egg noodles

1 teaspoon chopped fresh rosemary

MAKES 6 SERVINGS

To make the four-spice blend, in a small bowl, stir together the nutmeg, ginger, cloves, and 1 teaspoon pepper.

Coarsely chop the onion and carrot. Smash the garlic cloves with the flat side of a knife blade. In a large, nonreactive saucepan, combine the onion, carrot, garlic, thyme, parsley, juniper berries, coriander seeds, sage, and 1/4 teaspoon of the four-spice blend. (Reserve the remaining spice blend for another use.) Pour in the wine, place over high heat, and bring to a boil. Remove from the heat and let cool to room temperature. Trim the beef fillet of all visible fat and cut into 1 1/2-inch (4-cm) cubes. Pour the marinade into a nonreactive container and add the beef. Cover and marinate in the refrigerator for 24 hours.

Preheat the oven to 350°F (180°C). Remove the meat from the marinade, reserving the marinade, and pat the meat dry with paper towels. In a Dutch oven or other large, ovenproof pot over medium-high heat, warm the canola oil. Add the meat and cook, turning as needed, until brown on all sides, about 15 minutes total. Transfer to a plate. Add the marinade to the pot, stir to remove any browned bits from the bottom of the pot, and heat until the marinade begins to bubble slightly, about 5 minutes. Return the meat to the pot, cover, transfer to the oven, and bake until the meat is tender, about 1 hour.

Set a sieve over a large bowl. Drain the stew into the sieve. Using tongs, remove the meat from the other solids, place the meat in a bowl, cover, and set aside. Using the back of a wooden spoon, press against the solids to extract as much of their juices as possible. Discard the solids. Clean out the pot and pour the reserved liquid into it; you will have about 2 1/2 cups (20 fl oz/625 ml). Add the *glace de viande* to the cooking liquid and bring to a boil over high heat. Boil until the liquid is reduced to 1 1/2 cups (12 fl oz/375 ml), about 15 minutes. Reduce the heat to a simmer, return the meat to the pot, and add the olives. Simmer until the meat and olives are heated through, about 10 minutes.

About 20 minutes before the beef is ready, bring a large pot three-fourths full of water to a boil. Add 2 tablespoons salt and the noodles. Cook the fresh noodles just until tender, 3–4 minutes; cook the dried noodles according to the package directions until al dente. Drain the noodles and divide among individual plates. Using a slotted spoon, divide the meat and olives among the plates. Spoon 1/3 cup (3 fl oz/80 ml) of the hot liquid over each serving. Garnish with the rosemary and serve at once.

Adapted from a recipe by Alain Senderens, chef-owner of the three-star Lucas Carton restaurant in Paris, this lavish dish calls for a lean beef fillet trimmed of fat. The finer the wine, and the richer the beef broth used, the better this dish will be. For the broth, the ideal is *glace de viande,* the concentrated gelled beef stock sold at specialty-food stores and some supermarkets. The beef is served over noodles so that you can savor every drop of its deep, dark sauce. For dessert, offer Chocolate Meringues (page 222) and Peach-Mango Sorbet (page 241).

Grilled Beef Fillets with Mushrooms and Red Wine Sauce

Beef fits into a healthful diet if you serve a lean cut in reasonably sized portions and trim the meat of all visible fat. Here, grilled beef fillets are accompanied by meaty mushrooms and a coriander-spiced wine sauce. For guests who do not eat meat, grill a tofu steak or serve two mushrooms with the sauce. Heads of Belgian endive (chicory/witloof) and spears of asparagus, grilled alongside the mushrooms, make good accompaniments.

To make the sauce, in a small saucepan, combine the tomatoes, garlic, and broth. Bring to a boil and cook until most of the liquid has evaporated, about 4 minutes. Remove from the heat, pour in the wine, and add the coriander and peppercorns. Bring to a boil, reduce the heat to medium, and cook until reduced by one-third, about 8 minutes. Pour through a fine-mesh sieve into a bowl. Discard the solids. Whisk in the olive oil and ¹/₄ teaspoon salt. Season with pepper. Keep warm.

Prepare a CHARCOAL or GAS GRILL for direct-heat grilling over high heat. Oil the grill rack. Season the fillets with salt and pepper.

BY CHARCOAL GRILL: Using tongs, place the fillets directly over the hottest part of the fire and grill until grill marks are visible, about 2 minutes. Rotate 90 degrees and grill until cross-hatching is visible, about 1 minute. Turn the fillets and grill for about 1 minute longer for rare, about 2 minutes for medium, and about 3 minutes for well done.

BY GAS GRILL: Using tongs, place the fillets directly over the heat elements and grill until grill marks are visible, about 2 minutes. Rotate 90 degrees and grill until cross-hatching is visible, about 1 minute. Turn the fillets and grill for about 1 minute longer for rare, about 2 minutes for medium, and about 3 minutes for well done.

Transfer the fillets to a platter, tent loosely with aluminum foil, and let rest for about 10 minutes. Brush the mushroom caps with the olive oil.

BY CHARCOAL GRILL: Grill the mushrooms, cap side down, over the hottest part of the fire until grill marks are visible, about 2 minutes. Rotate 90 degrees and grill until cross-hatching is visible, about 2 minutes. Turn and grill until tender throughout when pierced in the center with a sharp, thin-bladed knife, 2–3 minutes.

BY GAS GRILL: Grill the mushrooms, cap side down, directly over the heat elements until grill marks are visible, about 2 minutes. Rotate 90 degrees and grill until cross-hatching is visible, about 2 minutes. Turn and grill until tender throughout when pierced in the center with a sharp, thin-bladed knife, 2–3 minutes.

Place a mushroom, cap side down, in the center of each plate. Set a fillet on top of the mushroom. Top with one-fourth of the wine sauce and serve.

For the Mushroom-Wine Sauce

2 plum (Roma) tomatoes, seeded and chopped

2 roasted garlic cloves (page 271), peeled and mashed

¹/₂ cup (4 fl oz/125 ml) mushroom broth

1 cup (8 fl oz/250 ml) fruity red wine such as Zinfandel

¹/₄ teaspoon coriander seeds, crushed

¹/₄ teaspoon peppercorns

1 teaspoon extra-virgin olive oil

Kosher salt and freshly ground pepper

4 beef fillets, about 6 oz (185 g) each, trimmed of all visible fat

Kosher salt and freshly ground pepper

4 large portobello mushrooms, about 5 oz (155 g) each, brushed clean and stems removed

2 teaspoons extra-virgin olive oil

MAKES 4 SERVINGS

Grilled Beef with Salsa Verde

For the Salsa Verde

³/₄ cup (³/₄ oz/20 g) loosely packed fresh flat-leaf (Italian) parsley leaves, chopped

4 teaspoons capers, rinsed, drained, and chopped

3 pitted green olives, finely chopped

2 or 3 anchovy fillets, rinsed, patted dry, and finely chopped

1 clove garlic, minced

1 tablespoon chopped fresh mint

2 tablespoons white wine vinegar

1 tablespoon extra-virgin olive oil

Kosher salt and freshly ground pepper

1 lb (500 g) flank steak

Kosher salt and freshly ground pepper

MAKES 4 SERVINGS

Italy is known for some memorable beef dishes, including *bistecca alla fiorentina,* grilled beef steak traditionally from the young Chianina cattle of eastern Tuscany, and *bollito misto,* a Piedmontese classic of boiled meat served with a sharply flavored *salsa verde* (green sauce). Here, the *salsa verde,* made with parsley, capers, and garlic, is perfect with thin slices of grilled flank steak. In this version, green olives add a pleasant savory note. Flank steak is one of the cuts of beef that is lowest in fat. Because it is fibrous, it can be tough. Be careful not to overcook it, and cut it across the grain into thin slices.

To make the *salsa verde,* in a small bowl, combine the parsley, capers, olives, anchovies, garlic, mint, vinegar, and olive oil. Using a fork, mix together until all the ingredients are evenly distributed. Stir in ¹/₄ teaspoon salt, or more to taste, and season with pepper. Set aside for 20–30 minutes to allow the flavors to blend.

Prepare a CHARCOAL or GAS GRILL for direct-heat grilling over high heat. Oil the grill rack. Season the flank steak on both sides with ¹/₂ teaspoon salt and ¹/₈ teaspoon pepper.

BY CHARCOAL GRILL: Using tongs, place the steak over the hottest part of the fire and grill, turning once, 5–7 minutes per side for medium-rare, 6–8 minutes for medium, and 8–10 minutes for well done. To test for doneness, cut into the steak at the thickest part.

BY GAS GRILL: Using tongs, place the steak directly over the heat elements and grill, turning once, 5–7 minutes per side for medium-rare, 6–8 minutes for medium, and 8–10 minutes for well done. To test for doneness, cut into the steak at the thickest part.

Transfer the steak to a platter and let rest for about 10 minutes to reabsorb the juices. Cut the steak across the grain into thin slices. Serve with the *salsa verde.*

Bread Crumb–Crusted Rack of Lamb with White Beans

For a special occasion, rack of lamb is as easy to make as it is elegant. Ask the butcher to french the bones, that is, scrape off any meat and fat from the top 1¹/₂ inches (4 cm) of each bone. To keep the meat juicy, it is first browned at a high temperature, then coated with a flavorful crust and roasted at a lower temperature. Cannellini beans, cooked in the roasting pan under the meat, come out creamy and aromatically seasoned. Leftover beans puréed and mixed with fresh herbs make a good spread for *crostini*.

Place the soaked, drained beans in a saucepan and add 4 cups (32 fl oz/1 l) water. Stick the clove into an onion half and add the onion halves, garlic, bay leaf, and thyme to the saucepan. Bring to a boil over high heat, reduce the heat to low, cover partially, and simmer gently until the beans are tender, 1–1¹/₂ hours. Drain the beans, reserving the liquid. Discard the bay leaf, both onion halves, and the clove.

Preheat the oven to 450°F (230°C).

Place the lamb, meaty side up, in a shallow 2-qt (2-l) baking dish. Pour in ¹/₂ cup (4 fl oz/125 ml) of the bean liquid. Roast the meat until lightly browned, about 10 minutes. Remove the dish from the oven and reduce the oven temperature to 400°F (200°C).

Place the lamb on a cutting board. Spread the mustard over the meaty side of the rack. In a small bowl, stir together the bread crumbs, parsley, thyme, rosemary, ¹/₂ teaspoon salt, and ¹/₈ teaspoon pepper. Using your hands, press the bread crumbs into the mustard, covering the meat in an even layer. Measure out 4 cups (1³/₄ lb/875 g) of the cooked beans and arrange on the bottom of the baking dish to cover completely. (Reserve the remaining beans for another use.) Pour in 2 cups (16 fl oz/500 ml) of the bean liquid. Set the lamb, crumb-coated side up, on the top of the beans.

Roast the lamb until the meat springs back to the touch or until an instant-read thermometer inserted into the thickest part of the meat registers 130°–135°F (54°–57°C) for medium-rare and 140°–150°F (60°–65°C) for medium, about 15 minutes for medium-rare and 20 minutes for medium. Remove from the oven, transfer the lamb to the cutting board, and tent loosely with aluminum foil. Let rest for 10 minutes.

Divide the beans among warmed individual plates. Carve the lamb into 8 chops. Place 2 chops on each plate and serve at once.

For the White Beans

2 cups (14 oz/440 g) dried cannellini beans, soaked and drained (page 278)

1 whole clove

1 yellow onion, halved

4 cloves garlic, smashed

1 bay leaf

¹/₂ teaspoon dried thyme

1 rack of lamb, 8 ribs or about 2 lb (1 kg), trimmed of any fat and frenched (see note)

2 tablespoons Dijon mustard

¹/₂ cup (1 oz/30 g) fresh white bread crumbs (about 2 slices) (page 278)

2 tablespoons chopped fresh flat-leaf (Italian) parsley

1 tablespoon chopped fresh thyme

1 teaspoon finely chopped fresh rosemary

Kosher salt and freshly ground pepper

MAKES 4 SERVINGS

Medallions of Venison with Cranberry-Port Sauce

1 small carrot

2 plum (Roma) tomatoes

4 teaspoons canola oil

2 cloves garlic, chopped

1 large shallot, chopped

1 can (15 fl oz/470 ml) reduced-sodium, fat-free beef broth

1/2 cup (4 fl oz/125 ml) cranberry juice

1/4 cup (2 fl oz/60 ml) red wine vinegar

1 tablespoon Worcestershire sauce

6 fresh flat-leaf (Italian) parsley sprigs

3 cardamom pods, crushed

2 teaspoons dried thyme

1 bay leaf

1 1/4 lb (625 g) venison tenderloin

1/3 cup (1 1/2 oz/45 g) dried cranberries

1/3 cup (3 fl oz/80 ml) ruby Port

Kosher salt and freshly ground pepper

2 tablespoons chilled unsalted butter

MAKES 4 SERVINGS

Peel and slice the carrot and chop the tomatoes. In a saucepan over medium-high heat, warm 2 teaspoons of the canola oil. Add the garlic, shallot, and carrot and sauté until the shallot starts to soften, about 3 minutes. Add the broth, cranberry juice, vinegar, Worcestershire sauce, tomatoes, parsley, cardamom, thyme, and bay leaf and bring to a boil. Reduce the heat to medium and boil gently for 10 minutes. Let the marinade cool to room temperature.

Cut the venison crosswise into slices 1 inch (2.5 cm) thick. Place in a nonreactive bowl and pour in the cooled marinade, including the vegetables, herbs, and spices. Cover and marinate the meat in the refrigerator for 24 hours.

When you are ready to cook the venison, place the cranberries in a bowl. Add the Port and set aside until the fruit is plump, 20–30 minutes.

Set a sieve over a large bowl. Drain the meat into the sieve. Using tongs, remove the venison from the other solids, place it on a plate, cover, and set aside. Using the back of a wooden spoon, press against the solids to extract as much of their juices as possible. Discard the solids. Reserve the liquid. Pat the meat dry with paper towels.

Preheat the oven to 200°F (95°C). In a large frying pan over medium-high heat, warm the remaining 2 teaspoons canola oil. Arrange the meat in the pan in a single layer, leaving 1 inch (2.5 cm) between the pieces. (If you do not have a pan large enough, cook the meat in 2 batches.) Cook the venison, turning once, until browned on both sides, 10–12 minutes total. The venison should be pink in the center. Transfer the meat to a plate, tent loosely with aluminum foil, and set it in the warm oven.

Pour the reserved marinade into the pan and bring to a boil over medium-high heat. Using a wooden spoon, scrape up all the browned bits from pan bottom. Boil until the liquid is reduced by one-third, about 10 minutes. Use a large, shallow spoon, skim off any foam that forms on the surface. Add the cranberries and any remaining Port and cook until the liquid is reduced by one-fourth, about 5 minutes. Add 1/2 teaspoon salt and season with pepper. Remove from the heat. Cut the butter into 8 equal pieces. Add the butter to the liquid and whisk until melted and blended into the sauce, 1–2 minutes.

Divide the meat among warmed individual plates. Spoon an equal amount of the sauce over each serving, dividing the cranberries evenly as well. Serve at once.

Venison is a naturally lean meat, and although most venison is farm raised, which means it is tender and mild flavored, it still benefits from long marination. It also has an affinity for the sweetness of fruit and the bold flavor of big wines. Here, it is marinated in a mixture that includes cranberry juice and is served with a sauce made from the marinade and dried cranberries plumped in Port. If you are using wild venison, marinate it for up to 48 hours.

Small Plates

About Small Plates

Snacks and light meals–typical trouble spots on the road to a healthful diet–take a nutritious turn. Here, sandwiches are made with whole-grain bread, and fillings and spreads are low in fat and high in vitamins, minerals, and protective phytochemicals.

Small plates, all of them perfect for serving as snacks or light meals, have in common a wrapper, sturdy base, or other element that encloses a filling or holds a topping or spread. Sandwiches immediately come to mind, and several wholesome and delicious examples are included here, but there are also pizzas, crepes, tacos, and Asian rolls. Each dish is an outstanding example of how to maximize health benefits and minimize health risks through careful selection of ingredients.

SHAPE AND STRUCTURE

All the sandwiches start with some type of whole-grain bread. In Vegetable Melts on Garlic Toast (page 155) and Tomato, Onion, and Goat Cheese Sandwiches (page 164), for example, slices of toasted whole-grain coarse country bread serve as the base. If you have time to bake, make Multigrain Yeast Bread (page 263), a versatile loaf that goes together easily, is a good source of fiber, and can be used for making these sandwiches and many others. If you buy bread, check the label to ensure the product is low in fat or contains one or more whole grains.

The wrappers and crusts in this chapter have the same healthful makeup as the breads. The dough used for both pizza recipes (pages 149 and 150) calls for whole-wheat (wholemeal) flour to lend nutrients and texture, while the batter for Buckwheat Crepes with Mushrooms (page 166) relies on buckwheat flour, a source of fiber, niacin, iron, zinc, and protein. The corn tortillas for Fish Tacos with Tomato and

Orange Salsa (page 152) are low in fat and cholesterol free, and the rice paper rounds that enclose the noodles, shrimp (prawns), herbs, and vegetables in Vietnamese-Style Summer Rolls with Dipping Sauce (page 169) are made from fat-free rice flour.

SPREADS AND FILLINGS

An array of tasty low-fat spreads contributes moisture and flavor to the various wrappers and crusts. In Roasted Red Pepper and Mozzarella Sandwiches (page 159), low-fat pesto delivers a rich vein of taste without a trace of cholesterol. Ahi Tuna and Cucumber Sandwiches with Tapenade (page 163) feature a heart-healthy olive, caper, and green onion paste. Spreads are versatile, too, easily transforming these same sandwiches and other recipes. Experiment with the following spreads or toppings to make new dishes, choosing them for their complementary flavors and good nutrient balance: Tomato and Basil Pesto (page 150), Caramelized Onions (page 164), Roasted Garlic (page 271), Tomato Chutney (page 272), Tzatziki (page 272), or Yogurt Cheese (page 273), as well as the tapenade.

Fillings and toppings can be nutritious if you keep each ingredient's health benefits in mind. Cheese regularly has a role in sandwiches and pizzas, but take care to use the right type and amount of cheese to avoid excess fat and cholesterol. Check out the amount and type of fat by reading the Nutrition Facts panel on the cheese package. Both the vegetable melts and the roasted pepper sandwiches in this chapter

rely on a sensible portion of low-fat mozzarella cheese combined with a generous measure of nutrient- and fiber-rich vegetables. Both of the pizzas also boast a minimum of highly flavored cheese along with a variety of vegetables.

Other examples of healthful fillings include the salmon in the fish tacos, which is high in omega-3 fatty acids and is grilled rather than fried, and burgers stacked with big portobello mushrooms, tomato, and lettuce (page 160) instead of higher-calorie (-kilojoule) and higher-cholesterol ground (minced) beef patties. Fresh goat cheese, which is typically lower in fat than cow's milk cheeses, is rolled up with crunchy nuts, fiber-rich dried figs, and other healthful ingredients in sheets of *lahvosh* (page 156) to make pinwheel sandwiches that please both the eye and the palate.

As with spreads, it is easy to improvise your own small plates with alternative healthful fillings and toppings. Try tucking lean cooked chicken breast strips into the buckwheat crepes along with the mushrooms, or replace the mushrooms with sautéed onions or a combination of other lightly cooked seasonal vegetables. You can fill the tacos with another type of fish, chicken or turkey breast strips, or cooked, peeled shrimp. The summer rolls can be filled with chicken breast strips, thin mango slices, and fresh basil leaves.

As you leaf through the pages in this chapter, you will see the same three steps repeated in many of the recipes: A dish starts with a wholesome wrapper, crust, or other base that will hold its ingredients in place. This base is then treated to a spread that is high in flavor and low in fat. Finally, nutrient-packed fillings or toppings, built on fresh vegetables and/or lean protein, are put in place. These three simple steps are the secret to making small plates that are nutritious and great tasting.

Pizza with Caramelized Red Onions, Olives, and Feta Cheese

Slivered red onion, feta cheese, and black olives on this pizza are a departure from the typical topping of tomato and cheese. The salty edge of the crumbled feta and the chopped black olives helps to balance the sweetness of the red onions, which have been slowly cooked until their natural sugars caramelize. A combination of whole-wheat (wholemeal) and white flours gives the pizza crust a pleasant, nutty flavor and chewy texture. Onions are rich in organosulfides, phytochemicals that aid the enzymes that detoxify carcinogens. Organosulfides have antibacterial properties as well. Onions also contain quercitin, a phytochemical that protects the heart.

Prepare the pizza dough as directed and set the dough aside to rise.

To make the caramelized onions, heat a large frying pan over medium heat until hot enough for a drop of water to sizzle and immediately evaporate. Add the olive oil and onions; reduce the heat to low. Add 2 tablespoons water and toss to coat. Cover and cook, stirring occasionally and adding more water if needed to prevent scorching, until the onions are tender, about 8 minutes. Uncover and raise the heat to medium-high. Cook, stirring, until all the moisture is evaporated and the onions begin to turn golden, about 5 minutes longer. Add the vinegar, oregano, a pinch of salt, and a grind of pepper and stir to mix. Cook for 1 minute, then remove from the heat. Let the onions cool to room temperature.

Punch the dough down and let rest for 10 minutes. (You can make the dough up to 1 day in advance, punch it down, place it in a plastic bag, and refrigerate it until ready to shape and bake.) If making individual pizzas, divide the dough into 4 equal portions.

Position a rack in the lowest position in the oven and preheat to 450°F (230°C). Lightly oil one 14-by-16-inch (35-by-40-cm) baking sheet, one 14-inch (35-cm) pizza pan, or four 9-inch (23-cm) pizza pans or cake or tart pans.

On a lightly floured work surface, gently stretch or roll out the dough to fit the prepared pan(s). Transfer to the pan(s). Spread all of the cheese on the large crust and top with the onions, or divide the cheese evenly among the 4 smaller crusts and top with the onions, again dividing evenly.

Bake the pizza(s) until the crust(s) are nicely browned, 20–25 minutes. Spray the bottom of the oven with water at regular intervals 3 times during the first 5–10 minutes of baking, and sprinkle the pizza(s) with the olive halves, dividing them evenly if making individual pizzas, during the last 5–10 minutes of baking. Remove the pan(s) from the oven. Cut the small pizzas in half and the large pizza into 8 wedges, and serve at once.

Pizza dough (page 150)

For the Caramelized Red Onions

1 tablespoon olive oil

1 lb (500 g) red onions, cut lengthwise into slices 1/8 inch (3 mm) thick

1 tablespoon red wine vinegar

1 teaspoon dried oregano

Kosher salt and freshly ground pepper

2 cups (10 oz/315 g) crumbled feta cheese

12 Kalamata olives, pitted and halved

MAKES 8 SERVINGS

Pizza with Potatoes, Mushrooms, and Tomato-Basil Pesto

For the Pizza Dough

1 tablespoon honey

2 teaspoons olive oil

1 envelope (2¹/₂ teaspoons) active dry yeast

1¹/₂ cups (7¹/₂ oz/235 g) all-purpose (plain) flour, or more as needed

¹/₂ cup (2¹/₂ oz/75 g) whole-wheat (wholemeal) flour

Kosher salt

For the Tomato-Basil Pesto

¹/₂ cup (1¹/₂ oz/45 g) dry-packed sun-dried tomato halves

Boiling water

2 firm, ripe plum (Roma) tomatoes, diced (about ¹/₂ cup/3 oz/90 g)

¹/₂ cup (³/₄ oz/20 g) packed fresh basil leaves

1 clove garlic, chopped

Kosher salt

2 tablespoons extra-virgin olive oil

To make the dough, in a small bowl, stir together 1 cup (8 fl oz/250 ml) luke-warm water, the honey, and 1 teaspoon of the olive oil until blended. Sprinkle the yeast on top and let stand until foamy, about 10 minutes.

BY HAND: In a large bowl, using a wooden spoon, stir together 1 cup (5 oz/150 g) of the all-purpose flour, the whole-wheat flour, and 1 tea-spoon salt. Pour in the yeast mixture and stir, adding enough of the remaining ¹/₂ cup (2¹/₂ oz/75 g) all-purpose flour, or more if needed, to form a soft dough. Turn the dough out onto a floured work surface and knead until the surface of the dough is very smooth, about 5 minutes, adding more all-purpose flour as needed. The dough should be soft, but not sticky.

BY FOOD PROCESSOR: In a food processor, combine 1 cup (5 oz/150 g) of the all-purpose flour, the whole-wheat flour, and 1 teaspoon salt and pulse a few times to blend. Pour in the yeast mixture and pulse until combined. Add enough of the remaining ¹/₂ cup (2¹/₂ oz/75 g) all-purpose flour, or more if needed, and pulse to form a soft dough. Turn the dough out onto a floured work surface and knead until the surface of the dough is very smooth, about 5 minutes, adding more all-purpose flour as needed. The dough should be soft, but not sticky.

Lightly oil a large bowl with the remaining 1 teaspoon oil. Form the dough into a ball and place in the bowl. Turn to coat with the oil. Cover the bowl with plastic wrap and let the dough rise in a warm place until doubled in bulk, about 1 hour.

To make the pesto, place the dried tomatoes in a heatproof bowl and add boiling water to cover. Let stand for 15 minutes, then drain. In a food processor, combine the reconstituted dried tomatoes, fresh tomatoes, basil, garlic, and ¹/₂ teaspoon salt and process until puréed. With the motor running, drizzle the olive oil through the feed tube and process just until the mixture is blended.

To make the topping, heat a large frying pan over medium heat until hot enough for a drop of water to sizzle and then immediately evaporate. Add the olive oil and the mushrooms and stir to blend. Reduce the heat to medium-low, cover, and cook until tender, about 5 minutes. Uncover, raise the heat to high, and cook, stir-ring, until any liquid has evaporated and the mushrooms are lightly browned, about 3 minutes. Add the parsley, garlic, ¹/₂ teaspoon salt, and a grind of pepper. Cook, stirring, for 2 minutes longer. Remove from the heat.

A thin layer of sliced Yukon gold potatoes makes an unusual, but delicious, topping for pizza, especially with the addition of sautéed mushrooms and the fresh, bright taste of tomato and basil pesto. You can use shiitake, cremini, oyster, or small portobello mushrooms, or a combination. This ver-sion of pesto, made with tomatoes, is lower in fat than the traditional sauce made with basil, nuts, and olive oil because the juice from the tomatoes stands in for some of the oil. Make a double batch of pesto and use the extra as a topping for baked potatoes or pasta.

Punch the dough down and let rest for 10 minutes. (You can make the dough up to 1 day in advance, punch it down, place it in a plastic bag, and refrigerate it until ready to shape and bake.) If making individual pizzas, divide the dough into 4 equal portions.

Position a rack in the lowest position in the oven and preheat to 450°F (230°C). Lightly oil one 14-by-16-inch (35-by-40-cm) baking sheet, one 14-inch (35-cm) pizza pan, or four 9-inch (23-cm) pizza pans or cake or tart pans.

Using a food processor fitted with the slicing blade, a mandoline, or a large, sharp knife, slice the potatoes paper-thin. Rinse and blot dry between a double thickness of kitchen towels.

On a lightly floured work surface, gently stretch or roll out the dough to fit the prepared pan(s). Transfer to the pan(s). Spread the potatoes on the large crust and scatter the mushrooms randomly on top, or divide the potatoes among the 4 smaller crusts and top with the mushrooms, dividing evenly. Sprinkle the cheese over the large pizza or divide evenly among the small pizzas.

Bake the pizza(s) until the crust(s) are nicely browned, 20–25 minutes. Spray the bottom of the oven with water at regular intervals 3 times during the first 5–10 minutes of baking. Remove the pan(s) from the oven. Cut the small pizzas in half and the large pizza into 8 wedges. Top each serving with a spoonful of pesto, and serve at once.

For the Topping

1 tablespoon extra-virgin olive oil

³/₄ lb (375 g) fresh mushrooms, brushed clean, tough stems removed, and caps coarsely chopped (see note)

2 tablespoons finely chopped fresh flat-leaf (Italian) parsley

1 clove garlic, finely chopped

Kosher salt and freshly ground pepper

1 lb (500 g) Yukon gold or other small boiling potatoes

¹/₂ cup (2 oz/60 g) grated Parmigiano-Reggiano cheese

MAKES 8 SERVINGS

Fish Tacos with Tomato and Orange Salsa

1/2 lb (250 g) salmon fillet

Kosher salt and freshly ground pepper

1/2 cup (2 1/2 oz/75 g) diced peeled English (hothouse) cucumber

2 tablespoons thinly sliced green (spring) onion

1/2–1 teaspoon minced jalapeño chile, or to taste

1/2 teaspoon grated orange zest

3 tablespoons fresh lime juice

For the Tomato and Orange Salsa

1 each large navel orange and tomato

2 tablespoons finely chopped fresh cilantro (fresh coriander)

1/2–1 teaspoon minced jalapeño chile, or to taste

1/2 teaspoon grated orange zest

1 tablespoon fresh lime juice

Kosher salt

4 soft, fresh white- or yellow-corn tortillas

1 cup (2 oz/60 g) loosely packed thin-chiffonade-cut romaine (cos) lettuce, outer leaves only (page 279)

MAKES 4 SERVINGS

Preheat the BROILER (GRILL), or preheat the OVEN to 425°F (220°C). Remove the skin from the salmon (page 276). Season the fish lightly on both sides with salt and pepper.

BY BROILER: Place the salmon on a broiler pan and slip it in the broiler about 3 inches (7.5 cm) from the heat source. Broil (grill), turning once, until the salmon is slightly translucent in the very center at the thickest part, about 4 minutes per side.

BY OVEN: Place the salmon in a baking pan in the oven and bake until slightly translucent in the very center at the thickest part, allowing slightly less than 10 minutes per inch (2.5 cm) of thickness.

Transfer the salmon to a plate and let cool to room temperature. (The fish will continue to cook away from the heat until opaque.) Flake into a large bowl, discarding any errant bones.

Add the cucumber, green onion, jalapeño, orange zest, and 1/4 teaspoon salt to the fish. Sprinkle with the lime juice and toss lightly to combine.

To make the salsa, cut a thick slice off the top and bottom of the orange to reveal the flesh. Stand the orange upright on a cutting board. Following the contour of the fruit and rotating it with each cut, slice downward to remove the peel, pith, and membrane. Holding the fruit over a bowl, cut along each side of the membrane between the sections, letting each freed section drop into the bowl. Cut the sections into bite-sized pieces and return them to the bowl.

Cut the tomato into 1/2-inch (12-mm) dice. Add the tomato, cilantro, jalapeño, orange zest, lime juice, and 1/2 teaspoon salt to the bowl holding the orange. Stir gently to combine.

To assemble the tacos, set each tortilla on a work surface. Place some lettuce on the tortilla, dividing it evenly. Add about 1/4 cup (2 fl oz/60 ml) of the salmon mixture to each tortilla, then top with 2 rounded tablespoons of the salsa. Fold or roll each tortilla, arrange on a platter, and serve.

The orange, lime, jalapeño, and cilantro add a quartet of bright, fresh tastes to this refreshing snack. Salmon is a good choice for the taco filling, as it is especially high in heart-healthy omega-3 fatty acids, but all fish are a nutritious source of easily digestible protein and are relatively low in fat. Pacific cod, halibut, or flounder would be excellent stand-ins for the salmon.

Vegetable Melts on Garlic Toast

Here is a new look at an old favorite, the melted-cheese sandwich. In this version, a stack of vegetables is made irresistible with a topping of melted mozzarella cheese. The sandwiches can be assembled ahead and placed in the broiler just before you serve them. This light meal will appeal to vegetarians and nonvegetarians alike.

Peel the eggplant and cut crosswise into 8 slices about 1/2 inch (12 mm) thick. Sprinkle both sides of each slice lightly with salt and layer them in a colander set over a plate. Place a second plate on top to weigh them down and let stand for 1 hour. Rinse the slices well and pat dry with paper towels.

Preheat the oven to 425°F (220°C). Halve the tomatoes lengthwise and remove the seeds. Arrange the tomatoes, cut side up, in a 9-inch (23-cm) square baking pan and drizzle with 1 tablespoon of the olive oil. Arrange the eggplant slices on a baking sheet and, using 1 tablespoon oil, brush both sides of each slice. Place both pans in the oven. Roast the eggplant for 15 minutes; using a wide spatula, turn and continue to roast until lightly browned and soft, about 10 minutes longer. Remove from the oven. Meanwhile, roast the tomatoes, turning them and rotating the pan so the tomatoes cook evenly, until the skins are shriveled and caramelized, 35–45 minutes. Remove from the oven, cover with aluminum foil, and let the tomatoes cool. Uncover and peel off any skins that are loosened from the flesh. Reduce the oven temperature to 350°F (180°C).

Place a large frying pan over medium heat until hot enough for a drop of water to sizzle and then immediately evaporate. Add 1 tablespoon of the olive oil and the onion and toss to coat. Sprinkle with 2 tablespoons water, cover, reduce the heat to low, and cook until the onion is wilted and tender, about 8 minutes. Meanwhile, wash the spinach carefully in 2 or 3 changes or water. Drain briefly in a colander. Uncover the pan, stir in the minced garlic, and cook for 1 minute. Add the still-damp spinach leaves and toss to distribute evenly. Re-cover and cook until the spinach is wilted, about 5 minutes. Remove from the heat and add the olives, a pinch of salt, and a grind of pepper. Stir to mix.

Rub 1 side of each bread slice lightly with the cut side of a garlic half. Arrange the slices on a baking sheet. Brush evenly with the remaining 1 tablespoon olive oil. Bake until lightly toasted, about 12 minutes. Remove from the oven. Preheat the broiler (grill).

Make a layer of the spinach mixture on each of the toasts, dividing it evenly. Top with 2 eggplant slices, slightly overlapping them, and then with 2 roasted tomato halves, cut side up. Sprinkle evenly with the basil. Arrange a layer of the cheese on top of each sandwich, dividing evenly. Slip the pan into the broiler about 4 inches (10 cm) from the heat source and broil (grill) until the cheese is hot and bubbly, about 4 minutes. Transfer to individual plates and serve at once.

1 eggplant (aubergine), about 3/4 lb (375 g)

Kosher salt

4 large, firm ripe plum (Roma) tomatoes, about 1 lb (500 g)

4 tablespoons (2 fl oz/60 ml) extra-virgin olive oil

1 cup (3 1/2 oz/105 g) thin lengthwise-cut sweet onion such as Maui or Vidalia

5 oz (155 g) spinach leaves, stems removed (about 4 cups loosely packed)

1 teaspoon minced garlic, plus 1 clove garlic, halved

1 tablespoon finely chopped pitted Kalamata olives

Freshly ground pepper

4 thick slices whole-grain coarse country bread, each about 6 inches (15 cm) long, 4 inches (10 cm) wide, and 3/4 inch (2 cm) thick

4 large fresh basil leaves, cut into chiffonade (page 279)

1/4 lb (125 g) low-fat mozzarella cheese, shredded

MAKES 4 SERVINGS

Lahvosh Filled with Goat Cheese, Walnuts, and Dried Figs

¹/₂ lb (250 g) fresh goat cheese, at room temperature

¹/₂ cup (about 4 oz/125 g) moist-packed dried figs, stems trimmed and finely chopped

¹/₄ cup (³/₄ oz/20 g) thinly sliced green (spring) onion, including tender green tops

¹/₄ cup (1 oz/30 g) finely chopped walnuts

Kosher salt

2 pieces soft *lahvosh*, each 12 by 6 inches (30 by 15 cm)

4 soft lettuce leaves, such as butter (Boston) or leaf lettuce

MAKES 4 SERVINGS

In a large bowl, combine the goat cheese, figs, green onion, walnuts, and ¹/₂ teaspoon salt. Mash together with a fork until well blended.

Place a dampened kitchen towel on a work surface. Lay 1 piece of the *lahvosh*, a short side facing you, on the towel. Using a teaspoon, drop half of the cheese mixture at regular intervals on the surface of the bread. Spread as evenly as possible, making sure to bring it all the way to the edge of the bread farthest from you. Place 2 lettuce leaves in a single layer on top of the cheese. Starting from the edge nearest you, roll the bread away from you in a tight roll, making sure that the edge is sealed. Using a sharp knife, trim each end of the roll. Immediately wrap in plastic wrap and refrigerate. Repeat with the remaining piece of *lahvosh*, filling, and lettuce.

Refrigerate for at least 30 minutes or for up to 8 hours. Cut each roll crosswise into 6 pieces each 1 inch (2.5 cm) wide. Serve cold.

Lahvosh, a thin flat bread that originated in Armenia, is available round or oblong, and crisp like a cracker or soft like pita bread. This recipe uses the soft type, which you will need to cut to the size specified. *Lahvosh* has a tendency to dry quickly when exposed to the air, so keep it covered with a damp towel once it is removed from its wrapping. Goat cheese looks rich but is usually lower in fat than cheese made from cow's milk. Figs have more dietary fiber than dried plums, bran flakes, or popcorn in equal weights. They are also rich in potassium and calcium.

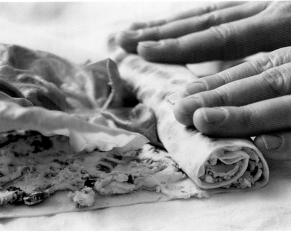

Roasted Red Pepper and Mozzarella Sandwiches

For this recipe, the ingredients in classic pesto have been altered to make a zesty sandwich spread with considerably fewer calories. The olive oil is reduced to make the sauce thicker. Walnuts or almonds, used in place of the pine nuts, add fiber and vitamins. Reserve leftover pesto to season soups or pasta or for future sandwiches.

Preheat the oven to 400°F (200°C).

To roast the bell peppers, spread the pepper quarters, skin side up, in a shallow 9-by-13-inch (23-by-33-cm) baking dish. Drizzle evenly with 1 tablespoon of the olive oil. Sprinkle lightly with salt and a grind of pepper. Roast, turning often, until the peppers are blackened and are tender when pierced with a knife, about 50 minutes. Remove from the oven and tightly cover the baking dish with a sheet of aluminum foil. Let stand until cool. Using a paring knife, remove any of the loosened skin and discard.

To make the pesto, in a food processor, combine the basil leaves, walnuts, cheese, and garlic and process until smooth. With the motor running, drizzle in the olive oil and then 2 tablespoons water through the feed tube. Process until creamy. Scrape into a small bowl.

To assemble the sandwiches, spread 1 tablespoon of the pesto on each of 4 of the toasted bread slices. (Spoon the remaining pesto into a container with a tight-fitting lid, pour a thin layer of olive oil onto the surface to prevent darkening, and refrigerate for up to 1 week.)

Divide the mozzarella evenly among the pesto-topped bread slices. Top each with 2 roasted pepper quarters and $1/2$ cup ($1/2$ oz/15 g) of the arugula leaves. Put the remaining toasted bread slices on top and cut each sandwich in half on the diagonal. Serve at once.

For the Roasted Peppers

2 large red bell peppers (capsicums), about $3/4$ lb (375 g) each, quartered lengthwise and seeded

4 tablespoons (2 fl oz/60 ml) extra-virgin olive oil

Kosher salt and freshly ground pepper

For the Pesto

1 cup (1 oz/30 g) loosely packed fresh basil leaves

$1/4$ cup (1 oz/30 g) chopped walnuts or almonds

1 tablespoon grated pecorino Romano or Asiago cheese

1 clove garlic, chopped

3 tablespoons extra-virgin olive oil

8 slices Multigrain Yeast Bread (page 263) or other whole-grain bread, toasted

$1/4$ lb (125 g) low-fat mozzarella cheese, thinly sliced

2 cups (2 oz/60 g) loosely packed arugula (rocket) leaves

MAKES 4 SERVINGS

Portobello Burgers

4 large portobello
mushrooms, 5–6 oz
(155–185 g) each, brushed
clean and stems removed

1 tablespoon extra-virgin
olive oil

4 whole-grain burger buns,
split

For the Herb Vinaigrette

2 tablespoons extra-virgin
olive oil

1 tablespoon red wine
vinegar

1 teaspoon Dijon mustard

1/2 teaspoon minced garlic

Kosher salt and freshly
ground pepper

1 teaspoon minced fresh
thyme

1 teaspoon minced fresh
rosemary

1 teaspoon minced fresh dill
or flat-leaf (Italian) parsley

5 oz (155 g) torn mixed salad
greens (about 4 cups loosely
packed)

4 thick slices beefsteak or
other large tomato

MAKES 4 SERVINGS

Portobello mushrooms, big and bursting with flavor, fill a sandwich bun almost as well as any other burger, and with far less fat and fewer calories. Look for mushrooms with smooth, blemish-free caps. Turn the caps over and make sure the gills are a dry, dull-looking brown. If they are damp and black-brown, the mushrooms are past their prime and will not be good for this dish. The burgers are topped off with salad greens in a tangy herb dressing and a thick slice of ripe tomato.

Prepare a CHARCOAL OR GAS GRILL for direct-heat grilling over medium heat or preheat the OVEN to 400°F (200°C). Oil the grill rack. Lightly brush the mushroom caps with the olive oil.

BY GRILL: Using tongs, place the mushrooms, cap side down, over the hottest part of the fire or directly over the heat elements and grill, turning once, until cooked through and tender when pierced with a knife, about 10 minutes. Transfer to a dish, cap side down. Using tongs, place the buns, cut side down, over the hottest part of the fire or heat elements and grill until toasted, 1–2 minutes.

BY OVEN: Place the mushrooms, cap side down, on a baking sheet and roast for 10 minutes. Turn the mushrooms and continue to roast until they are cooked through and tender when pierced with a knife, about 10 minutes longer. Transfer to a dish, cap side down. Turn on the BROILER (GRILL). Place the buns, cut side up, on a broiler pan and slip in the broiler about 3 inches (7.5 cm) from the heat source. Broil (grill) until toasted, 1–2 minutes.

To make the herb vinaigrette, in a small bowl, whisk together the olive oil, vinegar, mustard, garlic, 1/4 teaspoon salt, pepper to taste, and 1 tablespoon water until blended. Stir in the thyme, rosemary, and dill. Spoon 1/2 teaspoon of the dressing over each of the mushrooms.

Place the bottom half of each bun on an individual plate. Place the salad greens in a large bowl, add the remaining vinaigrette, and toss to coat evenly. Mound the salad greens on the bun halves on the plates, dividing them evenly. Top each with a tomato slice and then with a mushroom, cap side up. Put the tops of the buns in place and serve at once.

VARIATION

Portobello Burgers
with Red Bell Peppers
Substitute 2 roasted bell pepper (capsicum) quarters (page 277) for each tomato slice.

Ahi Tuna and Cucumber Sandwiches with Tapenade

Fish, olives, and olive oil offer a bonanza of heart-healthy fats. Whole grains and greens add plenty of fiber. Ahi, the Hawaiian name for yellowfin tuna, tastes best when cooked rare and then thinly sliced. If you prefer ahi cooked through, increase the time by seconds, not minutes, as it cooks quickly. If you overcook it, the delicate texture will be lost. (For advice about consuming raw seafood, see page 9.) Complementing the tuna are a piquant olive purée and a salad of bitter greens. You can use a combination of greens such as mizuna, mustard, arugula (rocket), beet greens, and spinach. You will need about 4 cups (6 oz/185 g). Any whole-grain coarse country bread may be substituted for the multigrain bread.

To cook the tuna, brush a large, heavy frying pan with the canola oil. Place over high heat until hot enough for a drop of water to sizzle and then immediately evaporate. Add the tuna and cook for exactly 1 minute. Turn the tuna and cook for 1 minute longer. Sprinkle 1 1/2 teaspoons of the soy sauce over the tuna, turn the tuna, and cook for 1 minute longer. The fish will be well browned on the exterior and rare inside. Sprinkle the remaining 1 1/2 teaspoons soy sauce over the tuna and transfer the tuna to a cutting board. Let stand while you prepare the remaining ingredients for the sandwiches.

To make the tapenade, in a food processor, combine the olives, green onion, garlic, and a grind of pepper; process until finely chopped. With the motor running, drizzle in the olive oil through the feed tube. Continue to process, stopping to scrape down the sides of the bowl as necessary, until the tapenade is creamy. Transfer to a small bowl.

To make the salad, in a large bowl, whisk together the rice vinegar, honey, and olive oil. Add the greens and toss to coat evenly.

Using a sharp knife with a thin blade, cut the tuna crosswise into slices 1/8 inch (3 mm) thick.

To assemble the sandwiches, arrange the bread on a platter. Spread with a thin layer of tapenade, using about 2 teaspoons for each slice. Place an equal amount of the salad on each slice of bread. Top half of the slices with a layer of overlapping cucumber slices. Top the remaining slices with a layer of overlapping tuna slices. Serve at once.

For the Ahi Tuna

1/2 teaspoon canola oil

1 ahi tuna steak, about 3/4 lb (375 g) and 3/4 inch (2 cm) thick

3 teaspoons reduced-sodium soy sauce

For the Tapenade

1/3 cup (1 1/2 oz/45 g) chopped pitted Kalamata olives

2 tablespoons thinly sliced green (spring) onion, including tender green tops

1 clove garlic, coarsely chopped

Freshly ground pepper

2 tablespoons extra-virgin olive oil

For the Salad

1 tablespoon rice vinegar

1 tablespoon honey

1 tablespoon extra-virgin olive oil

5 oz (155 g) mixed baby salad greens (see note)

8 slices Multigrain Yeast Bread (page 263)

1 cup (6 oz/185 g) thinly sliced English (hothouse) cucumber

MAKES 4 SERVINGS

Tomato, Onion, and Goat Cheese Sandwiches

For the Oven-Roasted
Tomatoes

**4 large, firm ripe plum
(Roma) tomatoes, about
1 lb (500 g) total weight,
halved lengthwise and
seeded**

**1 tablespoon extra-virgin
olive oil**

For the Caramelized Onions

1¹/₂ lb (750 g) yellow onions

¹/₂ teaspoon dried thyme

**Kosher salt and freshly
ground pepper**

2 teaspoons red wine vinegar

**4 thick slices Multigrain Yeast
Bread (page 263) or whole-
grain coarse country bread,
each about ³/₄ inch (2 cm)
thick, toasted**

**¹/₄ lb (125 g) fresh goat
cheese or soft farmer cheese,
at room temperature**

**1 teaspoon fresh thyme
leaves (optional)**

MAKES 4 SERVINGS

To make the oven-roasted tomatoes, preheat the oven to 325°F (165°C). Arrange the tomatoes, cut side up, in an 8-inch (20-cm) square baking pan. Drizzle with the olive oil. Roast the tomatoes, turning them and rotating the pan so they will cook evenly, until wrinkled and browned but still moist, 1–1¹/₂ hours. Remove the tomatoes from the oven, cover with aluminum foil, and let cool. Uncover and peel off any skins that are loosened from the flesh.

To make the caramelized onions, cut each onion in half lengthwise, then cut crosswise into thin half circles. (You will have about 5 cups/18 oz/560 g.) Heat a large nonstick frying pan over medium heat until warmed. Add the onions and 2 tablespoons water. (The onions will come to the top of the pan, but will reduce considerably in volume during cooking.) Cover and cook, stirring once or twice and adding more water if necessary to prevent scorching, until softened, about 10 minutes. Uncover and cook, stirring often, until the onions are a rich golden brown, about 15 minutes longer. Add the dried thyme, ¹/₂ teaspoon salt, and a grind of pepper and continue to cook, stirring, for 1 minute to blend. Stir in the vinegar. Remove from the heat and let cool.

To assemble the sandwiches, place 1 slice of toasted bread on each plate. Spread each slice with the cheese, dividing it evenly. Top with the onions, again dividing evenly. Top each portion with 2 tomato halves. Garnish with fresh thyme leaves, if using, and serve at once.

Tomato jam is the closest description to the flavors that result when plum tomatoes are oven roasted. The tomatoes are ready when they are wrinkled and darkened, but still fairly moist. They will take at least an hour to prepare, so it is wise to double the recipe and reserve the remainder for another day. They keep well frozen in a single layer in a heavy-duty plastic bag or airtight plastic container for up to one month. Tomatoes are rich in lycopene, a part of the carotenoid family. Lycopene has been found to reduce the risk of some cancers.

Buckwheat Crepes with Mushrooms

For the Buckwheat Crepes

1/2 cup (4 fl oz/125 ml) 1-percent-fat milk

1 large whole egg, plus 1 large egg yolk

1 tablespoon plus 1 teaspoon canola oil

1/3 cup (1 1/2 oz/45 g) all-purpose (plain) flour

1/4 cup (1 1/4 oz/40 g) buckwheat flour

Kosher salt

For the Mushroom Filling

1 1/2 lb (750 g) cremini mushrooms, brushed clean

1/2 lb (250 g) fresh shiitake mushrooms, brushed clean

1 tablespoon extra-virgin olive oil

2 tablespoons minced yellow onion

1 teaspoon minced fresh thyme or rosemary

Kosher salt and freshly ground pepper

1 teaspoon minced garlic

2 tablespoons nonfat or light sour cream

2 tablespoons regular sour cream

2 cups (2 oz/60 g) arugula (rocket) leaves (optional)

MAKES 4 SERVINGS

To make the crepe batter, in a bowl, whisk together the milk, whole egg, egg yolk, 1 tablespoon canola oil, and 1/2 cup (4 fl oz/125 ml) water until blended. In a separate bowl, stir together the all-purpose flour, buckwheat flour, and 1/4 teaspoon salt. Pour the wet ingredients over the dry ingredients and whisk until smooth. Pour through a fine-mesh sieve placed over a clean bowl, pressing on the contents of the sieve with the back of a spoon to dissolve any lumps of flour. Cover and refrigerate for 30–60 minutes before cooking the crepes.

To cook the crepes, place an 8-inch (20-cm) frying pan with low, sloping sides over medium heat until hot enough for a drop of water to sizzle and then immediately evaporate. Brush the pan with some of the 1 teaspoon oil, coating it with only a thin film. Stir the batter well and add a scant 1/4 cup (2 fl oz/60 ml) to the hot frying pan; tilt the pan so that the batter forms a thin layer on the bottom. Cook until the edges turn golden, 1–2 minutes. Using a spatula, carefully turn the crepe and cook for about 1 minute more. Turn out onto a plate and repeat, lightly brushing the pan with more oil if necessary. You will have 8 crepes.

To make the mushroom filling, remove the stems from the cremini and shiitake mushrooms, and discard. Thinly slice the caps. In a large frying pan over medium high heat, warm the olive oil until it is hot enough for a piece of mushroom to sizzle upon contact. Add the mushrooms, onion, thyme, 1/2 teaspoon salt, and a grind of pepper and stir to combine. Cover and cook over medium heat, stirring once or twice, until the mushrooms are tender, about 5 minutes. Uncover and raise the heat to medium-high. Cook, stirring, until any excess moisture is evaporated, about 1 minute. Add the garlic, reduce the heat to low, and cook for 1 minute. Remove from the heat. In a small bowl, stir together the nonfat and regular sour creams, then fold into the mushroom mixture.

Spread half of each crepe with about 1/4 cup (2 oz/60 g) of the filling. Top with a few arugula leaves, if using. Fold the uncovered half over the filling, then fold in half again, creating a triangle. Repeat until all the crepes are filled, then divide among individual plates, placing 2 crepes on each plate, and serve.

Buckwheat flour is used in France, especially in Brittany, for making savory crepes. The fresh thyme or rosemary in this hearty crepe filling reinforces the woodsy taste of the mushrooms. To satisfy diehard sour cream fans, equal amounts of the real thing and the light version are used. The taste and texture of real sour cream will be noticed, but the fat will be cut in half.

Vietnamese-Style Summer Rolls with Dipping Sauce

Once you have assembled the ingredients, these irresistible rolls are easy to make. The trick to making summer rolls that will not fall apart is not to stuff them too full and to roll them tightly. Serve the rolls as soon as possible, as the rice paper toughens the longer it stands.

To make the dipping sauce, in a small bowl, combine the lime juice, rice vinegar, soy sauce, and 1 tablespoon sugar. Stir to dissolve the sugar. Add the 2 teaspoons jalapeño, taste, and add more sugar and more jalapeño to taste. Divide evenly among small bowls for dipping. Set aside until ready to serve.

Place the mushrooms in a small saucepan with water to cover and bring to a boil over high heat. Remove from the heat, cover, and let stand until the shiitakes are softened, about 15 minutes. Drain, remove and discard the stems, and cut the caps into thin slices. Place in a small bowl.

Bring a large saucepan three-fourths of water to a boil over high heat. If the rice noodles are folded into a skein, cut at the fold. Add the noodles to the boiling water and boil, uncovered, until tender, 2–3 minutes. Drain, rinse with cold water, drain again, and set aside. Place in a bowl.

Peel the shrimp (page 277). Place the lettuce, carrot, green onion, cilantro, mint, and shrimp in separate bowls or arrange in mounds on a large tray.

When ready to make the summer rolls, fill a large, wide bowl with hot (about 120°F/49°C) water and place on a work surface. Dampen a clean kitchen towel, wring it out as dry as possible, and spread it out next to the bowl of hot water. Set the prepared ingredients alongside the towel.

Dip 1 rice-paper round in the hot water and let stand until soft and pliable, about 10 seconds. Lift from the water and lay flat on the towel. Place a lettuce leaf half in the center of the round, making sure it is at least 1 inch (2.5 cm) or more from the edges. Using about one-eighth of the noodles, spread them in a line across the bottom of the rice paper. Top with a few shiitake slices, a pinch each of the carrot, green onion, cilantro, and mint, and a shrimp.

Fold up the bottom of the rice paper round and then fold in the sides. Tightly roll the rice paper around the ingredients, sealing the seam against the roll. Place the roll, seam side down, on a platter. Repeat with the remaining ingredients.

Cut each roll in half on the diagonal and serve with the dipping sauce.

For the Dipping Sauce

$1/4$ cup (2 fl oz/60 ml) fresh lime juice

$1/4$ cup (2 fl oz/60 ml) rice vinegar

$2^1/2$ teaspoons soy sauce

1 tablespoon sugar, plus more to taste

2 teaspoons minced jalapeño chile, or more to taste

2 large dried shiitake mushrooms

$2^1/2$ oz (75 g) dried rice stick noodles or rice vermicelli

$1/4$ lb (125 g) medium shrimp (prawns), cooked

4 large butter (Boston) lettuce leaves, halved

$1/2$ cup ($1^1/2$ oz/45 g) coarsely shredded carrot

$1/4$ cup ($3/4$ oz/20 g) thinly sliced green (spring) onion

$1/2$ cup ($3/4$ oz/20 g) torn fresh cilantro (fresh coriander) leaves

$1/2$ cup ($3/4$ oz/20 g) torn fresh mint leaves

8 large rice-paper rounds, each 10–12 inches (25–30 cm) in diameter

MAKES 4 SERVINGS

Spinach Custard with Gruyère Topping

2–3 tablespoons fine dried bread crumbs

1 lb (500 g) fresh spinach or 1 package 10 oz (315 g) frozen spinach

1 tablespoon extra-virgin olive oil

$1/2$ cup (2 oz/60 g) chopped yellow onion

1 teaspoon minced garlic

4 dry-packed sun-dried tomato halves, snipped into small pieces with kitchen scissors (about 2 tablespoons)

Kosher salt and freshly ground pepper

$1/2$ cup (2 oz/60 g) shredded Gruyère cheese

3 large eggs

1 cup (8 fl oz/250 ml) 1-percent-fat milk

1 teaspoon Dijon mustard

MAKES 6 SERVINGS

Preheat the oven to 180°F (165°C). Spray the inside of six $3/4$-cup (6–fl oz/180-ml) custard cups or an 8-inch (20-cm) pie dish or round or square baking dish with canola-oil cooking spray. Lightly coat with the bread crumbs, then tap out the excess. If using individual cups, arrange them on a baking sheet.

If using fresh spinach, rinse it carefully in 2 or 3 changes of water, discarding the tough stems and any damaged leaves. Drain briefly in a colander and then transfer to a large saucepan with only the water that clings to the leaves. Place over medium-high heat, cover, and cook, turning the leaves a couple of times, until wilted, about 5 minutes. Drain well and chop finely. Squeeze the spinach with your hands to remove all excess moisture. If using frozen spinach, thaw and drain it, then squeeze to remove all excess moisture. Set aside.

In a frying pan over medium-low heat, warm the olive oil. Add the onion and cook until tender, about 5 minutes. Add the garlic and cook until fragrant, about 1 minute. Add the spinach, tomatoes, $1/2$ teaspoon salt, and a grind of pepper and cook, stirring, until all the ingredients are heated through, about 5 minutes.

Divide the spinach mixture evenly among the prepared cups, or spoon into the pie dish or baking dish. Smooth the mixture to create an even layer. Sprinkle the cheese on top, dividing it evenly if using custard cups.

In a large bowl, whisk the eggs until blended. Add the milk and mustard and stir until blended. Gently pour the egg mixture over the spinach filling, dividing it evenly if using custard cups.

Bake the custards until puffed and golden, 25–30 minutes for the custard cups and 30–35 minutes for the pie dish or baking dish. Transfer to a wire rack(s) and let cool for about 15 minutes.

Serve the individual custards in the cups or, if desired, run a knife around the inside edge of each cup and turn the custard out onto an individual dish. The custards will be firm enough to turn top side up. To serve the larger custard, cut into wedges or squares. Serve warm, or cover and refrigerate until cold before serving.

After years of criticism for their cholesterol content, eggs are now recognized for their high nutrient density and wide range of vitamins and minerals. A large egg has 6 grams of protein and 4.5 grams of fat, the majority of which is unsaturated. A large egg contains about 215 milligrams of cholesterol, all in the yolk. Current expert advice is to eat up to 5 egg yolks per week. This custard recipe has only $1/2$ egg yolk per serving.

Side Dishes

About Side Dishes

Nutritious ingredients, everyday cooking methods, a sure hand with seasoning, and only a small amount of added fat are at the heart of the best—and best for you—side dishes. Always use seasonal vegetables or fiber- and vitamin-rich whole grains for these companion plates.

Bursting with phytochemicals, fiber, vitamins, and minerals, fresh vegetables and whole grains are indispensable elements of every healthful eating plan. Here, they are used to make side dishes that share a commitment to nutritious ingredients, cooking methods that preserve the nutrients, and bold seasonings that will make you forget about the minimal use of fat. Nearly all of the dishes take less than an hour to prepare, and more than half can be ready in less than thirty minutes.

SEASONAL VEGETABLES, SIMPLY COOKED

Any vegetable that has been locally grown and ripened in its natural season will be much more flavorful than one that is prematurely picked and ripened during transportation. In other words, spring is the time to make Roasted Asparagus with Toasted Bread Crumbs (page 176), and the long, hot days of summer, when eggplants (aubergines) are plentiful and tomatoes are bursting with juice, are perfect for putting together Eggplant with Tomatoes, Ricotta, and Parmigiano-Reggiano (page 182).

Always choose the freshest vegetables you can find. Farmers' markets and roadside stands are great sources, but in their absence, seek out a store that specializes in organic produce and has a steady turnover of inventory to ensure freshness. For the best flavor and nutrition, eat the vegetables soon after you buy them, and wash and trim them just before cooking. Leave their skins on when feasible for an extra dose of nutrients and fiber.

Roasting is a particularly effective cooking method for vegetables, as the heat of the oven concentrates their juices and deepens their flavors. For example, the natural sugars in carrots caramelize during roasting, blending nicely with the spices in Roasted Carrots with Orange Zest and Cinnamon (page 186). Sweet peppers (capsicums) and Vidalia onions become even sweeter in the oven in Three-Pepper and Sweet Onion Roast with Kalamata Olives (page 178).

Stir-frying, or cooking foods rapidly in a small amount of oil, retains nutrients. Stir-fried vegetables take well to strong seasonings, too, such as fresh herbs, citrus zest, and garlic. The assertive flavorings in Stir-Fried Spinach with Garlic and Lemon Zest (page 187) and Stir-Fried Baby Greens with Ginger and Garlic (page 188) excite the taste buds, making you less likely to miss the fat that is usually found in such dishes.

Perhaps the most healthful way to cook vegetables is steaming, a technique that preserves their shapes, colors, textures, and nutrients. Although steaming does not require the addition of any fat, a touch of fragrant oil will make the vegetables taste richer without compromising the wholesomeness of the finished dish. The chile-infused olive oil in Broccoli with Red Pepper Flakes and Garlic Chips (page 190) is one example.

Potatoes, which contain vitamins, fiber, and other nutrients, are the base for countless old-fashioned side dishes, many of them laden with cheese, cream, and/or salt. A few of them

have been deliciously updated here. In Goat Cheese and Potato Gratin (page 200), a contemporary version of scalloped potatoes, goat's milk cheese and 1-percent-fat milk replace the traditional cow's milk cheese and heavy (double) cream. A thin film of heart-healthy oil and a sprinkle of fresh herbs flavor Roasted Russet Potatoes with Parsley and Garlic (page 203) and Roasted Sweet Potatoes with Cumin and Cilantro (page 205), a pair of healthful alternatives to french fries.

THE BENEFITS OF GRAINS

Side dishes fashioned from whole grains, which have their bran (full of fiber and vitamins) and germ (containing unsaturated fat, protein, iron, vitamins, and minerals) intact, will be more nutritious than those made from refined grains.

Brown rice is rich in magnesium and is a source of iron, phosphorus, and B vitamins. Its slightly chewy texture and nutty flavor enhance preparations such as Sesame Brown Rice (page 208). But even white rice has its virtues, being both fat free and a good source of complex carbohydrates. The flavor, aroma, and texture of rice vary according to variety. Basmati rice, for example, has a floral character, which is complemented by the exotic spices in Spiced Basmati Rice Pilaf (page 210). Other grains to consider for healthful side dishes are polenta, made from enriched cornmeal, and quinoa, a high-protein grain that is a good source of iron, niacin, zinc, potassium, phosphorus, and magnesium.

Making healthful side dishes is easy when you start with fresh, wholesome vegetables and grains, keep added fats to a minimum, and season the dishes boldly enough to delight the palate while preserving the ingredients' natural flavors.

Roasted Asparagus with Toasted Bread Crumbs

1 bunch asparagus, about 1 lb (500 g), tough ends removed

3 teaspoons extra-virgin olive oil

2 teaspoons minced fresh thyme

¹/₂ cup (1 oz/30 g) fresh, soft bread crumbs, made from day-old coarse country bread with crusts removed (page 278)

1 teaspoon grated lemon zest

Kosher salt and freshly ground pepper

MAKES 4 SERVINGS

Preheat the oven to 450°F (230°C).

Spread the asparagus in a baking dish large enough to hold them in a single layer. Drizzle with 1 teaspoon of the olive oil and sprinkle with 1 teaspoon of the thyme. Toss to coat the asparagus evenly.

Roast the asparagus, stirring once halfway through the roasting time, until tender-crisp, 7–10 minutes; the timing will depend on the thickness of the spears.

Meanwhile, place the bread crumbs in a small bowl and drizzle with the remaining 2 teaspoons oil; toss to coat. Place a frying pan over medium heat. When it is hot, add the bread crumbs, reduce the heat to medium-low, and toast, stirring, until they are golden, 3–4 minutes. Stir in the remaining 1 teaspoon thyme, the lemon zest, a pinch of salt, and a grind of pepper. Remove from the heat.

Arrange the asparagus on a warmed platter and sprinkle the hot bread crumbs over the top. Serve at once.

The best way to trim spears of asparagus is to bend the cut end of each spear until it breaks naturally. The bottom portion will be tough and fibrous; the balance of the spear will be tender. You can cut a thin slice from the base of each spear for a tidier finish. If you have purchased very thick spears, you may also want to peel them lightly to within 2 inches (5 cm) or so of the tip, as the outer skin is sometimes fibrous. Peeling asparagus does not reduce its dietary fiber.

Three-Pepper and Sweet Onion Roast with Kalamata Olives

1 large green bell pepper (capsicum), about $3/4$ lb (375 g)

1 large red bell pepper (capsicum), about $3/4$ lb (375 g)

1 large yellow bell pepper (capsicum), about $3/4$ lb (375 g)

1 large sweet onion such as Vidalia or Maui, about 10 oz (315 g)

1 tablespoon extra-virgin olive oil

Kosher salt and freshly ground pepper

8 Kalamata olives, pitted and coarsely chopped

1 tablespoon fresh rosemary leaves, chopped, or 1 teaspoon dried rosemary leaves

MAKES 4 SERVINGS

Preheat the oven to 400°F (200°C).

Cut the bell peppers into quarters and remove the seeds and ribs. Cut each quarter lengthwise into strips $1/2$ inch (12 mm) wide. Cut the onion into 8 wedges.

Combine the bell pepper strips and onion wedges in a shallow, 9-by-13-inch (23-by-33-cm) baking dish. Drizzle evenly with the olive oil and sprinkle with $1/4$ teaspoon salt and pepper to taste. (Take care when adding salt, as the olives are very salty.)

Roast the vegetables, turning them once or twice, until golden and tender, about 50 minutes. If using dried rosemary, sprinkle it over the vegetables halfway through the roasting time. When the vegetables are ready, sprinkle them with the olives and with the fresh rosemary, if using, and roast for 5 minutes longer.

Transfer the vegetables to a warmed bowl and serve at once.

Rosemary has a distinctive flavor that goes well with the sweetness of roasted peppers and onions and the tang of black olives. The red and yellow bell peppers are sweeter than the green peppers, but if you cannot find a yellow pepper, use one green and two red bell peppers. Bell peppers, especially red ones, are rich in antioxidants and phytochemicals that protect vision and increase immunity.

Roasted Tomatoes with Cannellini Beans and Capers

This vegetarian dish is a good source of protein and an excellent source of dietary fiber, vitamin C, and many phytochemicals. The creamy texture of the cannellini beans, the mild acidity of the roasted tomatoes, and the saltiness of the capers come together in a combination that mates well with grilled fish, or with green vegetables as part of a vegetarian meal. Use any leftover cooked dried beans for a soup, stew, or salad. The beans also make a delicious spread for toasted bread when mashed with a dash of olive oil, a little minced garlic, a pinch of kosher salt, and a generous grind of pepper.

If using dried beans, place the soaked, drained beans in a saucepan and add water to cover generously. Bring to a boil over high heat, reduce the heat to low, cover partially, and simmer gently until tender, 1–1 1/2 hours. Drain well, measure out 1 3/4 cups (12 1/2 oz/390 g), and set aside. Reserve any remaining beans for another use (see note). If using canned beans, drain well, rinse under running cold water, drain well again, and set aside.

Preheat the oven to 400°F (200°C).

Spread the tomatoes in a shallow, 9-by-13-inch (23-by-33-cm) baking dish and drizzle with the olive oil. Roast the tomatoes until they begin to brown on the edges, about 25 minutes. Remove from the oven.

Combine the parsley, dried herbs, and orange zest on a cutting board and chop together finely. Add the beans, capers, and parsley mixture to the tomatoes and stir gently just to blend. Return to the oven and roast until all the ingredients are heated through, about 10 minutes. Remove from the oven. Sprinkle with 1/4 teaspoon salt, or more to taste, and season with pepper.

Transfer to a warmed serving dish and serve at once.

1 cup (7 oz/220 g) dried cannellini beans, soaked and drained (page 278), or 1 can (15 oz/470 g) cannellini beans

1 1/4 lb (625 g) plum (Roma) tomatoes, cut into wedges 1/2 inch (12 mm) wide

1 tablespoon extra-virgin olive oil

1 tablespoon chopped fresh flat-leaf (Italian) parsley

1/2 teaspoon dried *herbes de Provence*

1/2 teaspoon chopped orange zest

1 tablespoon small capers, rinsed and patted dry

Kosher salt and freshly ground pepper

MAKES 4 SERVINGS

Eggplant with Tomatoes, Ricotta, and Parmigiano-Reggiano

1 globe eggplant (aubergine), about 1¹/₂ lb (750 g), trimmed

Kosher salt

4 teaspoons extra-virgin olive oil

2 tablespoons finely chopped yellow onion

¹/₂ teaspoon minced garlic

1 can (14¹/₂ oz/455 g) whole or diced plum (Roma) tomatoes with juice

¹/₄ cup (¹/₃ oz/10 g) torn fresh basil leaves

Freshly ground pepper

¹/₂ cup (4 oz/125 g) part-skim ricotta cheese

2 tablespoons grated Parmigiano-Reggiano cheese

2 tablespoons shredded part-skim mozzarella cheese

MAKES 6 SERVINGS

Eggplant is often associated with oil-and-cheese-rich eggplant Parmesan. This recipe takes all the elements of that classic dish and streamlines the preparation while cutting the fat substantially. For example, the eggplant is roasted in a hot oven with just a thin coating of oil, rather than fried in oil on the stove top, and fat calories are kept to a minimum by using part-skim-milk ricotta and mozzarella cheeses.

Cut off the stem end of the eggplant. Standing it upright on the cut end, cut the eggplant vertically into 8 slices, each about ¹/₂ inch (12 mm) thick. Finely chop the outer slices, which are mostly skin, and reserve. Sprinkle both sides of the 8 eggplant slices lightly with salt and layer them in a colander set over a plate. Place a second plate on top to weigh them down and let stand for 1–2 hours. Rinse the slices well and pat dry with paper towels.

Preheat the oven to 400°F (200°C).

Lightly brush both sides of each eggplant slice, using 2 teaspoons of the olive oil for all of the slices. Arrange the slices in a single layer on a baking sheet. Bake them until the bottoms are lightly browned, about 15 minutes. Remove from the oven.

Meanwhile, in a large, nonstick frying pan over medium heat, warm the remaining 2 teaspoons oil. Add the onion and reserved chopped eggplant and sauté, stirring, until tender, about 15 minutes. Add the garlic and sauté for 1 minute until fragrant. Add the tomatoes and their juice and half of the basil and bring to a boil, breaking up the tomatoes. Reduce the heat to medium-low and simmer, stirring, until the sauce thickens, about 10 minutes. Stir in ¹/₄ teaspoon salt and season with pepper. In a small bowl, combine the ricotta, Parmigiano-Reggiano, and a grind of pepper and stir to blend.

Have ready a shallow, 1¹/₂-qt (1.5-l) baking dish. Place 4 of the eggplant slices in a single layer in the dish. Divide the ricotta mixture evenly among the eggplant slices, spreading it slightly. Top with half of the tomato mixture, dividing it evenly among the slices, then top with the remaining 4 slices. Spoon the remaining tomato mixture over the top, dividing evenly. Sprinkle evenly with the mozzarella.

Cover the dish with aluminum foil. Bake until the sauce is bubbly and the eggplant is heated through, about 25 minutes. Remove from the oven and sprinkle with the remaining basil.

Artichokes Vinaigrette

You can boil the artichokes a day or two in advance and then roast them just before serving. This dish makes an elegant first course for a sit-down dinner. It can easily be doubled for a large party.

Trim the artichokes (page 278) and cut in half lengthwise.

Bring a saucepan three-fourths full of water to a boil over high heat. Add a pinch of salt and the halved artichokes. Reduce the heat so the water is at a gentle boil, cover, and cook until the artichoke bottoms are tender when pierced with the tip of a knife and the leaves are tender to the bite, 8–10 minutes. Using a slotted spoon, transfer the artichoke halves to a colander to drain.

When the artichokes are cool enough to handle, use a teaspoon to remove any prickly chokes at the center.

Preheat the oven to 400°F (200°C).

Arrange the artichoke halves in a single layer in a shallow, 9-by-13-inch (23-by-33-cm) baking dish. Drizzle evenly with the olive oil. Roast the artichokes, turning once, until lightly browned, 10–12 minutes.

Using a slotted spoon, transfer the artichokes to a serving dish. Add the vinegar, oregano, garlic, $^1/_4$ teaspoon salt, and pepper to taste to the oil in the baking dish and whisk to form a vinaigrette. Drizzle the vinaigrette evenly over the artichokes. Serve warm or at room temperature.

$1^1/_4$ **lb (625 g) baby artichokes**

Kosher salt

3 tablespoons extra-virgin olive oil

1 tablespoon red wine vinegar

2 teaspoons minced fresh oregano or $^1/_2$ teaspoon dried oregano

$^1/_4$ teaspoon minced garlic

Freshly ground pepper

MAKES 4 SERVINGS

Roasted Carrots with Orange Zest and Cinnamon

1 lb (500 g) carrots, peeled and trimmed

2 cloves garlic, smashed

2 orange zest strips, each 2 inches (5 cm) long and ¹/₂ inch (12 mm) wide, cut into julienne

1 tablespoon extra-virgin olive oil

Kosher salt and freshly ground pepper

1 cinnamon stick, broken in half

2 teaspoons fresh lemon juice

MAKES 4 SERVINGS

This unusual combination of flavors will be popular with everyone at your table. Oven roasting concentrates the natural sugar in the carrots, giving them an extra flavor dimension. The nutrient value of cooked carrots is higher than the same amount of raw carrots. Heat makes the vitamins in carrots more available for the body to absorb. Serve these carrots with roasted chicken or fish and a green vegetable, such as green beans, to balance the sweetness of the carrots.

Preheat the oven to 400°F (200°C).

Cut the carrots into 2-inch (5-cm) lengths; halve lengthwise any thick top portions so all the pieces will cook evenly. In a shallow, 9-by-13-inch (23-by-33-cm) baking dish, combine the carrots, garlic, and orange zest. Drizzle the vegetables with the olive oil and sprinkle with ¹/₄ teaspoon salt and pepper to taste. Add the cinnamon stick, toss to coat the vegetables evenly, and spread in an even layer in the dish.

Roast the carrots, stirring every 10 minutes, until tender and lightly browned, about 50 minutes. Remove from the oven and transfer to a warmed serving dish. Sprinkle the carrots with the lemon juice and serve at once.

VARIATION

Roasted Carrots with Orange Zest and Cumin
Omit the cinnamon stick. Sprinkle 1 teaspoon ground cumin over the carrots with the salt and pepper.

Stir-Fried Spinach with Garlic and Lemon Zest

Spinach is one of the most nutritious vegetables. When spinach is cooked, its nutrients become even more concentrated. In addition to abundant iron, potassium, and vitamins A and C, the leaves are rich in leutine and zeaxathin, phytochemicals that protect vision.

Rinse the spinach carefully in 2 or 3 changes of water, discarding the tough stems and any damaged leaves. Drain briefly in a colander.

In a deep sauté pan or a wok over medium-high heat, combine the olive oil, lemon zest, and garlic. When the garlic begins to sizzle, after about 30 seconds, immediately add the still-damp spinach and, using tongs or 2 wooden spoons, toss and stir quickly until wilted, 2–3 minutes.

Transfer the spinach to a warmed serving dish and sprinkle with a pinch of salt and a grind of pepper. Serve at once.

2 lb (1 kg) spinach

1 tablespoon extra-virgin olive oil

1 teaspoon grated lemon zest

1 teaspoon minced garlic

Kosher salt and freshly ground pepper

MAKES 4 SERVINGS

Stir-Fried Baby Greens with Ginger and Garlic

1 tablespoon canola or safflower oil

2 teaspoons peeled and minced fresh ginger

1 teaspoon minced garlic

1 lb (500 g) mixed baby greens, well rinsed and drained (see note)

Kosher salt

MAKES 4 SERVINGS

Mixed baby greens for stir-frying are available, either loose or in cellophane bags, in many grocery stores or by the pound at farmers' markets. The mixtures typically include young, tender leaves of Swiss chard, kale, beets, spinach, radicchio, and curly endive (chicory). Because these cooking greens are deeper in color than the baby greens used for salads, they typically have more vitamins than their lighter cousins. They are delicious quickly tossed with oil and then "steamed" in the rinsing water still clinging to the leaves.

Place a wide, deep saucepan over medium-high heat until hot enough for a drop of water to sizzle and then immediately evaporate. Add the oil, ginger, and garlic and heat just until the garlic begins to sizzle, about 10 seconds.

Add the greens all at once and, using tongs or 2 wooden spoons, toss and stir to coat with the oil and seasonings. Cover and allow the greens to steam in their own juices until tender, 9–12 minutes; the timing will depend on the varieties in the mix. Season with a pinch of salt.

Transfer the greens to a warmed serving dish and serve at once.

Broccoli with Red Pepper Flakes and Garlic Chips

2 tablespoons extra-virgin olive oil

1 tablespoon thin, crosswise-cut garlic slices

1/4 teaspoon red pepper flakes

1 bunch broccoli, about 1 1/2 lb (750 g)

MAKES 4 SERVINGS

In a small frying pan over medium-low heat, combine the olive oil, garlic, and red pepper flakes. Heat, stirring, just until the garlic begins to turn golden on the edges, 1–2 minutes. Remove from the heat. Place a small, fine-mesh sieve over a heatproof bowl and pour the oil through it. Reserve the oil and the contents of the sieve separately.

Trim off 1/2 inch (12 mm) from the stem ends of the broccoli stalks, then peel the tough outer layer from the stalks. Cut off the florets and the slender stems from the tops of the stalks, trimming them so that they are 1–2 inches (2.5–5 cm) long. Cut the large stalks crosswise into slices 1/4 inch (6 mm) thick.

Place all the cut broccoli in a steamer rack set over boiling water, cover tightly, and cook until tender, 4–6 minutes.

Transfer the broccoli to a warmed serving dish. Drizzle with 2 teaspoons of the reserved garlic oil and toss to coat. Reserve the remaining oil for another use. Sprinkle with the crisp garlic slices and red pepper flakes and serve.

Broccoli, a member of the cabbage family, is a cruciferous vegetable thought to reduce the risk of cancer. Containing lots of vitamins A and C and several minerals, it is one of the most healthful vegetables. This version is drizzled with spicy red pepper oil and garnished with crisp garlic chips. These robust flavors are an excellent substitute for the pat of butter or shake of salt traditionally added to broccoli.

Cauliflower with Orange Zest and Green Onion

Cauliflower is an excellent source of vitamin C and potassium. As a cruciferous vegetable, it also has cancer-fighting properties. Soaking the cauliflower in water before baking is an important step, as the moisture creates hot steam that helps the cauliflower cook to a tender and succulent finish. Advise each diner to squeeze a little lemon juice onto the cauli-flower at the table. The citrus heightens the flavors of this cool-weather dish.

Place the cauliflower florets in a large bowl and add cold water to cover. Let stand for 20–30 minutes, then drain.

Preheat the oven to 400°F (200°C).

Spread the cauliflower in a single layer in a shallow, 9-by-13-inch (23-by-33-cm) baking dish. Drizzle with the olive oil, sprinkle with 1/4 teaspoon salt, or more to taste, and season with pepper. Toss to coat. Bake the cauliflower, turning the florets every 10 minutes and sprinkling with 1–2 tablespoons cold water each time, until they are tender and lightly browned, about 30 minutes.

Combine the green onion, parsley, and orange zest on a cutting board and finely chop together. Remove the cauliflower from the oven and sprinkle evenly with the green onion mixture. Spoon the cauliflower into a warmed serving dish and garnish with the lemon wedges. Serve at once.

1 head cauliflower, about 1 3/4 lb (875 g), cored and cut into uniform-sized florets

1 tablespoon extra-virgin olive oil

Kosher salt and freshly ground pepper

2 tablespoons coarsely chopped green (spring) onion

2 tablespoons chopped fresh flat-leaf (Italian) parsley

2 teaspoons grated orange zest

4 lemon wedges

MAKES 4 SERVINGS

Maple-and-Soy-Glazed Acorn Squash

The sweetness of maple syrup, the saltiness of soy, and the subtle heat of ginger come together in a perfectly balanced glaze for thick slices of acorn squash. Other varieties, such as butternut and banana, can be prepared the same way. Winter squashes with firm orange flesh are great sources of beta-carotene and antioxidant phytochemicals. Serve this cool-weather dish with roasted meat or poultry.

Preheat the oven to 425°F (220°C). Line a large baking sheet with aluminum foil. Lightly coat the foil with the oil or spray with nonstick cooking spray.

Cut off both ends of each squash. Halve lengthwise and scoop out and discard the seeds and strings. Turn the squash halves cut side down and cut each half cross-wise into 4 or 5 slices each about $1/2$ inch (12 mm) thick. Arrange the slices in a single layer on the prepared baking sheet. Cover tightly with aluminum foil. Bake the squashes for about 15 minutes. Meanwhile, in a small bowl, whisk together the maple syrup, soy sauce, and ginger.

Remove the baking sheet from the oven and remove the foil. Brush half of the maple syrup mixture on the squash slices. Sprinkle with $1/4$ teaspoon salt, or more to taste, and season with pepper. Return the baking sheet to the oven and bake, uncovered, for 10 minutes. Remove the baking sheet from the oven and turn the squash slices. Brush the slices with the remaining maple syrup mixture. Return the baking sheet to the oven and bake until the squash slices are browned and tender when pierced with a knife, 5–10 minutes longer.

Transfer the squash slices to a warmed serving dish and serve at once.

1 teaspoon canola or safflower oil or canola-oil cooking spray

2 acorn squashes, each about $1^1/_2$ lb (750 g)

$1/_4$ cup (2 fl oz/60 ml) maple syrup

1 tablespoon reduced-sodium soy sauce

$1/_2$ teaspoon peeled and grated fresh ginger

Kosher salt and freshly ground pepper

MAKES 4 SERVINGS

Zucchini and Red Onions with Mint

1 red onion, halved lengthwise and thinly cut crosswise into half circles

1 tablespoon extra-virgin olive oil

4 small zucchini (courgettes), each 4–5 inches (10–13 cm) long, about 1¹/₂ lb (750 g) total weight, trimmed and halved lengthwise

Kosher salt and freshly ground pepper

¹/₄ cup (¹/₃ oz/10 g) finely chopped fresh mint

1 teaspoon red wine vinegar

MAKES 4 SERVINGS

Preheat the oven to 400°F (200°C).

Spread the onion slices in a shallow, 9-by-13-inch (23-by-33-cm) baking dish. Drizzle with the olive oil and stir to combine. Spread the onion slices again into an even layer.

Bake until the onion slices begin to brown on the edges, about 15 minutes. Remove from the oven.

Push the onion slices aside. Arrange the zucchini, cut side down, in the baking dish and spoon the onion slices on top. Sprinkle with ¹/₄ teaspoon salt, or more to taste, and season with pepper. Bake for 10 minutes, remove from the oven, and turn the zucchini cut side up. Bake until the zucchini are tender when pierced with a knife, 5–10 minutes longer.

Arrange the zucchini, cut side up, on a warmed serving plate. Add the mint and vinegar to the onion slices and stir to blend. Spoon the onion over the zucchini and serve at once.

Zucchini are mild-flavored squashes that taste best when they are small and young. Here, their understated flavor is heightened by two bold partners, roasted red onions and aromatic fresh mint. Serve this easy-to-assemble side dish with grilled or roasted lamb.

Steamed Sugar Snap Peas with Black Sesame Seeds

These crisp, bright green peas are delicious eaten raw as a snack, or parboiled for a few minutes and served hot as a side dish or cold in salads. Here, they are flavored with sesame oil and sesame seeds, to produce a fragrant side dish. The color is beautiful, the flavor is great, and each serving has only 70 calories.

Trim the stems and, if necessary, remove the strings from the sugar snap peas. To check if strings are present, cut or snap off a stem and then pull downward the length of the pod.

Arrange the sugar snap peas in a steamer rack set over boiling water, cover, and steam until tender-crisp, about 3 minutes. Transfer the peas to a serving bowl.

Cut the green onions, including the tender green tops, into slices $1/4$ inch (6 mm) thick. Add the green onions, sesame oil, sesame seeds, and a pinch of salt to the bowl holding the peas. Toss to coat the peas evenly.

Serve warm or at room temperature.

1 lb (500 g) sugar snap peas

2 green (spring) onions

$1^1/_2$ teaspoons Asian sesame oil

1 teaspoon black sesame seeds

Kosher salt

MAKES 4 SERVINGS

Stir-Fried Green Beans with Tamari Almonds

For the Tamari Almonds

¹/₄ cup (1¹/₂ oz/45 g) almonds, coarsely chopped

1¹/₂ teaspoons tamari or reduced–sodium soy sauce

1 lb (500 g) green beans

Kosher salt

2 teaspoons tamari or reduced-sodium soy sauce

2 teaspoons Chinese rice wine or dry sherry

¹/₂ teaspoon sugar

¹/₂ teaspoon Asian sesame oil

1 tablespoon peanut or canola oil

1 clove garlic, thinly sliced

MAKES 4 SERVINGS

This fresh-tasting dish complements pan-seared shrimp or chicken. Almonds provide some vitamin E and dietary fiber. Tamari, like soy sauce, is made from soybeans, but without the wheat that soy sauce contains. It is thicker and has a slightly milder, but more complex, taste. Reduced-sodium soy sauce may be substituted.

To make the tamari almonds, spread the almonds in a small, dry nonstick frying pan. Place over low heat and heat, stirring, until the pan is hot and the almonds begin to feel warm. Sprinkle the almonds with the tamari and stir quickly to coat and toast slightly, about 1 minute. Pour out onto a plate and let cool.

Bring a saucepan three-fourths full of water to a boil. Trim the green beans and cut into 2-inch (5-cm) lengths. Add the green beans and 1 teaspoon salt and cook, stirring, until tender-crisp, 4–6 minutes; the timing will depend on the size of the beans. Drain well.

While the beans are cooking, in a small bowl, stir together the tamari, rice wine, sugar, and sesame oil. Set aside.

Place a wok or large frying pan over medium-high heat until hot enough for a drop of water to sizzle and then immediately evaporate. Add the peanut oil and garlic and stir-fry just until the garlic sizzles, about 30 seconds. Add the drained green beans, a small handful at a time (be careful, as the beans will sizzle and may splatter you), and toss and stir just until the skins begin to blister slightly, about 3 minutes.

Add the tamari mixture to the beans and stir to coat. Spoon into a warmed serving bowl and garnish with the tamari almonds. Serve at once.

Roasted Mushrooms, Potatoes, and Green Beans

Oven roasting at a high temperature concentrates the moisture and flavor in vegetables and requires little or no additional fat. The olive oil in this recipe is used more for its rich taste than out of necessity. The vegetables are showered with a small amount of Parmigiano-Reggiano during the last few minutes of roasting. As long as you are using such a small amount, it is important to use the best and enjoy the maximum flavor benefit, as well as the boost in calcium.

Preheat the oven to 400°F (200°C).

Trim the ends of the stems from the mushrooms and discard. Cut the mushrooms in half throught the stems. Cut the potatoes into 1-inch (2.5-cm) pieces. Cut the onion into wedges ½ inch (12 mm) thick. Trim the green beans and cut into 1-inch (2.5-cm) lengths. Set the green beans aside.

In a shallow, 9-by-13-inch (23-by-33-cm) baking dish, combine the mushrooms, potatoes, and onion. Drizzle the vegetables with the olive oil, toss to coat evenly, and spread in an even layer in the dish.

Roast until the vegetables begin to brown on the edges, about 30 minutes. Remove the dish from the oven, add the green beans, and carefully turn and rearrange the vegetables in an even layer. Sprinkle with ¼ teaspoon salt and pepper to taste. Continue to roast until the vegetables are browned and tender when pierced with a knife, about 15 minutes longer. Sprinkle with the Parmigiano-Reggiano and thyme. Roast for 5 minutes longer to melt the cheese.

Serve the vegetables directly from the baking dish or transfer to a serving bowl.

8–10 white mushrooms, about ¼ lb (125 g) total weight, brushed clean

2 Yukon gold potatoes, about ½ lb (250 g) total weight

1 yellow onion

¼ lb (125 g) green beans

1 tablespoon extra-virgin olive oil

Kosher salt and freshly ground pepper

2 tablespoons grated Parmigiano-Reggiano cheese

1 tablespoon chopped fresh thyme

MAKES 4 SERVINGS

Goat Cheese and Potato Gratin

2 teaspoons extra-virgin
olive oil

1 1/2 lb (750 g) small, round
white potatoes

2 tablespoons finely chopped
fresh flat-leaf (Italian) parsley

1 teaspoon fresh thyme
leaves, plus extra leaves for
garnish

1 tablespoon all-purpose
(plain) flour

Kosher salt and freshly
ground pepper

3 oz (90 g) crumbled, very
cold fresh goat cheese
(about 3/4 cup)

1 1/4 cups (10 fl oz/310 ml)
1-percent-fat milk

1 tablespoon grated
Parmigiano-Reggiano cheese

MAKES 6 SERVINGS

Preheat the oven to 350°F (180°C). Brush an 8-inch (20-cm) square or other shallow, 1 1/2-qt (1.5-l) baking dish with the olive oil.

Using a mandoline, a food processor fitted with the slicing blade, or a large, sharp knife, slice the potatoes paper-thin.

In a small bowl, stir together the parsley and 1 teaspoon thyme. In another small bowl, stir together the flour, 1/4 teaspoon salt, and a grind of pepper. Place the goat cheese in a third bowl.

Arrange one-third of the potato slices, slightly overlapping them, in the prepared baking dish. Sprinkle evenly with half of the herb mixture, half of the flour mixture, and one-third of the goat cheese. Arrange half of the remaining potato slices on top, again overlapping them slightly. Sprinkle evenly with the remaining herb mixture, the remaining flour mixture, and half of the remaining cheese. Arrange the remaining potato slices in a layer on top and sprinkle evenly with the remaining goat cheese. Pour the milk evenly over the top.

Cover the baking dish tightly with aluminum foil. Bake the potatoes until tender when pierced with a knife, about 1 hour. Uncover, sprinkle the top lightly with the Parmigiano-Reggiano, and continue to bake until golden, about 15 minutes longer. Remove from the oven and let stand for 15 minutes before serving. The moisture in the dish will thicken and be reabsorbed by the potatoes.

Garnish the gratin with thyme leaves, cut into squares, and serve.

This is a modern version of a popular classic, scalloped potatoes. High-moisture fresh goat cheese delivers a lot of flavor with a bit less fat than hard grating cheeses. Look for soft fresh goat cheese as opposed to aged goat cheese covered by a rind. The fresh has a moderately creamy texture and can easily be crumbled when cold. It is typically sold in a disk or a log, sealed in plastic. Some varieties are seasoned with herbs or black or white pepper, but for this dish, plain unseasoned cheese is preferred.

Mashed Yukon Gold Potatoes

2 lb (1 kg) Yukon gold potatoes, peeled and cubed

4 cloves garlic

1 bay leaf

1 cup (8 fl oz/250 ml) 1-percent-fat milk

Kosher salt

2 tablespoons unsalted butter, melted and kept warm

MAKES 4 SERVINGS

Place the potatoes, garlic, and bay leaf in a large saucepan with water to cover by about 2 inches (5 cm). Bring to a boil over high heat, reduce the heat to medium-low, cover, and simmer until the potatoes are tender when pierced with a knife, about 15 minutes. Drain the potatoes and discard the bay leaf.

BY FOOD MILL OR RICER: Transfer the potatoes to a ricer or a food mill fitted with a medium disk, place it over the saucepan, and push the plunger or rotate the handle to purée the potatoes. Add the milk.

BY MIXER: Return the potatoes to the saucepan with the milk. Using a handheld electric mixer on high speed, beat the potatoes until smooth; take care not to overbeat or they will become gummy.

Using a wooden spoon, stir the puréed potatoes over low heat until thickened. Stir in 1/4 teaspoon salt, or more to taste.

Spoon the potatoes onto individual plates. Drizzle 1 1/2 teaspoons of the butter over each serving. Serve at once.

Traditional mashed potatoes require a stick of butter for flavor and creaminess. But this is unnecessary when using Yukon gold potatoes, naturally golden gems with a dense, creamy texture. Their flavor is enhanced in this recipe by adding a few garlic cloves and a bay leaf to the cooking water. The only butter used is a small amount that is melted and drizzled in a small pool on each serving, making a modest 6 grams of fat per serving seem like much more.

Roasted Russet Potatoes with Parsley and Garlic

Roasted potato strips are an excellent alternative to a plain baked potato and a healthful alternative to french fries. Not only do they cook faster, but they also allow you to keep the added fat (in the form of sour cream or butter) to a minimum by tossing the potatoes in just enough oil to give them a little flavor and encourage browning.

Preheat the oven to 400°F (200°C).

Cut the potatoes lengthwise into slices ¹/₂ inch (12 mm) thick. Stack half of the slices and cut lengthwise into strips ¹/₂ inch (12 mm) wide. Repeat with the remaining slices. Rinse the strips with cold water and spread on a clean kitchen towel; blot dry with a second kitchen towel.

Place the potatoes in a bowl. Drizzle with the olive oil and toss to coat evenly.

Preheat a nonstick baking sheet in the oven for 5 minutes. Remove from the oven and carefully arrange the potatoes in a single layer on the hot baking sheet. Roast the potatoes, turning every 10 minutes, until evenly browned and tender when pierced with a knife, 30–35 minutes. Meanwhile, combine the parsley and garlic on a cutting board and chop together finely.

Transfer the potatoes to a serving dish and sprinkle with ¹/₂ teaspoon salt and a grind of pepper. Add the parsley mixture and toss gently to coat. Serve at once.

2 long russet potatoes, about 1 lb (500 g) total weight

1 tablespoon extra-virgin olive oil

2 tablespoons finely chopped fresh flat-leaf (Italian) parsley

1 clove garlic

Kosher salt and freshly ground pepper

MAKES 4 SERVINGS

Roasted Sweet Potatoes with Cumin and Cilantro

Of the many varieties of sweet potatoes, the dark orange-fleshed tubers (often labeled "yams" in the United States) are especially popular, and are a healthful choice because they are high in vitamins A and C. You can also use a combination of varieties. In this simple recipe, sweet potato wedges are lightly seasoned with ground cumin before roasting and then dusted with chopped cilantro when served.

Preheat the oven to 400°F (200°C).

Cut the potatoes lengthwise into slices 1/2 inch (12 mm) thick. Stack half of the slices and cut lengthwise into strips 1/2 inch (12 mm) wide. Repeat with the remaining slices. Rinse the strips with cold water and spread on a clean kitchen towel; blot dry with a second kitchen towel.

Place the potatoes in a bowl. Drizzle with the oil, sprinkle with the cumin, and toss to coat evenly.

Preheat a nonstick baking sheet in the oven for 5 minutes. Remove from the oven and carefully arrange the potatoes in a single layer on the hot baking sheet. Roast the potatoes, turning every 10 minutes, until evenly browned and tender when pierced with a knife, 30–35 minutes.

Transfer the potatoes to a serving dish and sprinkle with 1/2 teaspoon salt, a grind of pepper, and the cilantro. Toss gently to coat. Serve at once.

2 orange-fleshed sweet potatoes, about 1 lb (500 g) total weight, peeled

1 tablespoon canola or safflower oil

1 teaspoon ground cumin

Kosher salt and freshly ground pepper

2 tablespoons finely chopped fresh cilantro (fresh coriander)

MAKES 4 SERVINGS

Sweet Potato and Cranberry Hash

3 orange-fleshed sweet potatoes, about 2 lb (1 kg) total weight

3 tablespoons unsalted butter

1 Fuji apple, peeled, cored, and cut into $^1/_2$-inch (12-mm) cubes

$^1/_2$ cup ($1^1/_2$ oz/45 g) sliced green (spring) onion

1 cup (4 oz/125 g) cranberries, coarsely chopped

$^1/_4$ teaspoon ground cinnamon

Pinch of ground allspice

Kosher salt and freshly ground pepper

MAKES 6 SERVINGS

Place a rack in the middle of the oven and preheat the oven to 350°F (180°C). Set the sweet potatoes directly on the rack and bake until they still feel slightly firm when pressed, 50–55 minutes. Remove from the oven and let cool to room temperature. Place the sweet potatoes on a plate, cover loosely, and refrigerate overnight. (Chilling them firms the flesh, making it hold together better in the hash.) The next day, peel the sweet potatoes and cut them into 1-inch (2.5-cm) pieces. Set aside.

In a nonstick frying pan over medium-high heat, melt 2 tablespoons of the butter. Add the apple cubes and sauté, stirring occasionally, until the butter browns and the apple cubes start to caramelize and brown around the edges, about 5 minutes. Add the remaining 1 tablespoon butter. When it melts, stir in the green onion and cranberries and cook until the green onion wilts, about 1 minute. Stir in the cinnamon and allspice, add the sweet potatoes, and cook, stirring frequently, until the sweet potatoes are heated through, about 4 minutes. They will break up somewhat, but try to smash them as little as possible. Add $^1/_4$ teaspoon salt, or more to taste, and season with pepper. Transfer to a serving dish and serve hot, warm, or at room temperature.

Surprisingly versatile, orange-fleshed sweet potatoes are good for making more than a savory candied side dish or a high-calorie dessert pie. Despite their name and flavor, sweet potatoes are not much higher in carbohydrates than white potatoes. Here, they are underbaked to keep their creamy flesh slightly firm, then are diced and combined with green onions, cranberries, and a touch of spice, to make a savory-sweet hash that is delicious served with poultry, pork, or game.

Lemon Orzo with Parsley

VARIATIONS

Lemon Orzo with Peas and Mint
Omit the parsley. Stir in 1 cup (6 oz/ 185 g) thawed, frozen English peas during the last 5 minutes of cooking. Sprinkle with 1 table-spoon minced fresh mint.

Lemon Orzo with Asparagus
Stir about ¼ lb (125 g) trimmed fresh asparagus, cut on the diago-nal into ¼-inch (6-mm) pieces (about 1 cup), into the orzo during last 3 minutes of cooking.

Orzo, which means "barley" in Italian, is a small, oval pasta shaped like its name-sake. It is delicious in soups, but also makes a good side dish for serving in place of potatoes or rice. The lemon juice and zest add a fresh, bright taste to the orzo, making it perfect to serve with seafood, especially pan-seared shrimp (prawns) or broiled salmon fillets.

In a large saucepan over high heat, bring 3 cups (24 fl oz/750 ml) water to a boil. Stir in the orzo and 1 teaspoon salt, cover, reduce the heat to medium, and cook until the water is absorbed and the pasta is tender, about 15 minutes.

Add the butter, lemon juice, lemon zest, and parsley and stir to blend. Spoon into a warmed serving dish and serve at once.

1½ cups (10½ oz/330 g) orzo

Kosher salt

2 tablespoons unsalted butter

2 tablespoons fresh lemon juice

2 teaspoons grated lemon zest

1 tablespoon finely chopped fresh flat-leaf (Italian) parsley

MAKES 6 SERVINGS

Sesame Brown Rice

1 cup (7 oz/220 g) medium-grain brown rice

Kosher salt

2 teaspoons sesame seeds

1 teaspoon Asian sesame oil

1 tablespoon thinly sliced green (spring) onion tops

MAKES 4 SERVINGS

In a saucepan over high heat, bring 2 3/4 cups (22 fl oz/680 ml) water to a boil. Add the rice and 1/2 teaspoon salt, stir once, reduce the heat to low, cover, and cook, without stirring, until all the water has been absorbed and the rice is tender, 35–45 minutes.

Meanwhile, in a small, dry frying pan over medium heat, toast the sesame seeds until they are fragrant and have taken on color, about 2 minutes. Pour the seeds onto a plate and set aside.

Carefully lift the cover of the saucepan so that no condensation drips into the rice. Drizzle the sesame oil evenly over the top and sprinkle on half of the sesame seeds. Gently fluff the rice with a chopstick or the handle of a wooden spoon.

Spoon the rice into a warmed serving dish. Sprinkle with the remaining sesame seeds and the green onion. Serve at once.

Medium-grain brown rice, often sold as short-grain brown rice, has a sticky texture and a lovely, nutlike aroma and taste. It is a whole grain with its bran intact, making it far more healthful than white rice. Asian sesame oil, which has a rich, toasted flavor, and sesame seeds complement the distinctive nature of the rice. If there are leftovers, transform them into a rice salad by adding grated carrot and a generous drizzle of rice vinegar.

Quinoa with Dried Cranberries and Toasted Pecans

VARIATION
Quinoa with Pine Nuts and Broccoli
Omit the pecans and substitute 2 tablespoons pine nuts, lightly toasted in a small, dry frying pan over low heat for about 3 minutes. Gently stir 2 cups (8 oz/250 g) chopped steamed broccoli florets into the quinoa during the last 1 minute of cooking.

Quinoa, a tiny, nutritious seed native to the Andes, is high in protein and loaded with niacin, iron, phosphorus, and potassium. The cooked seeds are crunchy and nutty, the perfect background for dried fruits and toasted nuts.

Preheat the oven to 350°F (180°C). Spread the pecans in a small baking pan, place in the oven, and toast until they are fragrant and have taken on color, about 15 minutes. Pour onto a plate and let cool.

Meanwhile, in a large, deep frying pan over medium-high heat, warm the olive oil until a quinoa seed dropped into it sizzles upon contact. Add the quinoa and cook, stirring, until the seeds are separate and golden, about 5 minutes. Add the garlic and cook for 1 minute until fragrant. Add 2 cups (16 fl oz/500 ml) water and $1/2$ teaspoon salt. Bring to a boil, reduce the heat to medium, cover, and cook until the liquid is absorbed, 15–18 minutes. Uncover and continue to cook until any excess moisture is cooked off, about 1 minute. Spoon the quinoa into a warmed serving dish. Top with the pecans and cranberries, and serve.

$1/4$ cup ($1^1/2$ oz/45 g) coarsely chopped pecans

1 tablespoon extra-virgin olive oil

1 cup (6 oz/185 g) quinoa, rinsed thoroughly in a sieve and well drained

1 clove garlic, minced

Kosher salt

2 tablespoons dried cranberries, coarsely chopped

MAKES 4 SERVINGS

Spiced Basmati Rice Pilaf

2 teaspoons extra-virgin olive oil

1 tablespoon minced yellow onion

1 cup (7 oz/220 g) basmati rice

1 cinnamon stick

1 cardamom pod

1 slice fresh ginger, ¹/₈ inch (3 mm) thick, peeled

Kosher salt

¹/₂ cup (2 oz/60 g) walnuts, coarsely chopped

MAKES 4 SERVINGS

In a large, deep frying pan or sauté pan over low heat, warm together the olive oil and onion. Cook, stirring, just until the onion is wilted, about 3 minutes. Add the rice and stir until the kernels are evenly coated with the oil and are warmed, about 3 minutes. Add 2 cups (16 fl oz/500 ml) water and the cinnamon, cardamom, ginger, and ¹/₂ teaspoon salt. Raise the heat to high, and bring to a boil. Stir once, reduce the heat to low, cover, and cook, without stirring, until small craters form on the surface of the rice, indicating that all the water has been absorbed, and the rice is tender, 15–18 minutes.

Meanwhile, spread the walnuts in a small, dry frying pan and place over medium-low heat. Toast the walnuts, stirring, just until they are fragrant and have taken on color, about 3 minutes. Remove from the heat and pour onto a plate.

Carefully lift the cover of the pan so that no condensation drips into the rice. Do not stir. Gently spoon the rice into a warmed serving dish. Sprinkle with the walnuts. Serve at once.

Basmati rice, meaning "queen of fragrance," is highly regarded for its aroma and taste. It is typically used in pilafs seasoned with spices and sautéed onion. These additions heighten the already aromatic character of the rice, and the pilaf technique—sautéing the grains in oil before steaming them—produces rice with a fine, delicate texture. Walnuts contain both polyunsaturated and monounsaturated fats. Recent research suggests that frequently eating moderate amounts of walnuts can lower blood cholesterol.

Baked Polenta with Mushrooms

Baked polenta layered with mushrooms is the perfect side dish with pot roast, beef stew, or braised chicken. This polenta is partially cooked on top of the stove and then is finished in the oven, which substantially reduces the amount of time required to stir the boiling polenta by hand. It will emerge from the oven soft and creamy with an attractive golden crown. Use any finely milled cornmeal, either the type for making corn bread or the Italian cornmeal often sold simply as polenta. Coarse-ground or stone-ground cornmeal is also suitable, but will require 1 cup (8 fl oz/250 ml) more water for the first stage of cooking.

Combine the parsley and garlic on a cutting board and chop together finely. Set aside.

Place a large frying pan over medium-high heat until hot enough for a drop of water to sizzle and then immediately evaporate. Add the 1 tablespoon olive oil and tilt the pan to coat the bottom evenly. Add all the mushrooms and cook, stirring, until lightly browned and softened, about 10 minutes. Add the parsley-garlic mixture and cook for 1 minute. Stir in the tomato paste until blended. Stir in $1/4$ teaspoon salt, or more to taste; season with pepper. Remove from the heat.

Preheat the oven to 400°F (200°C). Oil an 8-inch (20-cm) square or other shallow, $1^{1}/2$-qt (1.5-l) baking dish with the 1 teaspoon olive oil. Pour the milk into a large bowl. Gradually add the cornmeal, stirring until smooth.

In a saucepan over high heat, bring 3 cups (24 fl oz/750 ml) water to a boil. Gradually stir the cornmeal mixture into the water. Reduce the heat to medium-low and cook, stirring, until the cornmeal is very thick and pulls away from the sides of the pan, about 15 minutes. (Be careful, as the hot polenta can bubble and spatter.) Stir in 2 tablespoons of the Parmigiano-Reggiano. Remove from the heat.

Using a rubber spatula, spread half of the polenta evenly in the prepared baking dish. Spoon the mushrooms evenly on top. Spoon the remaining polenta on top and spread in a smooth layer. Sprinkle with the remaining 2 tablespoons cheese.

Bake the polenta until puffed and golden, about 30 minutes. Remove from the oven and let stand for 15 minutes before serving.

Serve the polenta directly from the baking dish, scooping it out with a large spoon or a spatula. The polenta will be soft, but will stiffen upon standing.

2 tablespoons chopped fresh flat-leaf (Italian) parsley

2 cloves garlic, chopped

1 tablespoon plus 1 teaspoon extra-virgin olive oil

$1/2$ lb (250 g) white mushrooms, brushed clean, stems removed, and caps coarsely chopped

$1/4$ lb (125 g) cremini mushrooms, brushed clean, stems removed, and caps coarsely chopped

$1/4$ lb (125 g) fresh shiitake mushrooms, brushed clean, stems removed, and caps coarsely chopped

1 tablespoon tomato paste

Kosher salt and freshly ground pepper

$1^{1}/2$ cups (12 fl oz/375 ml) 1-percent-fat milk

1 cup (5 oz/155 g) yellow cornmeal

4 tablespoons (1 oz/30 g) grated Parmigiano-Reggiano cheese

MAKES 6 SERVINGS

Desserts

About Desserts

A few savvy ingredient swaps can transform your favorite high-fat desserts into satisfying and healthful finales to everyday meals. For example, tofu can replace egg yolks in chocolate mousse, and oil or a fruit butter can be used instead of some of the butter in cakes and cookies.

Many people believe that eating dessert is always a high-calorie (-kilojoule), high-fat splurge—that cakes, cookies, and pies can never be part of a healthful eating plan. This chapter proves them wrong. Desserts can taste good and be good for you as long as you make them according to a handful of healthful guidelines. The same guidelines will help you make a smart dessert choice from nearly any restaurant menu.

FRUITS SET THE PACE

The most healthful desserts are usually made from fruits that have been minimally handled so that their nutrients and phytochemicals remain intact. Swirled Melon Soup (page 237), an ice-cold melon purée flavored with white wine and ginger and lightly sweetened with honey, is utterly simple, yet totally satisfying. White Wine–Poached Pears (page 244) and Red Wine–Poached Pears (page 245) call for simmering firm, ripe fruits in wine until tender, then reducing the now-alcohol-free liquid for use as a sauce for the finished dish. A trio of vitamin C–loaded summer berries, sweetened with only a few spoonfuls of jam, is topped with a "lean" buttermilk-biscuit crust to form Three-Berry Cobbler (page 230).

When shopping for these and other fruits, look for ripe specimens that are in season and preferably locally grown. Select ones that are heavy for their size and smell deeply of their characteristic aroma; wash and prepare them just before you plan to use them. If their peels are edible, leave them intact to boost fiber,

nutrients, flavor, and texture, as in the stuffed baked apples on page 235.

If you are fond of ice cream, sorbets are a flavorful, healthful alternative. Prepared without eggs and cream, sorbets are made by the incorporation of air into sweetened fruit purées as they freeze in an ice-cream maker. The process results in an intense flavor and light texture that make such recipes as Peach-Mango Sorbet (page 241) cool and refreshing treats. Sorbets are not always fashioned from fruit, however. Chocolate Sorbet (page 240) will satisfy the fussiest chocolate-ice-cream lover and be free of the saturated fat and cholesterol found in its rival.

IRRESISTIBLE GUILT-FREE CHOCOLATE DESSERTS

Chocolate fans will also appreciate Very Chocolate Mousse (page 246). But gone are the eggs, butter, and cream that keep any traditional mousse off the menus of health-conscious eaters. Puréed silken tofu replaces the egg yolks, providing body and richness, and whipped egg whites stand in for the whipped cream, contributing airiness. The rest of the recipe follows the classic, calling for the finest chocolate you can find and a splash of brandy for deep, rich flavor. It is an ideal dessert for an elegant dinner party.

Several other desserts in this chapter are also modified classics, developed to reduce the fat and cholesterol and/or increase the nutrition of their traditional counterparts. Apple butter replaces a portion of the fat in

old-fashioned Oatmeal-Raisin Cookies (page 221); the use of high-fiber oats and raisins keeps the cookies to a sensible splurge. Glazed Lemon Loaf (page 224) uses mono-unsaturated canola oil instead of butter for moisture, flavor, and tenderness. Low-fat milk and a tangy lemon syrup help keep the loaf moist. In Key Lime Chiffon Pie (page 228), nonfat condensed milk replaces regular condensed milk, whipped egg whites assume the role of the whipped cream, and a graham cracker crust is substituted for a pastry crust, reducing fats and calories to levels far below those of the original.

As the chocolate mousse and Key lime pie recipes demonstrate, fat-free egg whites can act as the foundation for healthful desserts. Whipped until stiff with sugar and flavorings, egg whites are transformed into meringue, a versatile base for such cookies as Chocolate Meringues (page 222) or such cakes as Angel Food Cake with Mocha Sauce (page 227). You can serve the cookies or the cake plain or with a healthful accompaniment: Raspberry Sauce (page 275) or its strawberry, blueberry, or mango variation; slices of Red Wine–Poached Pears (page 245); a scoop of Peach-Mango Sorbet (page 241) or Chocolate Sorbet (page 240); or a small mound of warm fruit compote.

Look for the same characteristics that define a healthful homemade dessert when selecting from a restaurant menu. Choose fruit-based desserts. Pass up—or share with several others so you have only a small portion—desserts that depend on egg yolks, cream, and butter for their flavor and texture. Finally, choose desserts made from an egg white base, such as a meringue, lady fingers, or angel food cake, to reduce fats. Follow these guidelines and eating dessert both at home and in restaurants will be a healthful pleasure.

Chocolate-Cherry-Almond Biscotti

Chocolate and cherries are a great combination. So are chocolate and almonds. Fortunately, almonds are among the lowest in fat of all the nuts, so you can use a fair amount of them in these long, slender cookies. Cherries contain flavonoids such as quercitin, a potent anti-oxidant that defends cells against cancer. As with many chocolate desserts, the biscotti taste better a day or two after they are made, when the flavors have had a chance to meld. The cookies ship well, too, so keep them in mind for holiday gift giving. If possible, use insulated baking sheets, which are constructed with an air pocket between two layers of metal, to protect against overbrowning.

Position racks in the upper third and lower third of the oven and preheat to 325°F (165°C). Line 2 baking sheets, preferably insulated sheets, with parchment (baking) paper.

In a large bowl, whisk together the flour, granulated sugar, cocoa, brown sugar, baking powder, baking soda, and 1/2 teaspoon salt until well mixed. Add the cherries and almonds and toss with your hands to distribute them evenly.

In another bowl, whisk together the whole eggs, egg white, and vanilla and almond extracts. Pour into the dry ingredients. Using a fork, mix together the dry and wet ingredients, taking care to work all the bits of dry ingredients into the dough. This will take about 5 minutes. The dough will be dense and sticky. Divide the dough in half.

Place a piece of plastic wrap 18 inches (45 cm) long on the countertop. Transfer half of the dough to the plastic wrap. Lightly moisten your hands with cold water to prevent the dough from sticking to them, then shape the dough into a flattened log 12 inches (30 cm) long by 2 1/2 inches (6 cm) wide by 1 inch (2.5 cm) high. Lifting the plastic wrap and cradling the dough, flip the dough onto the center of one of the prepared baking sheets. Repeat with the remaining dough, flipping it onto the second prepared baking sheet.

Bake the logs until they are dry to the touch and firm in the center when pressed with your fingers, about 30 minutes. They will spread considerably and may crack slightly on top. Transfer to wire racks and let the logs cool on the pans for 30 minutes. The logs will still be slightly warm to the touch.

Carefully transfer the logs to a cutting board and set the parchment-lined pans aside. Using a serrated knife, cut the logs crosswise on the diagonal into slices 1/2 inch (12 mm) wide.

Arrange the slices, cut side down, on the lined baking sheets, placing them close together but not touching. Bake for 15 minutes. Remove from the oven and, using tongs or a spatula, turn the biscotti. Continue to bake until dry and crisp, 10–15 minutes. Remove from the oven and transfer the biscotti to wire racks to cool completely. Store the biscotti in an airtight container at room temperature for up to 3 weeks.

1 3/4 cups (9 oz/280g) unbleached all-purpose (plain) flour

1 cup (8 oz/250 g) granulated sugar

1/2 cup (1 1/2 oz/45 g) Dutch-process cocoa powder, sifted

1/4 cup (2 oz/60 g) firmly packed light brown sugar

1 1/2 teaspoons baking powder

1/4 teaspoon baking soda (bicarbonate of soda)

Kosher salt

3/4 cup (3 oz/90 g) dried tart cherries, coarsely chopped

3/4 cup (4 1/2 oz/140 g) blanched almonds, coarsely chopped

3 large whole eggs, plus 1 large egg white

1 teaspoon vanilla extract (essence)

1/8 teaspoon almond extract (essence)

MAKES 4 DOZEN COOKIES

Oatmeal-Raisin Cookies

Nearly everyone loves a good oatmeal cookie. Oats are a healthful ingredient: they are high in thiamin and are a good source of riboflavin, vitamin E, and fiber; they contain more protein than most other grains. Reducing the fat while keeping the cookies crisp is an artful balancing act. Using apple butter is the secret in this recipe, along with an egg white. To keep down the cholesterol, canola oil is blended with only enough butter to ensure great flavor. For a softer cookie, do not flatten the dough as much before baking. Make the cookies large, or shape them into small coins and present them after dinner, with coffee and liqueurs.

Position racks in the upper third and the lower third of the oven and preheat to 350°F (180°C). Line 2 baking sheets, preferably insulated sheets, with parchment (baking) paper.

In a bowl, stir together the oats, flour, baking powder, baking soda, cinnamon, allspice, and $1/4$ teaspoon salt until well mixed. In a large bowl, using a wooden spoon, cream together the butter and canola oil until blended. The mixture will be oily. Add the brown sugar and beat with the spoon until the mixture is fluffy and clings together, about 3 minutes. Mix in the egg white, apple butter, vanilla, and raisins. The mixture may look slightly curdled. Add the dry ingredients and mix until a sticky dough forms.

Using 2 tablespoons, drop walnut-sized balls of the dough onto the prepared baking sheets, spacing them $2^{1}/2$ inches (6 cm) apart. For rustic cookies, dip the bottom of a glass in cold water and flatten each ball until it is $1/4$ inch (6 mm) thick. For a more elegant shape, moisten your fingers, then flatten each cookie while smoothing the sides, making neat, 2-inch (5-cm) rounds.

Bake the cookies for 7 minutes, then switch the position of the pans between the racks and rotate each pan 180 degrees. Continue to bake the cookies until they are cinnamon brown, about 8 minutes longer. Remove from the oven and, using a wide spatula, carefully transfer the cookies to wire racks. Let cool completely. The cookies will crisp as they cool. Store the cookies in an airtight container at room temperature for up to 2 weeks.

$2^{1}/2$ cups ($7^{1}/2$ oz/235 g) quick-cooking rolled oats

1 cup (5 oz/155 g) unbleached all-purpose (plain) flour

$1/2$ teaspoon baking powder

$1/2$ teaspoon baking soda (bicarbonate of soda)

1 teaspoon ground cinnamon

$1/8$ teaspoon ground allspice

Kosher salt

3 tablespoons unsalted butter, at room temperature

2 tablespoons canola oil

1 cup (7 oz/220 g) firmly packed light brown sugar

1 large egg white

$1/3$ cup (3 oz/90 g) apple butter

2 teaspoons vanilla extract (essence)

$2/3$ cup (4 oz/125 g) raisins

MAKES 40 COOKIES

Chocolate Meringues

¹/₄ cup (³/₄ oz/20 g) Dutch-process cocoa powder

1¹/₄ cups (10 oz/310 g) sugar

³/₄ cup (6 fl oz/180 ml) egg whites (about 6 large), at room temperature

Kosher salt

MAKES 40–48 COOKIES

Position 2 racks in the center of the oven and preheat to 250°F (120°C). Line 2 baking sheets, preferably insulated sheets, with parchment (baking) paper.

Combine the cocoa and ¹/₂ cup (4 oz/125 g) of the sugar in a sifter or the finest-mesh sieve possible and sift them into a bowl. Set aside.

In a bowl, using a stand mixer fitted with the whip attachment or a handheld mixer, beat the egg whites on medium speed until very frothy, about 1 minute. Add a pinch of salt and continue beating until soft peaks form, 2–3 minutes. Increase the speed to high and begin gradually adding the remaining ³/₄ cup (6 oz/185 g) sugar, 1 tablespoon at a time, always beating for about 10 seconds to dissolve the addition before adding the next spoonful. Continue beating until the whites form stiff peaks, about 2 minutes.

Sprinkle one-third of the cocoa-sugar mixture over the egg whites. Using a rubber spatula, gently fold the cocoa-sugar mixture into the whites until it is about two-thirds blended. Fold in the remaining cocoa-sugar mixture, in 2 additions, taking care to deflate the whites as little as possible.

Spoon the meringue into a medium-sized pastry bag fitted with a number 4 star tip. Grasping the bag firmly at the top with one hand and guiding it at the tip with the other hand, pipe the meringue onto the prepared baking sheets, making 3-inch (7.5-cm) long ladyfingers or figure-eights 2 inches (5 cm) round and 4 inches (10 cm) long. You can also pipe two 3-inch (7.5-cm) lengths side by side to make double-wide cookies. Space the cookies 2 inches (5 cm) apart on the sheets.

Bake the meringues until they are completely dry, about 2¹/₂ hours. Transfer to wire racks and let the meringues cool completely on the pans.

Carefully lift the meringues off the parchment paper and store in an airtight container at room temperature for up to 3 days.

Featherlight meringue produces deliciously elegant, fat-free, cholesterol-free cookies. Making meringue recipes, however, can be intimidating to many cooks. This one is very forgiving. The cocoa, which delivers a rich flavor, also eliminates concern that your meringue may turn beige during baking. These meringues are even delicious when the centers are still slightly chewy, which may happen if you bake on a humid day. If you do not want to pipe this thick meringue into shapes, omit the pastry bag and spoon dollops of the stiff batter onto baking sheets, shaping them into plump kisses.

Glazed Lemon Loaf

1¹/₂ cups (7¹/₂ oz/235 g) unbleached all-purpose (plain) flour

³/₄ cup (6 oz/185 g) sugar

1 teaspoon baking powder

¹/₄ teaspoon baking soda (bicarbonate of soda)

Finely shredded zest of 1 large lemon

Kosher salt

2 large eggs

¹/₂ cup (4 fl oz/125 ml) 1-percent-fat milk

¹/₄ cup (2 fl oz/60 ml) canola oil

1 teaspoon vanilla extract (essence)

For the Glaze

¹/₃ cup (3 oz/90 g) sugar

Juice of 1 large lemon (about 3¹/₂ tablespoons)

MAKES 12 SERVINGS

Preheat the oven to 350°F (180°C). Coat an 8¹/₂-by-4¹/₂-by-2¹/₂-inch (21.5-by-11.5-by-6-cm) loaf pan with canola-oil cooking spray.

In a large bowl, whisk together the flour, sugar, baking powder, baking soda, lemon zest, and a pinch of salt until well mixed. In another bowl, whisk together the eggs, milk, canola oil, and vanilla until blended. Pour the wet ingredients into the dry ingredients. Using a rubber spatula, mix until they are just combined, forming a thick, slightly lumpy batter. Pour the batter into the prepared pan, spreading it with the spatula to make it smooth and even on top. The pan will be about half full.

Bake the cake until it is deeply browned with some golden cracks on top and it feels springy to the touch when pressed lightly in the middle, about 40 minutes. For an alternative test, insert a knife into the center; it should come out clean. Transfer the pan to a wire rack and insert a thin knife vertically into the cake in 8–10 uniformly spaced places. (Alternatively, use a bamboo skewer.)

To make the glaze, in a small, heavy, nonreactive saucepan over medium-high heat, combine the sugar and lemon juice and bring to a boil. Continue to boil until the mixture is bubbling and frothy on the surface, about 3 minutes. Remove from the heat and immediately pour evenly over the surface of the hot cake.

Let the glazed cake cool completely in the pan on the rack. Run a thin-bladed knife around the inside edge of the pan to loosen the cake. Carefully invert the cake onto the rack and lift off the pan. Turn upright onto a serving plate, slice thinly, and serve. Store the cooled cake tightly wrapped at room temperature for up to 4 days.

This moist lemon cake is satisfying on its own, but is heavenly topped with a mix of blueberries, blackberries, and strawberries. Made without butter, and using just a fraction of the oil found in similar recipes, the cake keeps beautifully because it is bathed in tangy lemon syrup. It travels well, too, making it ideal for carrying to picnics and potlucks.

Angel Food Cake
with Mocha Sauce

Angel food cake seems rich, although it contains not one bit of fat. The trick is serving it with the right embellishment, like a generous drizzle of deep, dark mocha sauce. Another virtue of this cake is that it keeps for several days. Remember that egg whites contain lots of protein but no cholesterol, making them a very heart-healthy ingredient. Cake flour is milled finer than all-purpose flour and contains less gluten. This light flour is used for delicate cakes like this one.

Position a rack in the lower third of the oven and preheat to 350°F (180°C).

In a bowl, using a stand mixer fitted with the whip attachment or a handheld mixer, beat the egg whites on medium speed until very frothy, about 1 minute. Add the cream of tartar and continue beating until soft peaks form, 2–3 minutes. Increase the speed to high and begin gradually adding the sugar, 1 tablespoon at a time, always beating for about 10 seconds to dissolve the addition before adding the next spoonful. Continue to beat until the egg whites form stiff peaks, about 2 minutes longer. Add the flour, a pinch of salt, the vanilla extract, and the lemon juice to the whipped whites and, using a rubber spatula, fold in gently.

Gently scoop the batter into a 10-inch (25-cm) angel food cake pan with a removable bottom. Run a thin-bladed knife through the cake batter several times to eliminate any air pockets. Rap the pan firmly on a countertop 2 or 3 times.

Bake the cake until a thin knife inserted into the center comes out clean, about 30 minutes. Remove from the oven and immediately invert the pan to cool the cake upside down. If your pan does not have small legs on which to rest it, suspend it upside down by slipping its tube onto a wine bottle. Let cool completely, 1–2 hours.

While the cake is cooling, make the mocha sauce: In a small, heavy saucepan, whisk together the sugar, cocoa, condensed milk, corn syrup, and espresso until well blended. Place over medium heat and bring to a boil. Reduce the heat to low and simmer for 1 minute. Remove from the heat and stir in the chocolate and vanilla until the chocolate melts. Let cool to lukewarm or room temperature before using. It will thicken as it cools. You will have about 1 cup (8 fl oz/250 ml).

Run a thin-bladed knife around the inside edge of the pan to loosen the cake sides, then push up on the bottom of the pan to remove the sides. Slide the knife between the cake and the base of the pan, working it around to free the cake, then work the knife vertically around the center tube. Invert a serving plate over the cake and, holding the plate in place, invert the cake and plate together. Lift off the pan bottom.

Slice the cake with a serrated knife. Drizzle about 1 tablespoon of the sauce on each dessert plate. Top with a slice of cake and serve.

1 1/2 cups (12 fl oz/375 ml) egg whites (about 12 large), at room temperature

1 1/4 teaspoons cream of tartar

1 1/2 cups (12 oz/375 g) sugar

1 cup (4 oz/125 g) cake (soft-wheat) flour, sifted

Kosher salt

1 teaspoon vanilla extract (essence)

1 teaspoon fresh lemon juice

For the Mocha Sauce

1/2 cup (4 oz/125 g) sugar

1/3 cup (1 oz/30 g) Dutch-process cocoa powder

1/4 cup (2 fl oz/60 ml) nonfat condensed milk

3 tablespoons light corn syrup

1/4 cup (2 fl oz/60 ml) brewed espresso or 1/4 teaspoon instant espresso coffee powder dissolved in 1/4 cup (2 fl oz/60 ml) warm water

1 oz (30 g) bittersweet chocolate, chopped

1 teaspoon vanilla extract (essence)

MAKES 12 SERVINGS

Key Lime Chiffon Pie

For the Crust

1¹/₂ cups (4¹/₂ oz/140 g) graham cracker crumbs, made from reduced-fat cookies (about 12 whole cookies)

¹/₂ teaspoon ground ginger

Kosher salt

1 tablespoon canola oil

2 tablespoons nonfat milk

For the Filling

¹/₂ cup (4 fl oz/125 ml) Key lime juice

1 tablespoon (1 package) unflavored gelatin

³/₄ cup (6 oz/185 g) sugar

3 large egg yolks, beaten

Grated zest of 2 limes (about 1¹/₂ tablespoons)

¹/₄ cup (2 fl oz/60 ml) nonfat condensed milk

4 large egg whites, at room temperature

Kosher salt

MAKES ONE 9-INCH (23-CM) PIE, OR 8 SERVINGS

To make the crust, preheat the oven to 350°F (180°C). In a bowl, stir together the graham cracker crumbs, ginger, and a pinch of salt. Add the canola oil and milk. Starting with a fork, and then using your fingers, work the liquid into the crumbs until the mixture resembles fluffy, moist sand, about 3 minutes. Turn the mixture into a 9-inch (23-cm) pie pan. Using your fingers, press the crust mixture firmly and evenly over the bottom and up the sides of the pan.

Bake the pie crust until it is golden brown, about 8 minutes. Transfer to a wire rack and let cool completely.

To make the filling, pour the lime juice into a small, heavy, nonreactive saucepan. Sprinkle the gelatin over the juice and set aside until the gelatin softens, about 5 minutes. Add ¹/₄ cup (2 oz/60 g) of the sugar, the egg yolks, and 1 tablespoon of the zest. Place the pan over medium heat and whisk constantly until the mixture thickens to the consistency of a light cream soup and starts to steam, 4–5 minutes. To test if it has thickened sufficiently, dip a spoon into the mixture and then run your finger down the middle of the back of it; your finger should leave a clear path that does not flow back onto itself. Do not let the mixture boil.

Immediately pour the gelatin mixture into a nonreactive metal or heatproof glass bowl. Mix in the condensed milk, then cover and refrigerate the mixture, stirring occasionally with a rubber spatula to prevent it from congealing around the sides of the bowl, until it is the consistency of mayonnaise, 15–20 minutes.

In a bowl, using a stand mixer fitted with the whip attachment or a handheld mixer, beat the egg whites on medium speed until very frothy, about 1 minute. Add a pinch of salt and continue beating until soft peaks form, 2–3 minutes. Increase the speed to high and begin gradually adding the remaining ¹/₂ cup (4 oz/125 g) sugar, 1 tablespoon at a time, always beating for about 10 seconds to dissolve the addition before adding the next tablespoonful. When all the sugar has been added, continue to beat until the egg whites form stiff peaks, about 2 minutes longer.

Using the rubber spatula, gently stir one-fourth of the whites into the gelatin mixture. Pour over the beaten whites and fold gently just until no streaks of white remain. Spread the filling in the cooled pie crust and smooth and level the top with the spatula. Sprinkle the remaining grated lime zest over the surface. Refrigerate the pie until the filling sets, 1–2 hours. Chiffon pie is best served the day it is made.

Fortunately for those who like Key lime pie, condensed milk, an indispensable ingredient in the pie, comes in nonfat form. Egg whites stand in for the usual whipped cream, transforming this version into a light chiffon pie that tastes, and looks, deliciously old-fashioned. Key limes are the size of a very large grape. Far more tart than Persian limes, they are hard to find fresh. Bottled Key lime juice, sold in some grocery stores and at specialty-food stores, works just as well as fresh.

Three-Berry Cobbler

For the Filling

2 cups (8 oz/250 g) blueberries

4 cups (1 lb/500 g) raspberries

4 cups (1 lb/500 g) strawberries, stems removed and halved lengthwise

1/4 cup (2 1/2 oz/75 g) raspberry jam

1 tablespoon instant tapioca

For the Crust

1 cup (5 oz/155 g) unbleached all-purpose (plain) flour

2 teaspoons baking powder

1/4 teaspoon baking soda (bicarbonate of soda)

Kosher salt

3 tablespoons unsalted butter, at room temperature

1/3 cup (3 oz/90 g) sugar

1/3 cup (3 fl oz/80 ml) nonfat buttermilk

MAKES 6 SERVINGS

There is nothing like butter for producing a tender crust, but this biscuit-topped cobbler shows how to reduce the amount of butter used in most cobbler recipes by replacing part of it with buttermilk and other lean ingredients. The juices in the filling thicken slightly and almost become a sauce for the topping. Halving instead of slicing the strawberries keeps them from turning mushy in the filling. Berries are rich in vitamin C, potassium, dietary fiber, and protective phytochemicals.

Preheat the oven to 350°F (180°C). Coat an 8-inch (20-cm) square nonreactive metal pan or ceramic baking dish with canola-oil cooking spray. (Do not use a glass dish.)

In a bowl, combine the blueberries, raspberries, strawberries, jam, and tapioca. Using a rubber spatula, stir gently to coat the berries with the jam. Spread the fruit in an even layer in the prepared pan.

To make the crust, in a bowl, stir together the flour, baking powder, baking soda, and 1/2 teaspoon salt.

BY HAND: In another bowl, using a wooden spoon, cream together the butter and sugar until fluffy and pale, about 3 minutes. Mix in about half of the buttermilk. Add about half of the dry ingredients and stir until almost combined. Stir in the remaining buttermilk. Add the remaining dry ingredients and stir until a thick, sticky batter forms. Do not overmix.

BY MIXER: In a bowl, using a hand-held mixer, cream together the butter and sugar on high speed until fluffy and pale, about 3 minutes. Reduce the speed to medium and beat in about half of the buttermilk. Add about half of the dry ingredients and beat until almost combined. Beat in the remaining buttermilk. Add the remaining dry ingredients and beat until a thick, sticky batter forms. Do not overmix.

Drop the batter by heaping spoonfuls over the fruit. Spread it as evenly as possible, using the back of the spoon. Some fruit will be exposed.

Bake the cobbler until the crust is deep golden brown and the fruit juices bubble up around the edges and through any cracks, about 40 minutes. Transfer to a wire rack and let cool to lukewarm before serving. Scoop the cobbler from the dish onto dessert plates and serve.

Cinnamon-Raisin Bread Pudding with Maple Sauce

A luxurious bread pudding uses generous amounts of heavy (double) cream, eggs, and butter. Here, the eggs and butter in the challah or other egg bread provide that richness, while a puréed banana contributes creaminess without fat or cholesterol. Cinnamon sugar sprinkled over the top becomes a sparkling crust as the pudding bakes. The warm maple sauce, spiced with cinnamon and orange, adds a taste of New England. If possible, use dark grade B maple syrup, which has a wonderfully deep, intense flavor.

Place the bread in a large bowl. Add the raisins and mix with your hands to distribute them evenly.

Place the banana in a bowl and mash with a fork until it is puréed, 3–4 minutes. In another bowl, whisk the eggs until blended. Whisk in the milk, the puréed banana, all but 1 tablespoon of the sugar, 1 teaspoon of the cinnamon, and the vanilla, mixing well. Pour evenly over the bread. Set aside to soak for 30 minutes.

Preheat the oven to 350°F (180°C). Coat a 9-by-2-inch (23-by-5-cm) round cake pan with canola-oil cooking spray.

Spoon the soaked bread mixture into the prepared pan, smoothing the top to level it. It will reach the rim of the pan. In a small bowl, stir together the remaining 1 tablespoon sugar and the ¼ teaspoon cinnamon. Sprinkle the cinnamon sugar evenly over the top of the pudding.

Bake the pudding until it has puffed about 1 inch (2.5 cm) above the rim of the pan, the top is medium brown, and a knife inserted into the center of the pudding comes out clean, about 1 hour. Remove from the oven and let cool to lukewarm or room temperature.

To make the maple sauce, in a small frying pan, combine the maple syrup, marmalade, cinnamon sticks, and ½ cup (4 fl oz/125 ml) water. Bring to a boil over medium-high heat. Boil gently, reducing the heat if necessary, until the liquid is reduced by one-third, about 6 minutes. Remove from the heat. You will have about 1 cup (8 fl oz/250 ml). Let cool to warm or room temperature before serving. Remove the cinnamon sticks.

Cut the pudding into wedges and place on individual plates. Spoon 2 tablespoons of the sauce over each wedge. Serve at once.

1 loaf challah or other egg bread, about 1 lb (500 g), torn into 1½-inch (4-cm) pieces (about 10 cups)

¾ cup (4½ oz/140 g) raisins

1 very ripe banana, peeled

4 large eggs

3 cups (24 fl oz/750 ml) 2-percent-fat milk

1 cup (8 oz/250 g) sugar

1¼ teaspoons ground cinnamon

1 teaspoon vanilla extract (essence)

For the Maple Sauce

½ cup (5½ oz/170 g) maple syrup, preferably grade B

¼ cup (2½ oz/75 g) orange marmalade

2 cinnamon sticks, each 3 inches (7.5 cm) long

MAKES 8 SERVINGS

Baked Apples Filled with Apricots and Figs

Baked apples stuffed with dried fruits are an alluring dessert, especially when sweet apple cider is used to plump the fruits. Honey makes a sparkling glaze for the apples. Of the many varieties available, wildflower honey has a flavor that best complements the dried fruits. Blueberry or raspberry honey works well, too. When choosing apricots, avoid the Turkish variety, as they are too sweet. California dried apricots, if available, are a good choice. Also look for fruits dried without the use of sulfur. Heap the filling high in each apple to create an attractive presentation.

To make the filling, in a heatproof bowl, combine the apricots, figs, prunes, pears, cranberries, and raisins. In a small saucepan, bring the cider to a boil. Pour the hot liquid over the fruits. Let stand until the fruits have plumped, 30–60 minutes.

Preheat the oven to 350°F (180°C).

Using a sharp knife, cut a slice $^1/_2$ inch (12 mm) thick off the stem end of each apple. Using a melon baller, scoop out and discard the core from each apple, being careful not to puncture the base of the apple. Then, still using the melon baller, carve out the flesh to leave a shell $^1/_2$ inch (12 mm) thick. Discard the flesh or reserve for another use. Stand the apples in a baking dish just large enough to hold them upright.

Drain the plumped fruits in a sieve held over the baking dish. Spoon the fruits into the apple cavities, dividing them evenly and heaping them high. Cut out four 5-inch (13-cm) square pieces of aluminum foil and tent a piece over the stuffing in each apple. Bake the apples until a knife pierces the bottom with only slight resistance but the sides retain their shape, 35–40 minutes. Remove from the oven and lift off the foil.

When the apples are cool enough to handle, after about 20 minutes, use a slotted spoon to transfer them to a serving platter. Spoon any of the fruit stuffing that fell off back in place. Discard the liquid remaining in the dish.

While the apples are cooling, in a saucepan, combine the apple juice concentrate and honey. Bring to a boil over medium-high heat, reduce the heat to medium, and simmer until the liquid is syrupy and reduced by about one-third, about 8 minutes. Spoon the hot glaze over the stuffing and apples until it pools in the bottom of the platter. Serve warm or at room temperature.

For the Filling

16 dried apricots

4 dried Calimyrna figs

4 pitted soft prunes

2 dried pear halves, each cut into 4 pieces

$^1/_4$ cup (1 oz/30 g) dried cranberries

$^1/_4$ cup (1$^1/_2$ oz/45 g) raisins

1 cup (8 fl oz/250 ml) sweet apple cider

4 baking apples such as Rome Beauty, Fuji, or Jonagold

$^2/_3$ cup (5 fl oz/160 ml) thawed, frozen apple juice concentrate

$^1/_3$ cup (3 oz/90 g) honey

MAKES 4 SERVINGS

Cranberry-Apple Crisp

4 sweet, firm apples

3 cups (12 oz/375 g) fresh or frozen cranberries

2 tablespoons chopped candied ginger

1/3 cup (3 fl oz/80 ml) thawed, frozen apple juice concentrate

2/3 cup (3 1/2 oz/105 g) unbleached all-purpose (plain) flour

1/3 cup (1 3/4 oz/50 g) whole-wheat (wholemeal) pastry flour

3/4 cup (6 oz/185 g) firmly packed light brown sugar

4 tablespoons (2 oz/60 g) chilled unsalted butter

MAKES 8 SERVINGS

Preheat the oven to 400°F (200°C). Coat a deep, 2-qt (2-l) baking dish with canola-oil cooking spray.

Peel the apples, then cut in half; remove the cores and cut into thin wedges. Place the apples, cranberries, ginger, and apple juice concentrate in the prepared baking dish and stir with a rubber spatula to distribute evenly.

In a bowl, using a fork, stir together the all-purpose and pastry flours and the brown sugar. Add the butter and work it into the dry ingredients with the fork until the mixture resembles moist sand. Sprinkle the topping evenly over the filling, leaving a 1/2-inch (12-mm) border uncovered around the edge. Using your fingers, pat the topping firmly to make a crust.

Bake the crisp for 10 minutes. Reduce the heat to 375°F (190°C) and continue to bake until the fruit is bubbly around the edges of the crust and the crust is nicely browned, 35–40 minutes. Transfer to a wire rack and let cool to lukewarm. Scoop the crisp from the dish onto dessert plates and serve.

Candied ginger and apple juice sweeten the filling in this juicy crisp. Its thin crust includes whole-wheat pastry flour, which lends a nutty flavor that complements the brown sugar. Be sure to use a sweet, firm apple that will hold its shape during baking, such as Fuji, Delicious, or Crispin. A small scoop of vanilla frozen yogurt makes a nice accompaniment.

Swirled Melon Soup

A bold-flavored dessert fruit soup is a clever way to add another serving of fruit to the day. Offer the soup as soon as it is ice-cold, while the melon purée still has a just-picked melon flavor. If your melons are very ripe, you may not need the honey, so taste the melon purées before adding it. Wildflower or blueberry honey would complement the melons.

In a blender, combine the honeydew, wine, lime juice, and 2 teaspoons of the honey and purée until frothy, 3–4 minutes. Taste the purée and adjust with additional honey. Pour into a nonreactive bowl, cover, and refrigerate to chill thoroughly, 1–2 hours.

Just before serving, in the blender, combine the cantaloupe, apricot nectar, lemon juice, ginger, and remaining 1 teaspoon honey. Purée until smooth, 2–3 minutes.

Stir the chilled honeydew purée to redistribute the foam, then divide it evenly among individual bowls. Using a large, shallow spoon, gently swirl some of the cantaloupe purée over the surface of the honeydew purée. Sprinkle with mint, if desired. Serve at once.

6 cups (1½ lb/750 g) peeled and diced, chilled ripe honeydew melon

⅔ cup (5 fl oz/160 ml) fruity white wine

Juice of 1 lime

About 3 teaspoons honey

2 cups (8 oz/250 g) peeled and diced cantaloupe

¼ cup (2 fl oz/60 ml) apricot nectar

2 teaspoons fresh lemon juice

¼ teaspoon ground ginger

Slivered fresh mint for garnish (optional)

MAKES 4 SERVINGS

Summer Fruit Parfaits

VARIATION

Winter Fruit Parfaits

Substitute 1 Golden Delicious or Fuji apple, cored and thinly sliced; 1 Bosc pear, cored and thinly sliced; 1 ripe Fuyu persimmon, thinly sliced; 1 small banana, sliced; and $^1/_2$ cup (3 oz/90 g) seedless red grapes, halved lengthwise, for the nectarine, strawberries, peach, kiwifruit, and blueberries. Use nonfat vanilla yogurt flavored with 1 teaspoon ground cinnamon in place of the lemon yogurt.

Ripe, fresh fruits layered with yogurt in elegant balloon wineglasses make a deceptively simple dessert. Thyme and lemon zest add intriguing flavors to the seasonal mix of fruits. Bruising the thyme sprigs helps bring out their volatile oils. Honey encourages the ripe fruits to release their juices. A mild-flavored honey that complements, rather than overpowers, their flavors is preferred. Wildflower or raspberry honey is a good choice.

Place the thyme sprigs on a cutting board and whack them 2 or 3 times with the side of a heavy knife or cleaver to bruise the leaves. Place the thyme in the bottom of a wide, shallow dish. Arrange the nectarine slices in a single layer over the thyme. Arrange the strawberry slices over the nectarine slices. Arrange the peach slices over the berries. Sprinkle the lemon zest evenly over the fruit, then drizzle with the honey. Set aside for $1^1/_2$–2 hours at room temperature. During this time the fruits will release more juices, which will mix with the honey to form a light syrup in the bottom of the dish.

Halve the kiwifruit lengthwise. Cut each half crosswise into thin slices. Add the kiwifruit slices and blueberries to the macerated fruits and, using a fork, gently mix all the fruits to coat evenly with the honey syrup. Remove the thyme.

To assemble each parfait, use a slotted spoon to scoop up $^1/_4$ cup (1 oz/30 g) of the fruit, pausing to allow it to drain well over the bowl, and place it in the bottom of a balloon wineglass. Stir the yogurt until it is creamy. Spoon $^1/_3$ cup ($2^1/_2$ oz/85 g) of the yogurt over the fruit in an even layer. Using the slotted spoon, scoop up $^1/_2$ cup (2 oz/60 g) of the fruit, again making sure it is well drained, and arrange it on top of the yogurt. Layer another $^1/_3$ cup of the yogurt on top. Finally, place $^1/_4$ cup well-drained fruit in the center. Repeat to make 3 more parfaits.

Serve the parfaits immediately or cover with plastic wrap and refrigerate for up to 2 hours. Let stand for 20 minutes at room temperature, then garnish each parfait with a fresh mint sprig, if desired, before serving.

4 fresh thyme sprigs

1 large nectarine, pitted and thinly sliced

8 large strawberries, stems removed and each cut lengthwise into 4 slices

1 large peach, peeled if desired, pitted, and thinly sliced

2 teaspoons grated lemon zest

$^1/_4$ cup (3 oz/90 g) wildflower or raspberry honey

1 kiwifruit, peeled

1 cup (4 oz/125 g) blueberries

$2^2/_3$ cups (20 oz/680 g) nonfat lemon yogurt

4 fresh mint sprigs (optional)

MAKES 4 SERVINGS

Chocolate Sorbet

1¹⁄₃ cups (11 oz/345 g) sugar

3 tablespoons dark corn syrup

¹⁄₂ cup (1¹⁄₂ oz/45 g) Dutch-process cocoa powder

1¹⁄₂ oz (45 g) bittersweet chocolate, finely chopped

2 teaspoons vanilla extract (essence)

MAKES 1 QT (1 L), OR 6 SERVINGS

In a heavy saucepan over high heat, combine the sugar, corn syrup, and 3 cups (24 fl oz/750 ml) water and bring to a boil. Reduce the heat to medium and simmer for 1 minute.

Remove from the heat and whisk in the cocoa until the mixture is smooth. Add the chocolate and vanilla and whisk until the chocolate melts. Let cool, cover, and refrigerate to chill thoroughly, at least 4 hours or preferably overnight.

Pour the chocolate mixture into an ice-cream maker and freeze according to the manufacturer's instructions. Transfer the sorbet to a tightly covered freezer container just large enough to hold it and freeze until firm, at least 2 hours.

Let the sorbet stand at room temperature for 10–20 minutes to soften slightly before serving. The sorbet will keep for up to 4 days in the freezer.

If you crave chocolate, you will surely like this easy-to-make sorbet. Intense in chocolate flavor, it is low in both total fat and saturated fat and has no cholesterol. Using top-quality cocoa powder and bittersweet chocolate ensures the most satisfying result. Because the sorbet base is rich and thick, it is essential to chill it well, preferably overnight. If desired, garnish it with fresh raspberries.

Peach-Mango Sorbet

This creamy, intensely flavored sorbet is loaded with beta-carotene and vitamins C and E. Together, they enhance immunity, help prevent cataracts and cancer, and promote heart health. Using frozen fruit means you can enjoy the dessert year-round. If using fresh fruit, you will need 1¼ lb (625 g) peaches, peeled, pitted, and sliced, and 1½ lb (750 g) mangoes, peeled, pitted, and cubed (page 279).

In a small, heavy saucepan over high heat, combine the sugar, corn syrup, and ½ cup (4 fl oz/125 ml) water. Bring to a boil. When the sugar has dissolved, after about 1 minute, reduce the heat to medium and boil gently for 1 minute. Remove from the heat and let cool to room temperature. Use immediately, or cover and refrigerate for up to 5 days.

In a food processor, combine the peaches and mangoes. Add the sugar mixture and lime juice, and process until a smooth, thick purée forms, 2–3 minutes.

Immediately pour the purée into an ice-cream maker and freeze according to the manufacturer's instructions. Transfer the sorbet to a tightly covered freezer container just large enough to hold it and freeze until firm, at least 2 hours. Let the sorbet stand at room temperature for 10–20 minutes to soften slightly before serving. The sorbet is best served within 24 hours, or it may become icy.

½ cup (4 oz/125 g) sugar

¼ cup (2½ oz/75 g) light corn syrup

1 package (1 lb/500 g) frozen unsweetened sliced peaches

1 package (1 lb/500 g) frozen cubed mangoes

Juice of ½ lime (about 1 tablespoon)

MAKES 1 QT (1 L), OR 6 SERVINGS

Tropical Fruit Kabobs with Rum Sauce

For the Rum Sauce

Juice of 1 orange (about 1/2 cup/4 fl oz/125 ml), strained

1/2 cup (4 fl oz/125 ml) dark rum

1/4 cup (2 oz/60 g) firmly packed dark brown sugar

4 cardamom pods

3 orange zest strips, each 3 inches (7.5 cm) long and 1 inch (2.5 cm) wide

2 lemon zest strips, each 2 inches (5 cm) long and 1/2 inch (12 mm) wide

1 whole clove

2 pineapple slices, each 1 inch (2.5 cm) thick, cut into 1-inch (2.5-cm) cubes

2 bananas, peeled and cut into 1-inch (2.5-cm) pieces

1 large peach or nectarine, halved, pitted, and cut into 8 equal pieces

1 large mango, peeled, pitted, and cut into eight 1 1/4-inch (3-cm) cubes (page 279)

8 bamboo skewers, each 8 inches (20 cm) long, soaked in water for 30 minutes and drained

MAKES 4 SERVINGS

At the end of a barbecue, use the still-hot fire to grill these succulent kabobs. Brief searing transforms the taste of each fruit by caramelizing its sugars. Select under-ripe fruits so they will hold together on the grill. The rum sauce spooned generously over the grilled fruit is so rich that you will not believe it is fat free. The distinctive flavor of the sauce comes from aromatic cardamom, a distant relative of ginger. Coffee-bean-sized cardamom pods are pistachio green or white. The former, although superior, are also costly; use the white if you prefer.

Prepare a CHARCOAL or GAS GRILL for direct-heat grilling over medium-high heat. Oil the grill rack.

Meanwhile, to make the rum sauce, combine the orange juice, rum, brown sugar, cardamom, orange and lemon zests, and clove in a small saucepan. Bring to a boil over high heat, stirring to dissolve the sugar. Reduce the heat to medium and boil gently until the liquid is reduced by half, about 10 minutes. Remove from the heat and let the sauce steep for 10 minutes. Using a slotted spoon, lift out the whole spices and citrus zests, reserving 2 strips of the orange zest and discarding the rest. Chop the orange zest and stir into the warm sauce.

Thread onto each skewer in the order given: 1 pineapple cube, 1 banana piece, 1 peach piece, 1 mango cube, 1 banana piece, and 1 pineapple cube.

BY CHARCOAL GRILL: Using tongs, place the kabobs over the hottest part of the fire and grill, turning them as needed, until lightly marked on each side, about 3 minutes total. Transfer to a serving plate.

BY GAS GRILL: Using tongs, place the kabobs directly over the heat elements, and grill turning them as needed, until lightly marked on each side, 3–4 minutes total. Transfer to a serving plate.

To serve, place 2 kabobs on each individual plate. Spoon the warm sauce liberally over the kabobs, using 3–4 tablespoons (1 1/2–2 fl oz/45–60 ml) for each serving. Serve lukewarm.

VARIATION

Tropical Fruit Kabobs with Coconut Sorbet
Divide the warm sauce evenly among shallow serving bowls. Place a scoop of coconut sorbet in each bowl, and slide the fruit off the skewer onto the sorbet. Serve at once.

White Wine–Poached Pears

4 Bartlett (Williams') pears, peeled, with stem intact

1 bottle (3 cups/24 fl oz/ 750 ml) Pinot Grigio or other fruity white wine

$^3/_4$ cup (6 oz/185 g) sugar

2 strips lemon zest, each 2 inches (5 cm) long and $^3/_4$ inch (2 cm) wide

Juice of 1 lemon (about 3 tablespoons)

6 peppercorns

4 thin slices fresh ginger

4 fresh mint sprigs (optional)

MAKES 4 SERVINGS

Place the pears in a nonreactive saucepan just wide enough to hold them standing upright. Add the wine, sugar, lemon zest and juice, peppercorns, ginger, and 3 cups (24 fl oz/750 ml) water.

Place the pan over medium-high heat and bring to a boil. Reduce the heat to medium-low, set a heatproof plate on top of the pears to keep them submerged in the liquid, and simmer gently until a thin knife inserted into the widest part of a pear easily pierces to the center, about 25 minutes. Remove the plate covering the pears. Let the pears cool to room temperature in the liquid.

Using a slotted spoon, lift the pears from the liquid. Cut them in half and, using a melon baller, remove the cores. Set 2 halves in each shallow individual bowl. Bring the cooking liquid to a boil over high heat and boil until it is reduced by two-thirds, about 20 minutes. Pour the liquid through a fine-mesh sieve held over the pears and let the pears cool in the liquid. Serve at room temperature, garnished with the mint sprigs, if using.

Tender, fragrant Bartlett pears poached in white wine with peppercorns, ginger, and lemon are appealing during late summer and fall as an alternative to the traditional winter pears simmered in red wine. In the cooler months, serve these aromatic pears when pork or roasted poultry is on the menu. Like apples, pears are good sources of fiber. Thin, crisp oatmeal cookies (page 221) make a good accompaniment.

Red Wine–Poached Pears

Pinot Noir, along with raspberries and vanilla, updates this classic fruit dessert. Bosc pears, with their spicy flavor and creamy texture, are the best variety to use. To serve the pears, cut them in half and use a melon baller to remove the cores, then divide the pear halves among individual bowls. Pass thin wafers of bittersweet chocolate as an accompaniment for these ruby pears.

Place the pears in a nonreactive saucepan large enough to hold them lying down. Add the wine, sugar, lemon zest, vanilla bean, and 1½ cups (12 fl oz/375 ml) water. In a food processor or blender, purée the 1 cup fresh or frozen berries until smooth. Pass the purée through a fine-mesh sieve held over the pan holding the pears, pressing with the back of a wooden spoon to push as much of the purée through the sieve as possible. Discard the contents of the sieve.

Place the pan over medium-high heat and bring to a boil. Reduce the heat to medium-low, set a heatproof plate on top of the pears to keep them submerged in the liquid, and simmer gently until a thin knife inserted into the widest part of a pear pierces easily to the center, 35–40 minutes. Remove the plate covering the pears. Let the pears cool to room temperature in the liquid.

Using a slotted spoon, lift the pears from the liquid. Set each pear in a shallow individual bowl, or place all 4 pears on a deep platter. Bring the cooking liquid to a boil over high heat and boil until it is reduced by half, about 10 minutes. Pour the liquid over the pears and let the pears cool in the liquid. Remove the zest and vanilla bean and discard. Serve at room temperature, sprinkling the fresh raspberries evenly around the pears, if desired.

4 Bosc pears, peeled, with stem intact

2½ cups (20 fl oz/625 ml) Pinot Noir or other light, fruity red wine

½ cup (4 oz/125 g) sugar

1 lemon zest strip, 2 inches (5 cm) long by ¾ inch (2 cm) wide

2-inch (5-cm) piece vanilla bean

1 cup (4 oz/125 g) fresh or thawed, unsweetened frozen raspberries

½ cup (2 oz/60 g) fresh raspberries (optional)

MAKES 4 SERVINGS

Very Chocolate Mousse

4 oz (125 g) bittersweet chocolate, finely chopped

¹/₂ cup (4 oz/125 g) silken tofu, at room temperature

2 teaspoons brandy or orange-flavored liqueur

4 large egg whites, preferably organic, at room temperature

4 tablespoons (2 oz/60 g) sugar

Candied orange peel (page 275) for garnish (optional)

MAKES 4 SERVINGS

Dense and decadent, this ultrarich dessert could be called Chocolate Fool because it tricks everyone into thinking it is laden with egg yolks and whipped cream, rather than puréed tofu. It is so easy to make that you can treat friends and family to it anytime. Look for tofu sold sealed in a plastic tub and labeled *kinugoshi* in Asian food markets and "silken" or "soft silken" tofu in Western markets. If both silken and soft silken are available, use the latter type. The darker the chocolate you use, the more intense the flavor of your mousse will be. If you like chocolate, you will be pleased to know that it contains the same heart-healthy flavonoids and antioxidants as green tea and many vegetables.

Place the chocolate in the top of a double boiler set over (not touching) barely simmering water and heat until the chocolate melts, stirring often. Remove it from over the water and set aside to cool to room temperature (If the chocolate is too warm or the tofu too cold, the mousse will have a grainy texture). Place the tofu in a blender or food processor and purée until smooth, 1–2 minutes. Stir the puréed tofu and brandy into the melted chocolate until well blended. Set aside.

In a bowl, using a stand mixer fitted with the whip attachment or a handheld mixer, beat the egg whites on medium speed until they are frothy and opaque, about 2 minutes. Increase the speed to high and beat until soft peaks form, 2–3 minutes, then begin gradually adding the sugar, 1 tablespoon at a time. Beat for about 10 seconds to dissolve the addition before adding the next spoonful. When all the sugar has been added, continue to beat until the egg whites are stiff and glossy, 2–3 minutes longer.

Using a rubber spatula, gently fold one-third of the beaten whites into the chocolate mixture. Pour this lightened mixture over the remaining whites, then fold into the whites just until incorporated. Spoon the mousse into individual dishes, dividing it evenly, or into a serving bowl. Cover and refrigerate until the mousse is well chilled, about 3 hours. Remove the mousse from the refrigerator 15 minutes before serving. Garnish with candied orange peel, if desired.

VARIATION

If you are concerned about serving raw egg whites, you can use dehydrated egg whites, which will produce a slightly spongier mousse. In an impeccably clean bowl, sprinkle 2 tablespoons egg white powder over 6 tablespoons (3 fl oz/90 ml) lukewarm water, then stir for 1 minute. The powder will remain lumpy. Set the bowl aside for 20 minutes, then whip as directed in the recipe. Dehydrated whites will take up to 5 minutes longer by hand and 3 minutes longer by machine to whip to the desired result.

Breakfasts

About Breakfasts

You can easily update old-fashioned breakfast recipes by substituting whole grains for refined white flour in muffin, pancake, and waffle batters. You can also add aged cheese and vegetables to scrambled eggs and omelets to increase the nutrient count and boost the flavor.

Breakfast has long been called the most important meal of the day. Nutrition professionals insist that eating a good breakfast jump-starts the metabolism, increases energy, and fuels the brain. A wholesome breakfast can be anything from a quick fruit-and-yogurt smoothie for a meal-on-the-run to a vegetable omelet for brunch guests.

KEEPING FIBER HIGH AND SATURATED FATS LOW

Eating a muffin for breakfast can start you off with a healthy dose of fiber. But many muffins contain large amounts of fat and lots of sugar. Most muffins sold at coffee shops are oversized, and some provide almost 500 calories (2,100 kilojoules). Baking your own muffins allows you to control portion size and ingredients. First, look for recipes that call for whole grains, such as Fresh Corn and Cornmeal Muffins (page 253), which combine whole-wheat (wholemeal) flour and cornmeal. Oat bran, another whole grain, is touted for its high fiber content and link to the reduction of blood cholesterol levels in those who eat it regularly. It contributes plenty of flavor, too, as in Date-Apple Oat Bran Muffins (page 254). This same recipe calls for unsweetened applesauce and canola oil in place of the butter commonly used in preparing muffins.

Buttermilk is another health-savvy addition to muffin batter, as the Banana-Buttermilk Muffins (page 256) illustrate. Despite its rich-sounding name, buttermilk is low in fat, and its natural acidity aids in leavening, yielding light and fine-textured baked goods. To keep muffins healthful, choose toppings with care. Fruit butters, fresh-fruit spreads, or Yogurt Cheese (page 273) are all delicious stand-ins for high-fat butter or cream cheese.

Like muffins, pancakes and waffles can be high in fat and saturated fat. They are also typically topped with butter and sugary syrup. The pancake and waffle recipes that follow have been modified from their traditional counterparts to increase nutrients and/or fiber, reduce fat and cholesterol, and heighten flavor.

Ricotta-Lemon Pancakes (page 259) use part-skim ricotta cheese, low-fat milk, and whipped egg whites, yielding calcium-packed pancakes. Waffles with Strawberry and Honey Sauce (page 260) are prepared with whole-wheat flour, which not only provides more nutrients and fiber than all-purpose (plain) flour, but also results in a more interesting texture and a nutty taste. The sauce is made from fresh strawberries, which are high in vitamin C, and honey, an unrefined sweetener that marries well with the wheaty flavor of the waffles.

THE VERSATILE EGG

Nutritionally balanced, inexpensive, and remarkably versatile, eggs are valued breakfast staples. After years of criticism for their cholesterol content, they are now recognized for their high nutrient density and broad range of vitamins and minerals. Free of fat and high in protein, egg whites are particularly healthful. The egg yolks, on the other hand, contain both substantial fat and cholesterol. Current nutritional guidelines advise eating no more than five whole eggs (or egg yolks) per week. Medically prescribed diets may recommend fewer or more eggs.

This chapter offers two delicious ways to prepare eggs. Both the omelet (page 264) and the scrambled eggs (page 266) use a high proportion of vegetables and/or fresh herbs and a small amount of strong-flavored cheese to create satisfying dishes. Cooking an omelet or scrambled eggs is an easy way to get a healthful breakfast on the table quickly. They take well to improvisation, too. Here are four simple ideas for adapting egg dishes:

■ Add vegetables to scrambled eggs to increase the amount of nutrients and phytochemicals. Avoid using too much of any vegetable with a high water content, such as tomatoes, or the eggs will be too runny.

■ Add an aged grating cheese, such as Parmigiano-Reggiano or sharp cheddar. Aged cheeses are full flavored, so a little can go a long way.

■ Whisk chopped fresh herbs (about 1 teaspoon per egg) into the beaten eggs before cooking. Good choices are basil, tarragon, dill, or flat-leaf (Italian) parsley. Herbs not only are nutritious, but also are known to stimulate the appetite and aid in digestion.

■ To reduce the fat and cholesterol of an egg dish but still retain the egg flavor and texture, substitute two egg whites for every other whole egg called for in any recipe using two or more eggs.

When planning your daily meals, always remember to include a health-conscious start. You will have an easier time meeting your nutrition goals for the day, you will be less likely to overeat at other meals, and you will continue to feel energetic long after you leave the breakfast table.

Fresh Corn and Cornmeal Muffins

The addition of yogurt not only makes these sunny yellow muffins moist and delicate, but also adds calcium. The corn kernels deliver a pleasing chewiness and some fiber. The muffins are especially good halved, toasted, and spread with a little fruit jam.

Preheat the oven to 375°F (190°C). Spray 12 standard muffin cups with canola-oil cooking spray, or use paper liners.

If using fresh corn, husk the ears and carefully remove all of the silk. Hold 1 ear upright, stem end down, on a cutting board. Using a sharp knife, slice straight down between the kernels and the cob, rotating the ear a quarter turn after each cut. Repeat with the second ear. Measure out 1 cup (6 oz/185 g) kernels; reserve the remainder for another use. If using frozen corn, thaw and pat dry with paper towels. Set aside.

In a large bowl, stir together the all-purpose flour, cornmeal, whole-wheat flour, sugar, baking powder, baking soda, cinnamon, and $1/2$ teaspoon salt. Add the corn kernels and toss to combine.

In another bowl or a large, glass measuring pitcher, whisk together the yogurt, milk, canola oil, and eggs. Pour the wet ingredients over the dry ingredients and stir just until blended. Do not overmix. Spoon the batter into the prepared muffin cups, filling each about three-fourths full.

Bake the muffins until they are lightly browned and a toothpick inserted into the center of a muffin comes out clean, 20–25 minutes. Let cool in the pan on a wire rack for 15 minutes, then turn out onto the rack and let cool completely. The muffins will keep in a zippered plastic bag at room temperature for 2 or 3 days, or in the freezer for up to 2 months.

2 ears corn or 1 cup (6 oz/ 185 g) frozen corn kernels

$1^{1}/_{4}$ cups ($6^{1}/_{2}$ oz/200 g) all-purpose (plain) flour

$1/_{2}$ cup ($2^{1}/_{2}$ oz/75 g) yellow cornmeal

$1/_{4}$ cup ($1^{1}/_{2}$ oz/45 g) whole-wheat (wholemeal) flour

$1/_{3}$ cup (3 oz/90 g) sugar

1 tablespoon baking powder

1 teaspoon baking soda (bicarbonate of soda)

$1/_{2}$ teaspoon ground cinnamon

Kosher salt

1 cup (8 oz/250 g) low-fat plain yogurt

$1/_{4}$ cup (2 fl oz/60 ml) 1-percent-fat milk

$1/_{4}$ cup (2 fl oz/60 ml) canola oil

2 large eggs

MAKES 12 MUFFINS

Date-Apple Oat Bran Muffins

1 cup (5 oz/155 g)
all-purpose (plain) flour

1 cup (2¹/₂ oz/75 g) oat bran

¹/₂ cup (3¹/₂ oz/105 g) firmly
packed light brown sugar

¹/₄ cup (1 oz/30 g) nonfat dry
milk (milk powder)

2¹/₂ teaspoons baking powder

1 teaspoon ground cinnamon

Kosher salt

1 small apple such as pippin,
Granny Smith, or Golden
Delicious, halved, peeled,
cored, and finely diced

¹/₂ cup (3 oz/90 g) chopped
pitted dates

¹/₂ cup (4 fl oz/125 ml)
1-percent-fat milk

¹/₂ cup (4¹/₂ oz/140 g)
unsweetened applesauce

¹/₄ cup (2 fl oz/60 ml)
canola oil

1 large egg

1 teaspoon vanilla extract
(essence)

MAKES 10 MUFFINS

Preheat the oven to 375°F (190°C). Spray 10 standard muffin cups with canola-oil cooking spray, or use paper liners. Fill the unused cups one-third full with water to prevent the muffin pan from warping.

In a large bowl, stir together the flour, oat bran, brown sugar, nonfat dry milk, baking powder, cinnamon, and ¹/₂ teaspoon salt. Add the apple and dates and toss to coat with the dry ingredients.

In another bowl or a large, glass measuring pitcher, whisk together the milk, applesauce, canola oil, egg, and vanilla until blended. Pour the wet ingredients over the dry ingredients and stir just until blended. Do not overmix. Spoon the batter into the prepared muffin cups, filling each about three-fourths full.

Bake the muffins until they are lightly browned and a toothpick inserted into the center of a muffin comes out clean, 20–25 minutes. Let cool in the pan on a wire rack for 15 minutes, then turn out onto the rack and let cool completely. The muffins will keep in a zippered plastic bag at room temperature for 2 or 3 days, or in the freezer for up to 2 months.

The apple and applesauce add moisture, the dates and oat bran add fiber, and the nonfat dry milk adds calcium to these moist, flavorful muffins. Scientific research has found that fiber works to lower cholesterol and reduce the risk of heart disease. The muffins are delicious toasted and served with apple butter.

Banana-Buttermilk Muffins

1 cup (5 oz/155 g)
unbleached all-purpose
(plain) flour

³/₄ cup (4 oz/125 g)
whole-wheat (wholemeal)
flour

¹/₂ cup (4 oz/125 g) sugar

2 teaspoons baking powder

1 teaspoon baking soda
(bicarbonate of soda)

1 cup (8 fl oz/250 ml)
low-fat buttermilk

1 cup (8 oz/250 g) mashed
ripe banana (see note)

2 tablespoons canola oil

1 large egg

1 teaspoon vanilla extract
(essence)

¹/₂ cup (2 oz/60 g) chopped
walnuts

MAKES 12 MUFFINS

Preheat the oven to 375°F (190°C). Spray 12 standard muffin cups with canola-oil cooking spray, or use paper liners.

In a large bowl, stir together the all-purpose and whole-wheat flours, sugar, baking powder, and baking soda.

In another bowl or a large, glass measuring pitcher, whisk together the buttermilk, banana, canola oil, egg, and vanilla. Pour the wet ingredients over the dry ingredients and stir just until blended. Do not overmix. Spoon the batter into the prepared muffin cups, filling each about three-fourths full. Sprinkle the tops evenly with the walnuts.

Bake the muffins until they are lightly browned and a toothpick inserted in the center of a muffin comes out clean, 15–20 minutes. Let cool in the pan on a wire rack for 15 minutes, then turn out onto the rack and let cool completely. The muffins will keep in a zippered plastic bag at room temperature for 2 or 3 days, or in the freezer for up to 2 months.

Despite its name, buttermilk is made from cultured skim milk, not butter, and is low in fat. Although its unique tang is barely discernible in baked goods, it contributes to a tender, light crumb. The combination of the delicate texture, the moist banana flavor, and the crunchy walnuts will make this a favorite muffin recipe. Be sure to mash the bananas well with a fork to avoid lumps in the batter.

Ricotta-Lemon Pancakes

Light and delicate, these pancakes are moist, rich, and lemony on the inside and have a crisp, browned exterior. The texture comes from using lightly beaten egg whites instead of butter, and the calories are reduced by using part-skim ricotta cheese rather than whole-milk ricotta. Part-skim ricotta cheese has more calcium than whole-milk ricotta. When you open the ricotta cheese container, pour off any liquid sitting on the top. If desired, serve the pancakes with maple syrup in place of the confectioners' sugar and fresh berries.

Preheat the oven to 250°F (120°C).

Place the ricotta in a large bowl. Add the milk, egg yolks, and granulated sugar and whisk together until blended. Add the flour, lemon zest, and 1/4 teaspoon salt and, using a rubber spatula, fold just until blended.

In a separate bowl, combine the egg whites and the cream of tartar and, using a whisk or a handheld electric mixer set on medium speed, beat until soft peaks form. Using the rubber spatula, carefully fold the beaten whites into the ricotta mixture just until blended.

In a bowl, combine the berries and lemon juice and stir gently to blend. Set aside.

Place a large nonstick griddle or frying pan with low sloping sides over medium heat until hot enough for a drop of water to sizzle and then immediately evaporate. Brush the surface with a thin film of canola oil. For each pancake, ladle a scant 1/3 cup (3 fl oz/80 ml) batter onto the hot surface. Reduce the heat to medium-low and cook until small bubbles appear around the edges of the pancakes and the bottoms are lightly browned, 4–5 minutes. Carefully turn and cook until the other sides are lightly browned, 2–3 minutes longer. Transfer to an ovenproof platter and place in the oven to keep warm; do not cover the pancakes, or they will get soggy. Repeat with the remaining batter. You will have enough batter to make 12 pancakes, each about 3 inches (7.5 cm) in diameter.

Using a fine-mesh sieve, dust the warm pancakes generously with confectioners' sugar to taste. Serve the pancakes with the berries on the side.

1 cup (8 oz/250 g) part-skim ricotta cheese (see note)

1/4 cup (2 fl oz/60 ml) 1-percent-fat milk

3 large eggs, separated

2 tablespoons granulated sugar

1/3 cup (2 oz/60 g) all-purpose (plain) flour

1 tablespoon grated lemon zest

Kosher salt

Pinch of cream of tartar

4 cups (1 lb/500 g) mixed berries such as whole blueberries and raspberries and trimmed and sliced strawberries

1 tablespoon fresh lemon juice

About 1 teaspoon canola oil

1–2 tablespoons confectioners' (icing) sugar

MAKES 4 SERVINGS

Waffles with Strawberry and Honey Sauce

For the Strawberry and
Honey Sauce

¹/₂ cup (6 oz/185 g) honey

**¹/₄ cup (2 fl oz/60 ml) fresh
lemon juice**

**1 cup (4 oz/125 g) diced
strawberries**

**³/₄ cup (4 oz/125 g)
all-purpose (plain) flour**

**³/₄ cup (4 oz/125 g)
whole-wheat (wholemeal)
flour**

2 tablespoons wheat bran

1 tablespoon baking powder

1 teaspoon ground cinnamon

Kosher salt

**1¹/₂ cups (12 fl oz/375 ml)
1-percent-fat milk**

2 large eggs

**2 tablespoons unsalted
butter, melted**

**2 tablespoons wildflower or
orange blossom honey**

1 teaspoon canola oil

MAKES 4 SERVINGS

This recipe, with its complement of whole wheat, cinnamon, and honey, produces waffles with a crunchy texture and a nutty, whole-grain taste. Whole-wheat flour contains the germ and bran of wheat, as well as the starchy endosperm. It is slightly higher in protein than white flour and many times higher in fiber and some minerals, especially phosphorus and potassium. If you like, serve the waffles with maple syrup in place of the strawberry and honey sauce.

To make the sauce, in a small saucepan over low heat, warm the honey, stirring, until thinned but not hot, about 1 minute. Remove from the heat. Add the lemon juice and strawberries and stir until blended. Cover and let stand at room temperature until ready to serve. (The sauce will keep tightly covered in the refrigerator for up to 2 days; bring to room temperature before serving.)

In a large bowl, stir together the all-purpose and whole-wheat flours, bran, baking powder, cinnamon, and ¹/₂ teaspoon salt. In a separate bowl or large, glass measuring pitcher, whisk together the milk, eggs, and butter until blended. To make the honey easier to mix, warm it in a small saucepan over low heat for about 30 seconds or in a bowl in a microwave for about 10 seconds. Add to the milk mixture and whisk until blended.

Make a well in the center of the dry ingredients and add the wet ingredients. Stir just until blended; do not overmix. The batter will be thick.

To cook the waffles, preheat a waffle iron for 5 minutes, then brush with the canola oil. Ladle about ¹/₂ cup (4 fl oz/125 ml) of the batter into the center of the waffle iron, and spread with a small spatula to fill all the holes. Close the waffle iron and cook until the steam stops escaping from the sides and the top opens easily, or according to the manufacturer's directions, 4–5 minutes. The timing will depend on the specific waffle iron used. The waffle should be browned and crisp.

Transfer the waffle to a warmed platter and repeat with the remaining batter. Serve the waffles with the strawberry and honey sauce.

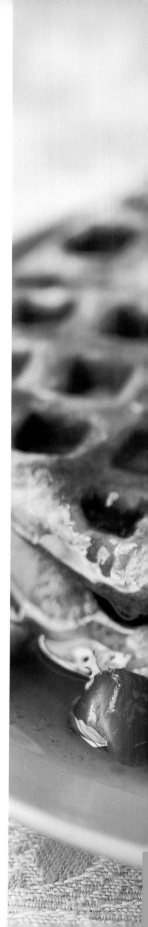

Multigrain Yeast Bread

This picture-perfect, crusty loaf will satisfy both the novice and the experienced baker. Use it for breakfast toast, spreading it with 1-percent-fat cottage cheese and then topping the cottage cheese with a little ground cinnamon. It also makes great sandwiches.

In a saucepan over low heat, combine the milk and molasses and heat to 105°–115°F (41°–46°C). Remove from the heat and sprinkle the yeast on top. Let stand until foamy, about 10 minutes.

BY HAND: In a large bowl, stir together the 2 cups all-purpose flour, whole-wheat flour, $^1/_2$ cup rolled oats, and 1$^1/_2$ teaspoons salt. Whisk the egg yolk into the yeast mixture, then slowly stir into the flour mixture. Beat with a wooden spoon until a sticky dough forms. Then add small amounts of all-purpose flour until the dough comes together in a smooth ball. Turn the dough out onto a lightly floured work surface and knead until smooth and elastic, about 10 minutes, adding all-purpose flour as needed to reduce stickiness.

BY MIXER: In the bowl of a stand mixer fitted with the paddle, stir together the 2 cups all-purpose flour, whole-wheat flour, $^1/_2$ cup rolled oats, and 1$^1/_2$ teaspoons salt. Whisk the egg yolk into the yeast mixture and add to the bowl. Beat on medium speed until a sticky dough forms. Continuing to beat, add small amounts of all-purpose flour until the dough comes together in a smooth ball. Switch to the dough hook and knead the dough on medium speed until smooth and elastic, 6–8 minutes, adding all-purpose flour as needed to reduce stickiness.

1$^1/_2$ cups (12 fl oz/375 ml) nonfat milk

$^1/_4$ cup (2$^3/_4$ oz/80 g) dark molasses

1 envelope (2$^1/_2$ teaspoons) active dry yeast

2 cups (10 oz/315 g) all-purpose (plain) flour, plus more as needed

1 cup (5 oz/155 g) whole-wheat (wholemeal) flour

$^1/_2$ cup (1$^1/_2$ oz/45 g) plus 1 tablespoon rolled oats

Kosher salt

1 large egg, separated

$^1/_3$ cup (1$^1/_2$ oz/45 g) plus 1 tablespoon hulled unsalted toasted sunflower seeds

MAKES 16 SERVINGS

Form the dough into a ball and place in a lightly oiled bowl. Turn to coat with the oil. Cover the bowl with plastic wrap and let the dough rise in a warm place until doubled in bulk, about 1 hour.

Lightly oil a 9-by-5-inch (23-by-13-cm) loaf pan. Punch the dough down and let rest for 10 minutes. Turn the dough out onto a floured work surface and sprinkle with the $^1/_3$ cup sunflower seeds. Fold the dough over and knead until the seeds are evenly distributed. Flatten the dough into a 12-by-7-inch (30-by-18-cm) rectangle. Beginning with a short side, loosely roll up the dough rectangle and pinch the seam to seal. Transfer, seam side down, to the prepared pan. Cover the pan with plastic wrap and let the dough rise in a warm place until doubled in bulk, about 30 minutes. While the dough is rising, preheat the oven to 350°F (180°C).

In a small bowl, lightly beat the egg white. Remove the plastic wrap and brush the top of the loaf with the egg white. Sprinkle the remaining 1 tablespoon each rolled oats and sunflower seeds evenly over the top. Bake the bread until the top is golden and the bottom sounds hollow when tapped, 40–45 minutes. Let cool in the pan for 5 minutes, then turn out onto a wire rack and let cool completely. The loaf can be cut into 16 slices.

Roasted Red Pepper, Spinach, and Feta Omelet

1 red bell pepper (capsicum), about ¹/₂ lb (250 g)

3 teaspoons extra-virgin olive oil

³/₄ cup (1 oz/30 g) loosely packed spinach leaves, stems removed

Kosher salt and freshly ground pepper

4 large eggs

2 tablespoons crumbled feta cheese

MAKES 2 SERVINGS

Roast the bell pepper as directed on page 277. Remove the stem, cut the pepper in half lengthwise, and remove the seeds, ribs, and blackened skin. Cut each half lengthwise into strips ¹/₂ inch (12 mm) wide. Measure out ¹/₂ cup (2¹/₂ oz/75 g) for the omelet filling. Reserve the remainder for another use.

In a frying pan over medium heat, combine the roasted pepper strips and 2 teaspoons of the olive oil and stir until hot, about 1 minute. Add the spinach and heat just until wilted, about 30 seconds. Transfer to a bowl and add a pinch of salt and a grind of pepper.

In a large bowl, whisk together the eggs, 2 tablespoons water, a pinch of salt, and a grind of pepper just until blended.

Heat a 9- or 10-inch (23- or 25-cm) frying pan with low, sloping sides, preferably well seasoned or nonstick, over medium heat for 2 minutes. Add the remaining 1 teaspoon oil and tilt the pan to coat evenly. Heat the oil until a drop of egg sizzles upon contact, then pour the eggs into the center of the pan and immediately reduce the heat to medium-low. Cook, without stirring, just until the bottom is set, about 10 seconds. Using a heatproof rubber spatula, gently pull the set edges in toward the center, and then tilt the pan so that the uncooked egg in the center runs toward the edges. Adjust the heat so that the eggs will set, but not brown. Cook until softly set with just a thin layer of moist egg on the surface, about 2 minutes total cooking time.

Spoon the red pepper mixture onto the side of the omelet closest to the handle of the frying pan. Sprinkle the mixture with the feta cheese. Using the spatula as a guide, fold the third of the omelet closest to the handle over the center third. Then, holding the pan by the handle, tilt the pan so that the omelet rolls out onto a warmed platter, seam side down.

Cut the omelet in half, arrange each half on a plate, and serve at once.

An omelet is one of the fastest dishes to prepare: four eggs and a few choice ingredients for the filling, and breakfast is quickly on the table. The small amount of water added to the eggs turns into steam when exposed to the heat of the frying pan, making the eggs tender and fluffy. It is best to use a frying pan that is either nonstick or well seasoned and has low, sloping, rather than straight, sides so that the finished omelet will be easy to turn out of the pan. Finally, do not attempt to make an omelet with more than four eggs. Serve the omelet with toasted whole-wheat (wholemeal) bread.

Scrambled Eggs with Tomato, Cheddar, and Basil

6 large eggs

1 tablespoon extra-virgin olive oil

$^1/_4$ cup (1 oz/30 g) chopped sweet onion such as Vidalia or Walla Walla

1 tomato, about 7 oz (200 g), diced (about 1 cup)

2 tablespoons chopped fresh basil

Kosher salt and freshly ground pepper

$^1/_4$ cup (1 oz/30 g) coarsely shredded cheddar cheese

MAKES 4 SERVINGS

In a bowl or large, glass measuring pitcher, whisk together the eggs and 2 table-spoons water until well blended.

In a large frying pan over medium heat, warm the olive oil. Add the onion and cook, stirring, until golden, about 5 minutes. Raise the heat to high and add the diced tomato, basil, $^1/_2$ teaspoon salt, and a grind of pepper. Cook until the tomato is heated through and any juices have evaporated, about 1 minute.

Add the beaten eggs all at once, reduce the heat to medium, and cook the eggs, without stirring, for 1 minute. Using a rubber spatula, stir the eggs from the edges of the pan toward the center. Continue to cook and stir gently until the eggs are almost cooked, but are still moist, about 3 minutes.

Sprinkle the cheese over the eggs and cook for 1 minute longer. Divide the eggs evenly among warmed plates. Serve at once.

Eggs and tomatoes are such a popular pairing that as many different dishes as there are cooks seem to exist. This simple recipe is a favorite preparation through-out Spain, where a local hard grating cheese would be used. In this version, coarsely grated sharp cheddar is the choice. Serve the eggs for breakfast with toasted bread drizzled with olive oil. For brunch or lunch, add a mixed green salad or a garnish of watercress sprigs.

Mango-Yogurt Smoothies

Banana-Strawberry Smoothies

Substitute $^1/_2$ cup (3 oz/90 g) sliced banana for half of the mango; add $^1/_2$ cup (2 oz/60 g) strawberries, stems removed and halved lengthwise, and 2 tablespoons whole natural almonds (optional).

Mango-Buttermilk Smoothies

Substitute 1 cup (8 fl oz/250 ml) low-fat buttermilk for the yogurt.

Fresh mango and cranberry juice, along with yogurt, make an unusual and refreshing smoothie. Mango is an excellent source of beta-carotene, and both mangoes and cranberries contain vitamin C.

To cut the mango, stand the fruit on one of its narrow sides, with the stem end facing you (page 279). Using a sharp knife, and positioning it about 1 inch (2.5 cm) from the stem, cut down the length of the fruit, just brushing the large, lengthwise pit. Repeat the cut on the other side of the pit. One at a time, holding each half cut side up, score the flesh in a grid pattern, forming $^1/_4$-inch (6-mm) cubes and stopping just short of the skin. Push against the skin side to force the cubes outward, then cut across the base of the cubes to free them. Measure out 1 cup (6 oz/185 g) mango cubes; reserve the remainder for another use.

In a blender, combine the 1 cup mango, cranberry juice, yogurt, and ice cubes. Blend until frothy and smooth. Divide between 2 tall glass and serve.

1 mango

1 cup (8 fl oz/250 ml) sweetened cranberry juice

1 cup (8 oz/250 g) nonfat plain yogurt

$^1/_2$ cup (4 oz/125 g) ice cubes

MAKES 2 SERVINGS

Basic Recipes

In addition to two stocks and two sauces used in this book, these basic recipes include flavorful condiments and seasonings that will enhance a variety of dishes. Low in fat and calories, they range from a chutney and a salsa to salad dressings and dessert sauces.

Rich Chicken Stock

1 chicken, about 3¹/₂ lb (1.75 kg)

1 lb (500 g) chicken wings

1 large carrot, peeled and quartered crosswise

1 celery stalk, quartered crosswise

1 leek, including 6 inches (15 cm) of the greens

1 large yellow onion, quartered

1 parsnip, peeled and quartered

12 fresh flat-leaf (Italian) parsley sprigs

1 teaspoon peppercorns

In a large stockpot, combine the whole chicken and chicken wings, carrot, celery, leek, onion, parsnip, parsley, peppercorns, and 6 qt (6 l) water. Place the pot over high heat. As soon as tiny bubbles start rising to the surface, after about 10 minutes, reduce the heat to medium and watch carefully. When scum starts to form and small bubbles break the surface, reduce the heat further. The stock should bubble so gently that the surface is almost still. If the stock boils, the fat will emulsify and make the stock cloudy.

Using a large spoon, skim off any scum and foam as soon as they form. For the first 30 minutes, the stock may require frequent skimming. After that, skimming can be done occasionally. Cook, uncovered, until the liquid is reduced by half and the flavor is concentrated, 3–4 hours. The chicken will be falling apart.

Remove from the heat and let stand until the liquid is almost room temperature, about 1 hour. Lift out the chicken and the chicken wings, and, if desired, remove the meat and reserve for other uses. Pour the stock through a fine-mesh sieve into 1 or more containers with tight-fitting lids. Discard the solids.

Let the stock cool to room temperature, then cover and refrigerate. When the stock is completely chilled, using a spoon, lift off the congealed layer of fat on top. Store in the refrigerator for up to 3 days or freeze for up to 2 months.

Makes 3 qt (3 l)

Roasted Vegetable Stock

3 teaspoons extra-virgin olive oil

1¹/₂ lb (750 g) plum (Roma) tomatoes, halved lengthwise

2 carrots, each quartered crosswise

1 leek, white part only, halved lengthwise

1 yellow onion, quartered

1 parsnip, peeled and cut into 4 pieces

1 large shallot, halved lengthwise

1 zucchini (courgette), halved lengthwise and cut crosswise into 4 pieces

¹/₃ medium celery root, cut into 2 pieces

¹/₄ cup (³/₄ oz/20 g) chopped celery leaves

Fresh peel from 1 small potato

4 fresh thyme sprigs

2 bay leaves

¹/₄ teaspoon peppercorns

Preheat the oven to 425°F (220°C). Coat 2 baking sheets with 1 teaspoon of the olive oil.

Place the tomatoes, carrots, leek, onion, parsnip, shallot, and zucchini in a bowl. Drizzle with the remaining 2 teaspoons oil and toss to coat. Arrange the tomatoes, cut side down, on a prepared baking sheet. Arrange the other vegetables in one layer in the remaining space and on the second prepared sheet.

Roast until the tomatoes are soft but still hold their shape, about 35 minutes. Using a slotted spoon, transfer them to a stockpot. Continue to roast the remaining vegetables until they are lightly colored, 5–10 minutes longer. Transfer to the stockpot.

Add the celery root pieces, celery leaves, potato peel, thyme, bay leaves, peppercorns, and 3 qt (3 l) water to the vegetables. Bring to a boil over medium-high heat, reduce the heat to medium-low, and simmer, uncovered, until the vegetables are very soft, about 1 hour.

Let the stock cool to room temperature. Pour the stock through a fine-mesh sieve into a bowl. Return all but 2–3 cups (16–24 fl oz/ 500–750 ml) of the roasted vegetables to the pot. Press the vegetables in the sieve firmly with the back of a wooden spoon to extract as much liquid as possible. Do not press so hard that pulp goes through the strainer, which will make the stock cloudy. Discard the contents of the sieve and repeat with the remaining roasted vegetables. Transfer the stock to containers with tight-fitting lids. Store in the refrigerator for up to 3 days or freeze for up to 2 months.

Makes 3 qt (3 l)

SERVING TIP

This low-fat vegetarian stock can be used in place of meat or chicken stock in soups, stews, and many other recipes.

Spicy Tomato Sauce

1 teaspoon freshly ground white or black pepper

¹/₂ teaspoon freshly grated nutmeg

¹/₄ teaspoon ground ginger

¹/₈ teaspoon ground cloves

2 tablespoons extra-virgin olive oil

1¹/₂ cups (7¹/₂ oz/235 g) finely chopped yellow onion

1 clove garlic, minced

1 can (28 oz/875 g) whole plum (Roma) tomatoes with juice

1 can (28 oz/875 g) chopped tomatoes with juice

2 cups (16 fl oz/500 ml) tomato sauce

In a small bowl, stir together the pepper, nutmeg, ginger, and cloves. Set aside.

In a large Dutch oven or other deep, heavy pot over medium-high heat, warm the olive oil. Add the onion and sauté until beginning to soften, about 4 minutes. Reduce the heat to medium-low, cover, and cook the onion until it releases its juices, about 5 minutes. Stir in the minced garlic.

Add the plum tomatoes and their juice. Using a wooden spoon, break up the tomatoes into 1-inch (2.5-cm) chunks. Add the chopped tomatoes and their juice and the tomato sauce, and then stir in the spice mixture. Raise the heat to medium-high and bring the sauce to a boil. Reduce the heat to medium-low and simmer, uncovered, until the sauce has the thickness of tomato purée, 15–20 minutes.

Remove from the heat and use immediately, or let cool, cover, and refrigerate for up to 1 week or freeze for up to 2 months.

Makes about 3 qt (3 l)

VARIATION

Add 2 orange zest strips, each 2 inches (5 cm) long by 1 inch (2.5 cm) wide, along with the tomatoes.

SERVING TIP

Use this almost fat-free sauce with meat loaf, on pasta, and over polenta.

Lean Béchamel Sauce

2¹/₂ cups (20 fl oz/625 ml) 1-percent-fat milk

2 or 3 gratings fresh nutmeg

1¹/₂ teaspoons canola oil

2 tablespoons all-purpose (plain) flour

Kosher salt and freshly ground white or black pepper

In a saucepan over medium heat, warm the milk until it begins to steam, about 5 minutes. Remove from the heat and add the nutmeg. Keep hot.

In a heavy, nonstick saucepan over medium heat, warm the canola oil. Using a wooden spoon, stir in the flour. Then, using a mashing motion, stir constantly until the flour mixture begins to become fluffy and looks shiny, 3–4 minutes. Cook for 30 seconds longer, taking care not to let the flour color.

While whisking vigorously, pour in ¹/₂ cup (4 fl oz/125 ml) of the hot milk. When the mixture is as smooth as you can get it, pour in the remaining milk while whisking constantly. Cook over medium heat until the lumps have dissolved and the sauce comes to a boil. Then, reducing the heat as needed to prevent scorching, cook, stirring often, until the sauce has the consistency of light whipping (double) cream, about 5 minutes. Add ¹/₂ teaspoon salt and season to taste with pepper.

Pour the sauce into a bowl, passing it through a fine-mesh sieve if lumps are visible. Use immediately, or cover the hot sauce with a piece of plastic wrap, pressing it against the surface to prevent a skin from forming. Set the sauce aside to cool, then refrigerate for up to 2 days before using.

Makes 3 cups (24 fl oz/750 ml)

Roasted Garlic

1 head garlic

1 teaspoon extra-virgin olive oil

Kosher salt

Preheat the oven to 400°F (200°C).

Pull off the papery outer layers from the head of garlic. Break the head into individual cloves, or slice the head crosswise at the root end to expose all of the cloves.

Lay a 12-inch (30-cm) square of aluminum foil on a work surface. Place the garlic in the center, drizzle with the olive oil, and using your fingers, rub the oil evenly over the garlic. If using the garlic head intact, place cut side down and make sure that the cut portion is well oiled. Sprinkle with 2 pinches of salt. Bring the 4 corners of the foil up over the garlic, twist, and press to seal the packet.

Roast until the garlic is very soft, 50–60 minutes. Remove from the oven and serve hot or at room temperature. The garlic will keep in its foil packet for up to 5 days in the refrigerator. Use the garlic as directed in recipes, squeezing the roasted cloves from their papery peels.

Makes 4 servings

Tomato Chutney

6 cups (2¼ lb/1.1 kg) chopped firm tomatoes

1 yellow onion, chopped

4 pitted dates, chopped

½ cup (3 oz/90 g) golden raisins (sultanas)

½ lemon, chopped

1 cup (7 oz/220 g) firmly packed brown sugar

½ teaspoon ground allspice

½ teaspoon freshly ground white pepper

¼ teaspoon ground cloves

¼ teaspoon ground mace

¼ teaspoon red pepper flakes

½ cup (4 fl oz/125 ml) sherry vinegar

Place the tomatoes, onion, dates, raisins, and lemon in a deep, heavy, nonreactive pot. Add the brown sugar, allspice, white pepper, cloves, mace, red pepper flakes, and vinegar and stir to combine. Bring to a boil over medium-high heat, reduce the heat to medium-low, and cook uncovered, stirring occasionally with a wooden spoon to prevent sticking, until the chutney plops when dropped from a spoon, 35–40 minutes.

Spoon the hot chutney into sterilized glass containers with tight-fitting lids. Let the chutney cool completely, 3–4 hours. The chutney will keep in the refrigerator for up to 2 months.

Makes 4½ cups (36 fl oz/1.1 l)

SERVING TIP
Offer the tomato chutney with low-fat cream cheese and low-sodium crackers as a starter, or serve it as a condiment for grilled poultry or meat. The chutney can also be used in or on an omelet and in sandwiches.

Gremolata

⅔ cup (1 oz/30 g) minced fresh flat-leaf (Italian) parsley

Finely grated zest of 1 lemon

2 cloves garlic, minced

In a small bowl, stir together the parsley, zest, and garlic.

Makes ¾ cup (1½ oz/45 g)

SERVING TIP
Sprinkle the *gremolata* over cooked fish or chicken, or steamed vegetables.

Preserved Lemons

4 lemons, about 1 lb (500 g) total weight

Kosher salt

2 cups (16 fl oz/500 ml) fresh lemon juice or as needed

Scrub each lemon thoroughly under running cold water to remove any dirt or wax. Cut each lemon lengthwise into quarters, leaving them attached at the stem end. Gently spread apart the quarters and sprinkle 1 tablespoon salt into the center of each lemon. Place 1 tablespoon salt into a sterilized jar large enough to hold the lemons. Add the lemons, pour in enough lemon juice to cover them, and close with a tight-fitting lid.

Store the lemons in a cool, dry place for 3 weeks, turning the jar occasionally to distribute the lemon juice and salt evenly. Before using the lemons, rinse well to remove any white film. Squeeze the lemons to expel the juice, cut away the pulp, and thinly slice the peel or cut as directed in individual recipes. Store the opened jar of lemons in the refrigerator for up to 3 months.

Makes 4 preserved lemons

SERVING TIP
Finely chop or slice the preserved lemon peel and use to season chicken or fish as it cooks. Or sprinkle on cooked chicken, fish, or vegetables as a garnish.

Tzatziki

1 large English (hothouse) cucumber, peeled, seeded, and cut into ¼-inch (6-mm) dice

Kosher salt

¾ cup (6 oz/185 g) low-fat plain yogurt

½ cup (4 oz/125 g) light sour cream

1 tablespoon fresh lemon juice

1 teaspoon red wine vinegar

2 tablespoons finely chopped fresh dill or mint

Freshly ground white pepper

1 teaspoon extra-virgin olive oil

Place the diced cucumber in a colander and sprinkle lightly with salt. Set the colander in a bowl and refrigerate for 30 minutes. Pat the cucumber dry with paper towels and put in a bowl.

In another bowl, whisk together the yogurt, sour cream, lemon juice, vinegar, and dill. Season to taste with pepper. Pour over the cucumber and stir gently to combine. The *tzatziki* can be covered and refrigerated at this point for up to 2 hours.

Just before serving, transfer the *tzatziki* to a serving bowl and drizzle with the olive oil.

Makes 2½ cups (20 fl oz/625 ml)

SERVING TIP
Serve with grilled meat, fish, or vegetables. Or offer it as a dip accompanied with wedges of toasted whole-wheat (wholemeal) pita bread.

Yogurt Cheese

4 cups (2 lb/1 kg) low-fat plain yogurt, preferably without added stabilizers

Line a fine-mesh sieve with a double layer of cheesecloth (muslin) and set over a bowl. Spoon the yogurt into the lined sieve, cover with plastic wrap, and place the bowl and sieve in the refrigerator. Let the yogurt drain for at least 8 hours or for up to overnight. Discard the liquid in the bowl. Transfer the yogurt cheese to a clean container and discard the cheesecloth. Cover tightly and store in the refrigerator for up to 10 days.

Makes about 2 cups (1 lb/500 g)

SERVING TIP

Offer this smooth, tangy cheese for spooning on pancakes (page 259) or waffles (page 260) or as a topping for baked potatoes and other vegetables. Finely chopped herbs added to the cheese transform it into a dip for vegetables and crackers. Stir in finely chopped candied lemon peel (page 275) to make an accompaniment for muffins and other baked goods.

Pico de Gallo

2 ripe tomatoes, seeded and chopped

4 green (spring) onions, white part only, thinly sliced

1 jalapeño or serrano chile, seeded and finely chopped

1/4 cup (1/3 oz/10 g) chopped fresh cilantro (fresh coriander)

Juice of 1/2 lime (about 1 tablespoon)

Kosher salt and freshly ground pepper

Combine the tomatoes, green onions, chile, cilantro, and lime juice in a bowl. Stir in 1/4 teaspoon salt, or more to taste, and season with pepper. Serve within 1 hour.

Makes 1 1/4 cups (10 fl oz/310 ml)

SERVING TIP

Offer this simple fresh salsa with baked corn chips as a starter. Or serve it to accompany grilled poultry or meat, or quesadillas, tacos, or burritos.

Aioli

1/2 cup (4 fl oz/125 ml) low-fat mayonnaise

4 cloves garlic, chopped

2 teaspoons fresh lemon juice

1/2 teaspoon extra-virgin olive oil

Kosher salt and freshly ground pepper

Place the mayonnaise and garlic in a food processor or blender. Process until blended, about 1 minute, stopping 3 or 4 times to scrape down the sides of the bowl. Add the lemon juice, olive oil, 1/4 teaspoon salt, and 1/8 teaspoon pepper. Process until smooth and creamy, about 1 minute.

Use the aioli immediately, or refrigerate, tightly covered, for up to 1 hour, before using, to allow the flavors to meld. Aioli is best used shortly after it is made.

Makes 1/2 cup (4 fl oz/125 ml)

SERVING TIP

This pungent condiment goes well with fish and roasted vegetables, and is also excellent on vegetable or fish sandwiches.

Buttermilk, Yogurt, and Herb Dressing

1/3 cup (1/2 oz/15 g) lightly packed, coarsely chopped fresh flat-leaf (Italian) parsley

2 tablespoons lightly packed, coarsely chopped fresh dill

1 tablespoon coarsely chopped fresh mint

1 green (spring) onion, including tender green tops, thinly sliced

1/2 cup (4 fl oz/125 ml) low-fat buttermilk

1/2 cup (4 oz/125 g) low-fat plain yogurt

1 tablespoon extra-virgin olive oil

Kosher salt

In a food processor, combine the parsley, dill, mint, and green onion and process until finely chopped. Add the buttermilk, yogurt, olive oil, and 1/2 teaspoon salt and process until the ingredients are thoroughly emulsified.

Pour the dressing into a container with a tight-fitting lid and refrigerate for several hours or for up to overnight before serving; it will thicken during this time. Shake or stir well before serving. The dressing will keep for up to 3 days.

Makes 1 1/4 cups (10 fl oz/310 ml)

SERVING TIP

Use this tangy dressing on mixed greens, thickly sliced ripe tomatoes, steamed vegetables, or poached chicken or fish.

Citrus-Mustard Dressing

$1/4$ cup (2 fl oz/60 ml) extra-virgin
olive oil

2 tablespoons fresh lemon juice

2 teaspoons Dijon mustard

$1/2$ teaspoon grated orange zest

$1/2$ teaspoon minced garlic

$1/2$ teaspoon sugar

Kosher salt

In a bowl, whisk together the olive oil, lemon
juice, mustard, orange zest, garlic, sugar,
$1/2$ teaspoon salt, and 1 tablespoon water until
blended. Use immediately or refrigerate, tightly
covered, for up to 3 days.

Makes $1/2$ cup (4 fl oz/125 ml)

SERVING TIP
This dressing is excellent on bitter greens such
as watercress, Belgian endive (chicory/witloof),
or chicory (curly endive) and on a salad with
greens and thinly sliced pears or apples.

Green Goddess Dressing

1 cup (8 oz/250 g) low-fat plain
yogurt

1 cup ($1^1/2$ oz/45 g) loosely packed
watercress leaves and tender stems

2 tablespoons chopped fresh dill

1 green (spring) onion, including
tender green tops, thinly sliced

$1/2$ teaspoon sugar

Kosher salt

Dash of hot-pepper sauce

In a food processor or blender, combine the
yogurt, watercress, dill, green onion, sugar,
$1/2$ teaspoon salt, and hot-pepper sauce and
process until smooth. Pour the dressing into a
container with a tight-fitting lid and refrigerate
for several hours or for up to overnight. The
dressing will be thin when first made, but it will
thicken, and the flavors mellow, when refrigerated. Shake or stir well before serving. The
dressing will keep for up to 3 days.

Makes 1 cup (8 fl oz/250 ml)

SERVING TIP
Toss the dressing with crisp romaine (cos) lettuce
leaves, or use it for dressing a salad made with
chicken or shrimp (prawns).

Honey and Cider Vinaigrette

$1/4$ cup (2 fl oz/60 ml) cider vinegar

$1/4$ cup (3 oz/90 g) honey such as
orange blossom or thyme

Kosher salt and freshly ground pepper

Pour the vinegar into a small bowl. Slowly add
the honey, whisking until blended. Whisk in
$1/2$ teaspoon salt and a grind of pepper. Use
immediately or refrigerate, tightly covered, for
up to 3 days.

Makes $1/2$ cup (4 fl oz/125 ml)

SERVING TIP
Use this simple dressing on salad greens, on a
shredded cabbage and apple salad, or on a
chicken and celery salad.

Lime-Ginger Vinaigrette

$1/3$ cup (3 fl oz/80 ml) canola oil

3 tablespoons fresh lime juice

1 teaspoon peeled and grated fresh
ginger

$1/2$ teaspoon minced garlic

Kosher salt

In a small bowl, whisk together the canola oil,
lime juice, ginger, garlic, and $1/2$ teaspoon salt
until blended. Use immediately or refrigerate,
tightly covered, for up to 3 days.

Makes $1/2$ cup (4 fl oz/125 ml)

Herb and Cheese Croutons

1 teaspoon extra-virgin olive oil

$1/4$ cup (1 oz/30 g) grated
Parmigiano-Reggiano cheese

1 teaspoon dried basil

1 teaspoon dried oregano

$1/2$ teaspoon dried thyme

Kosher salt and freshly ground pepper

1 large egg white

$1/2$ loaf whole-wheat (wholemeal) or
multigrain bread, about $1/2$ lb (250 g),
unsliced

Preheat the oven to 350°F (180°C). Brush a
baking sheet with the olive oil.

Place the cheese in a large bowl. Rub the
basil with your hands to release its oil, letting
it fall over the cheese. Repeat with the oregano
and then the thyme. Add $1/4$ teaspoon salt
and $1/8$ teaspoon pepper. Mix with a fork to
combine the cheese and seasonings.

In another large bowl, whisk the egg white until frothy, about 30 seconds.

Using a serrated knife, cut the crust from the bread. Cut the bread into slices $^3/_4$ inch (2 cm) thick. Stack the slices, 2 or 3 at a time, and cut into strips $^3/_4$ inch (2 cm) wide. Cut the strips crosswise to make $^3/_4$-inch (2-cm) cubes. Add the bread cubes to the egg white and, using the fork, toss to coat lightly with the egg white.

Using a slotted spoon, transfer the bread to the bowl with the cheese mixture. Toss until well coated, about 1 minute. If necessary, use your fingertips to help the cheese mixture adhere. Spread the coated bread cubes in one layer on the prepared baking sheet.

Bake the bread cubes for 5 minutes. Remove from the oven and turn the bread cubes, then bake for 5 minutes longer. Repeat 2 more times until the croutons are golden brown on all sides, about 10 minutes longer.

Remove from the oven and let the croutons cool completely on the baking sheet. Some will be soft to the touch but will become firm as they cool. Store the croutons in an airtight container in a cool, dry place for up to 2 days. Do not refrigerate them.

Makes 3$^1/_2$ cups (5 oz/155 g)

SERVING TIP
Add these croutons to salads, or use them to garnish pea soup (page 59) or winter squash soup (page 55). They are also good with thick dips or on their own as a snack.

Candied Lemon Peel

3 lemons

1 cup (8 oz/250 g) sugar, plus more for coating

2 tablespoons light corn syrup

Scrub the lemons thoroughly to remove any dirt and wax. Working with 1 lemon at a time, cut a thin slice from the blossom and stem ends. Make 4 equally spaced cuts from end to end and remove the peel in 4 sections. Repeat with the remaining 2 lemons. Place in a saucepan, add water to cover, and bring to a boil. Reduce the heat to low and simmer, uncovered, for 20 minutes. Drain the peel and repeat the process, and then drain again. When the sections of peel are cool to the touch, cut into strips $^1/_4$ inch (6 mm) wide.

In a saucepan over medium-high heat, combine the lemon strips, the 1 cup sugar, the corn syrup, and $^3/_4$ cup (6 fl oz/180 ml) water. Bring to a boil, stirring to dissolve the sugar. Reduce the heat to low and cook, stirring occasionally and adjusting the heat to prevent scorching, until the peel is translucent and has absorbed most of the syrup, about 45 minutes.

Remove from the heat and drain the peel. When the peel has cooled enough to handle but is still warm, spread sugar on a plate or piece of parchment (baking) paper. Working in batches, roll the strips in the sugar. Transfer the strips to a wire rack, spacing them so they do not touch. Let the candied peel dry for 1–2 hours. Store in a tightly covered container between sheets of parchment paper at room temperature for 3–4 weeks.

Makes about 1$^1/_4$ cups (5 oz/155 g)

VARIATION
To make candied orange peel, use 2 oranges, cutting them as directed for the lemons.

SERVING TIP
Finely chopped citrus peel can be stirred into fruit salads or used to top fruit and other desserts.

Raspberry Sauce

2 cups (8 oz/250 g) raspberries

2$^1/_2$ tablespoons orange blossom or wildflower honey

1$^1/_2$ teaspoons fresh lemon juice

In a food processor, combine the raspberries and honey and pulse just until the berries are puréed. Pour the purée through a fine-mesh sieve set over a bowl, pressing on the purée with the back of a wooden spoon to remove the seeds. Stir in the lemon juice. Cover and refrigerate for up to 5 days.

Makes 2 cups (16 fl oz/500 ml)

VARIATION
Substitute strawberries, blueberries, or mango cubes for the raspberries.

SERVING TIP
Use this versatile sauce to accompany pancakes (page 259) or waffles (page 260) or to spoon over slices of lemon loaf (page 224) or fresh fruit and yogurt.

Basic Techniques

BONING AND SKINNING A CHICKEN BREAST

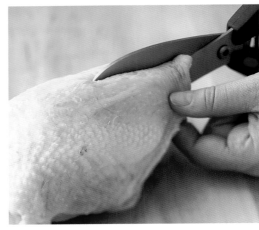  

1 Place the whole chicken breast on a cutting board. Using poultry shears, carefully cut lengthwise through the center of the breast to make 2 halves, splitting the breastbone and severing tough sinews between the halves.

2 Working with 1 breast half at a time, place it skin side down on the board. Insert a boning knife or other thin-bladed knife, between the bones and meat, then cut the bones away from the meat.

3 With your fingers, pull off the skin from each breast half. You may need to use the knife to free any tough sections. Trim away the white tendon and any large bits of fat and skin on the undersides of the breast halves.

BONING AND SKINNING FISH

1 Place the fish skin side down on a cutting board. Run your finger down the length of the fish to locate the small pin bones, which usually lie in a straight line. With needle-nose pliers or sturdy tweezers, remove the pin bones.

2 Using a long-bladed knife, cut a bit of the flesh away from the skin. Grasp the skin firmly and position the knife at a slight angle toward the board. Wiggle the knife back and forth as you cut the flesh away from the skin.

3 Discard the skin and move the fish to a clean area on the cutting board. Cut straight down at regular intervals to create portion-sized fillets. Use a scale to make sure that all the portions are the correct weight.

PEELING AND DEVEINING SHRIMP

1 Cut off the head of each shrimp (prawn), or leave it intact if directed in a recipe. Using your fingers, pull off the legs along the inside curve of the shrimp.

2 Starting at the head of the shrimp and using your fingers, carefully peel off the shell. Also remove the tail segments, or leave intact if required in a recipe.

3 Make a shallow cut along the shrimp's back, exposing the dark vein. Lift out with the tip of a knife. Rinse the shrimp under running cold water. Drain on paper towels.

ROASTING A BELL PEPPER

 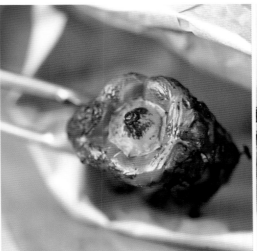 

1 Roast the bell pepper (capsicum) over the flame of a gas burner or in a preheated broiler (grill), turning with tongs as needed, until the skin is blistered and charred black on all sides, about 10–15 minutes.

2 Slip the pepper into a paper bag and fold over the top of the bag to create a closed environment. The steam created by the hot pepper will soften the flesh and skin and also allow the skin to be easily removed.

3 Remove the stem and discard. Slit the pepper open, then remove and discard the seeds and ribs. Place the pepper on a cutting board and remove the blackened skin with a paring knife or your fingers. Do not rinse.

Basic Techniques

SOAKING DRIED BEANS

Pick over the beans, discarding any misshapen beans or grit. Rinse the beans, put in a bowl, add water to cover by about 3 inches (7.5 cm), and let soak for at least 4 hours or for up to overnight. (For a quick soak, combine the beans and water in a saucepan and simmer rapidly for 2 minutes; remove from the heat, cover, and let stand for at least 1 hour.) Drain the beans.

MAKING FRESH BREAD CRUMBS

Cut slices from coarse country bread, whole-wheat (wholemeal) bread, or a baguette. Let stand overnight to dry out slightly. You can also place the bread in a 200°F (95°C) oven until they dry out, about 1 hour. Cut the crusts off the bread and tear the bread into large pieces. Place in a food processor, and process until they form crumbs of the desired consistency.

ZESTING CITRUS

Scrub the fruit well to remove any wax. Gently pull a citrus zester over the surface to produce fine shreds of colored zest. Or push the fruit against the fine rasps of a handheld grater or the razor-edged holes of a Microplane grater. Do not grate the bitter white pith beneath the zest. If you also need to use the juice of the lemon, remove the zest before juicing.

TRIMMING ARTICHOKES

1 Squeeze the juice from ¹/₂ lemon into a bowl of cold water. Using a paring knife, slice off the top ¹/₂ inch (12 mm) of the leaves to remove the prickly tips. If desired, trim the stem of each artichoke even with the base.

2 Pull off and discard the tough outer leaves until you reach the pale green inner leaves. Trim the bottom of the artichokes to remove the tough outer layers. Leave the artichoke whole or cut as directed.

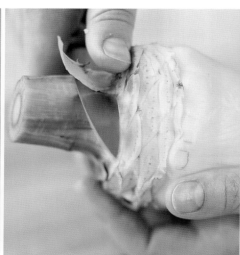

3 Place the trimmed artichokes in the lemon water to prevent the cut portions from turning brown. If you are preparing tender baby artichokes and will be eating the stems, use the paring knife to remove the tough outside flesh.

CHIFFONADE-CUTTING LETTUCE AND LEAFY HERBS

1 Remove and discard the stems from firm leafy vegetables or herbs. Stack 3–5 leaves on top of each other on a cutting board. Be sure to cut out any firm ribs, such as those found on romaine (cos) lettuce leaves.

2 Working from a long or short side, gently but firmly roll the leaves into a cylinder. Grasp the cylinder securely with one hand, allowing enough room to make cuts (it will be hard to move your hand once the roll is made).

3 Carefully cut the rolled leaves crosswise at $^1/_8$-inch (3-mm) intervals to make thin strips. It is especially important to use a sharp knife to prevent the leaves from blackening at the cut edges.

CUTTING A MANGO INTO CUBES

1 Stand the mango on an end on a cutting board. Positioning a sharp knife about 1 inch (2.5 cm) from the stem, cut the mango lengthwise, lightly brushing the large pit. Repeat on the other side of the mango.

2 Place each mango half cut side up on the board and use the knife to score the flesh in a grid pattern, forming cubes of the size specified in the recipe. As you work, be careful not to puncture the skin.

3 Holding the mango half with both hands, push against the skin side of the half to force the cubes outward. Carefully cut across the base of the cubes to free them. Repeat with the remaining half.

Glossary

ARUGULA Peppery green with markedly notched leaves averaging 3 inches (7.5 cm) in length. Good source of vitamin A. Look for bunches with bright green leaves. Also known as rocket.

BACON, PRESERVATIVE-FREE Uncured bacon with no nitrites or nitrates added to preserve the meat. Bacon is typically 50 percent fat. To lower the fat content of recipes, seek out leaner bacon, which can be as low as 33 percent fat.

BEANS, DRIED Nutritional powerhouses, dried beans are a beneficial source of complex carbohydrates, protein, and dietary fiber. They are also rich in vitamins, including the B vitamin folate, and are naturally low in fat, calories, and sodium. For convenience, canned beans may be used in most recipes. Rinse canned beans to remove added sodium.

Black Small and uniformly black with a shiny surface. Used widely in Latin American cooking to make pot beans, soups, and dips.

Borlotti Rosy beige bean with maroon speckles, used in Italian cooking. Similar to cranberry bean, below, and also available fresh.

Cannellini Ivory-colored bean with a smooth texture. Popular in salads, side dishes, and soups, including classic Italian minestrone.

Chickpea Large beige bean with a rich, nutty flavor and a firm texture. Also known as garbanzo bean or ceci bean.

Cranberry Mild-flavored bean with reddish flecks. The color fades when the beans are soaked and cooked. Also called Roman bean or borlotti bean. Sold fresh as well as dried.

French lentils Quick-cooking, disk-shaped legumes that include Le Puy, a small, dark green variety with a mild flavor.

Pinto Pale brown bean with darker, sometimes pinkish streaks that disappear during cooking. The full, earthy flavor of pinto beans is appreciated in the cuisine of the American Southwest.

White kidney Sometimes mistaken for cannellini, this mild-flavored variety is used often in Italian dishes and is a good substitute for cannellini in most recipes.

BRAN Outer covering of a grain that is removed during milling. Sold in bulk in supermarkets and health-food stores, wheat bran and oat bran impart robust flavor and texture to breads, muffins, and other baked goods. Bran is a rich source of dietary fiber and other nutrients.

BROTHS Whether a recipe calls for chicken, vegetable, or mushroom broth, the best choice for healthful cooking is a broth that is fat free and low in sodium. Various reduced-sodium, fat-free broths are widely available canned or in aseptic packaging. Fat and sodium content can easily be limited when preparing homemade stocks (page 270).

BUTTER, UNSALTED Also labeled "sweet butter," unsalted butter is preferred by many cooks who want a lower-salt alternative to regular salted butter. Some cooks prefer unsalted butter made from organic milk for its fresher, more pronounced flavor. Because the salt in butter acts as a preservative, unsalted butter in its original wrapping should be kept in the refrigerator for no longer than 6 weeks.

CAPERS A Mediterranean shrub is the source of these small unopened flower buds. The buds are bitter when raw; once they are dried and packed in brine or salt, they are used to add a pleasantly pungent flavor to a variety of dishes. Capers should be rinsed before use to remove excess brine or salt.

CHEESES The fat and sodium content of cheeses can vary greatly, but by making informed selections—choosing lower-fat types, using small amounts of strongly flavored or hard grating cheeses—you can enjoy a world of flavor and benefit from a rich source of protein, calcium, and other nutrients.

Asiago Italian cow's milk cheese that, when semifirm, has a pleasantly sharp taste. Fresh (mild) and aged (sharper) varieties are also available. American Asiago is very mild.

Feta Young cheese traditionally made from sheep's milk and used in Greek cuisine. It is known for its crumbly texture; some versions are also creamy. Feta's saltiness is heightened by the brine in which the cheese is pickled. Feta is also produced from cow's or goat's milk. Reduced-fat feta is also available.

Fresh goat Made from pure goat's milk or sometimes a blend of goat's and cow's milk. Fresh goat cheese is creamy in texture and mild or slightly tangy in flavor. Also called by its French name, chèvre.

Fromage blanc Fresh cheese made from skim or whole milk, appreciated for its soft, smooth texture and slightly tangy flavor.

Gruyère Firm, smooth-textured cow's milk cheese produced in Switzerland and France, noted for its mild nutty flavor.

Jarlsberg, reduced-fat Lighter version of the Norwegian cow's milk cheese produced from part-skim milk but still possessing a slightly nutty flavor. The interior has a network of holes.

Mozzarella, part-skim Mild-flavored cow's milk cheese with a smooth texture. The best Italian mozzarella is made from water buffalo's milk. Cheese labeled "part skim" has less fat than whole-milk mozzarella.

Parmigiano-Reggiano Trademarked name for Parmesan cheese from the Emilia-Romagna region of northern Italy. Made from partially skimmed cow's milk, the aged, firm cheese is mild, salty, and fragrant. One of the most prized grating cheeses.

Pecorino romano Italian grating cheese made from sheep's milk. It has a grainy texture and is pleasantly salty.

Ricotta, part-skim Soft cheese made by heating the whey that remains from producing cow's milk cheeses. Some ricottas are derived from sheep's or goat's milk. Part-skim ricotta contains less fat than whole-milk ricotta. Fat-free ricotta is also available, but part-skim is often preferred for its somewhat richer flavor.

Ricotta salata Aged Italian sheep's milk cheese. Lightly salted and low in fat, with a firm texture ideal for grating.

Romano A term that refers to several hard grating cheeses originating in Italy but now also produced outside the country. Pecorino romano, above, is one of the better known of the romano cheeses.

Stilton Strong-flavored blue-veined cow's milk cheese from England.

CHILES Low in calories, these pungent pepper pods are a good source of vitamin C (in green chiles) and vitamin A (in red chiles). They also have beneficial antioxidant properties.

Chipotle chile powder Ground seasoning made from chipotle chiles, the name for jalapeño chiles that have been dried and smoked. These dark brown chiles are very hot and have a smoky, slightly sweet flavor.

Jalapeño Fleshy chile that ranges from slightly hot to fiery and measures 2–4 inches (5–10 cm) long. Green jalapeños are the most common form; red jalapeños are also available.

Serrano Slightly slimmer than a jalapeño and about 2 inches (5 cm) long. Serranos have as much heat as jalapeños and may be used in place of them in recipes.

CHINESE RICE WINE Sweet golden wine made from glutinous rice. Resembling sherry, it is often served warm for drinking and is used extensively in Chinese cooking. The best-known Chinese rice wine is labeled "Shaoxing," after the city in eastern China.

COARSE COUNTRY BREAD General term that covers a variety of free-form rustic loaves, usually made from unbleached flour and using whole grains. The crumb is a bit rougher compared with that of other yeast breads, such as white bread.

COOKING SPRAY Oil packed in cans or sprayers, sometimes under pressure, used to coat baking sheets and other pans. The spray can also be applied directly on food to prevent sticking during cooking. Sprays are often a healthier option than liquid oils because they use less oil compared with pouring or brushing oil over a surface. Look for nonaerosol sprays that deliver a fine mist of olive or canola oil free of additives. Reusable misters, sold in cookware stores, can be filled with the oil of your choice.

CORNMEAL, YELLOW Dried corn kernels that have been ground to a fine, medium, or coarse consistency. The color of the corn determines the color of the cornmeal. Yellow and white cornmeal can be used interchangeably, but the yellow variety contains more vitamin A. Look for cornmeal labeled "water ground" or "stone ground," which contains the nutritious germ of the corn and has a slightly nutty flavor. More perishable than degerminated cornmeal, stone-ground cornmeal should be stored in the refrigerator. It will keep for up to 4 months.

DAIKON Asian radish, also known as Chinese turnip, with a long, white cylindrical body and crisp-textured flesh. It carries some heat, which comes from the skin, and a slightly sweet flavor. Daikon is purported to have several health benefits, one of which is aiding the digestion of fatty foods.

EDAMAME Soybeans harvested while still young. The pods are picked when plump but still green. *Edamame* are sold frozen or already cooked in their pods, and also shelled and frozen. The beans are often steamed in the shell, salted, and served for snacking. Low in fat and a good source of protein, calcium, iron, potassium, zinc, and many B vitamins.

ENDIVE, BELGIAN Member of the chicory family cultivated to form small, compact, elongated heads. The leaves are white with tinges of yellow and sometimes pale red tips. Their texture is crunchy, and their flavor is pleasantly bitter. Less commonly available is a deep-red variety. Also known as chicory or witloof.

FENNEL BULB This popular Mediterranean vegetable has the flavor of anise and is celery-like in appearance, with stalks, feathery leaves, and a thick, rounded base. Its distinctive taste complements fish dishes. Also known as sweet fennel, Italian fennel, and *finocchio*.

FILO PASTRY Large, paper-thin sheets of dough, also known as phyllo, commonly used to create flaky layers of pastry for Middle Eastern and Greek dishes both savory and sweet. In healthful cooking, filo pastry can be used to replace time-consuming, butter-rich puff pastry. Freshly made filo is sold in Middle Eastern markets; packages of frozen filo are available in many supermarkets. When working with filo, remember to bring the filo to room temperature, work quickly, and keep the sheets covered to prevent them from drying.

FLOURS Produced by grinding grains, seeds, nuts, or vegetables into a fine powder, flour is an essential ingredient in baked goods and noodles and is also used to thicken sauces and coat fried or baked foods.

Buckwheat Ground from the seeds of a plant. Firm-textured dark flour with a nutty, slightly sweet flavor. It is frequently called for in recipes for crepes, waffles, and various pancakes.

Cake Low in protein and high in starch, cake flour is milled from soft wheat to which cornstarch (cornflour) is added. Finer than all-purpose (plain) flour, it gives baked goods a light crumb. Also known as soft-wheat flour.

Unbleached all-purpose Flour made from both soft and hard wheats, from which the bran and germ have been removed. Unlike regular all-purpose, or plain, flour, it has not been bleached chemically and, in the opinion of some bakers, has a better flavor. All-purpose flour is versatile enough to use in a wide range of recipes, from sauces to pizza dough and pancakes.

Whole-wheat Also known as wholemeal flour, whole-wheat flour is milled from whole grains of wheat, including the bran and germ. As a result, whole-wheat flour is a darker color than all-purpose flour, is more nutritional, is denser after baking, and contains more fat. Regular whole-wheat flour is made from whole hard wheat berries; whole-wheat pastry flour is milled from whole soft-wheat berries. The latter is preferred for making more delicate baked goods, such as cakes and pie crusts. To prevent rancidity, both varieties of whole-wheat flour should be wrapped tightly and refrigerated until ready to use; they will keep for up to 6 months.

GINGER This staple of the Asian kitchen is not a root, as it is often called, but a rhizome, or underground stem. It is noted for its clean taste and is an essential aromatic ingredient in a wide range of dishes. Besides its power in the kitchen, its reputed medicinal qualities have long been revered in Asia.

Candied Ginger cooked in sugar syrup and then coated with granulated sugar. At once sweet and spicy, it is chopped and added to dessert fillings, cake batters, chutneys, or fruit salad. Also called crystallized ginger.

Fresh Gnarled and knobby in appearance with a thin brown skin that is easily removed with a paring knife or vegetable peeler. Fresh ginger has a refreshing and slightly sweet flavor and is also quite spicy. Select pieces that are firm and smooth, with slightly shiny skin.

Pickled Thin slices of ginger pickled in a mixture of vinegar, sugar, and water. Traditionally, pickled ginger is tinted pink. Also available is a white variety free of artificial dyes, sweeteners, and preservatives.

HERBES DE PROVENCE Mixture of dried herbs typical of those used in the Provence region of France. It usually contains lavender, thyme, basil, fennel seed, and summer savory. The blend is often sold in charming, small clay pots with lids.

JICAMA Round tuber shaped like a turnip but much larger, with light golden skin and juicy white flesh valued for its crunchy texture and sweet flavor. The flesh is shredded for use in salads, where it pairs well with citrus fruits and chiles, and is cut into sticks or strips and offered on a platter of crudités.

KALE Dark green with firm, tightly crinkled leaves on long stems. Like other dark leafy greens, this member of the cabbage family is rich in vitamins, such as A and B, and also contains calcium and iron. It retains its texture well when cooked. Several types of kale, with different leaf shapes and colors, are cultivated. Look for *cavolo nero* (black cabbage), dinosaur kale, Russian kale, and other varieties at farmers' markets and specialty-produce stores.

MANGO Juicy, sweet-fleshed fruit originally grown in India and now also cultivated in other tropical regions. Rich in beta-carotene, vitamin C, and many protective phytochemicals, mangoes are also a low-fat source of vitamin E. When shopping for ripe mangoes, choose fruits that are aromatic at their stem end and have uniformly smooth skin. They should give slightly to gentle pressure.

MILK A nutrient-dense food, milk is a good source of protein and an excellent source of calcium and vitamins A and D. It also supplies vitamin B_{12}, riboflavin, and potassium. The nutritional value of milks with reduced fat, including buttermilk and nonfat milk, is equivalent to that of whole milk. While adults monitoring their fat intake may want to drink nonfat milk, moderate amounts of whole milk are often desirable for cooking and baking.

1-percent-fat, 2-percent-fat In contrast to whole milk, which gets nearly half of its calories from fat, 1-percent-fat milk derives about 23 percent of its calories from fat; 2-percent-fat milk, about 35 percent of its calories from fat.

Buttermilk Traditionally the liquid left after butter is churned from cream. Today, buttermilk is commercially cultured from skim milk to develop its distinctive tangy flavor and creamy texture. It is much thicker than nonfat milk and is also higher in sodium than other milks. Both nonfat and low-fat forms are available.

Condensed Evaporated milk with a high proportion of sugar. Ivory in color and thick in consistency, it is available in nonfat form.

Evaporated Produced by using heat to remove about 60 percent of the water from milk. Nutrients are thus concentrated, making $\frac{1}{2}$ cup (4 fl oz/125 ml) evaporated milk similar nutritionally to 1 cup (8 fl oz/250 ml) whole milk. Evaporated milk is pale ivory and has a very slight caramelized flavor. It is sealed and sterilized in cans and cartons. It can be heated without curdling, making it ideal for use in sauces and puddings.

Nonfat Also called skim milk. It contains .5 percent fat or less.

Nonfat dry milk Made from pasteurized milk that has been dehydrated, with nearly all of the fat removed. It has about half the calories of whole milk. Dry milk must be reconstituted with water. It is added to recipes to boost the nutritional value of foods and is also used in baking and to thicken sauces. Also called milk powder or dry milk.

MUSHROOMS, DRIED Appreciated for their intense flavors and firm textures, dried mushrooms, after rehydrating, may be substituted for fresh in most cooked dishes, although they may need to cook longer to become tender.

Porcino Also known as cèpe and bolette. Porcini have a full, sweet fragrance and earthy flavor. Excellent in risottos and pasta sauces.

Shiitake Once imported from Japan or China but now cultivated outside Asia. Dried shiitakes have a rich, meaty flavor and texture.

MUSHROOMS, FRESH Containing only traces of various nutrients, mushrooms are valued primarily for their rich, woodsy flavor.

Cremini Brown-capped mushroom that may be substituted in recipes calling for button, or white, mushrooms. Cremini have a firmer texture and fuller flavor.

Oyster Fan-shaped mushroom named for its subtle shellfish flavor and creamy to pale gray color. Formerly found only in the wild, oyster mushrooms are now cultivated.

Portobello Mature cremini mushroom allowed to grow until the cap is up to 6 inches (15 cm) wide and dark brown. It has a smoky flavor and meaty texture that make it well suited to vegetarian dishes and for grilling.

Shiitake Most popular mushroom in Japan. Buff to dark brown in color and meaty in texture. Select shiitake mushrooms that have smooth, plump caps.

White The ubiquitous, all-purpose variety sold in grocery stores. The term refers specifically to young, tender specimens with closed caps.

OILS Cooking oils, fats that are liquid at room temperature, play an essential role in the kitchen. A recipe's other ingredients and its heat requirements usually will suggest which oil is most appropriate to use. For information on the function of fats in the diet and the nutrient content of fats, see page 287.

Asian sesame Deep amber-colored oil pressed from toasted sesame seeds. Used sparingly to add a rich, nutty flavor to recipes.

Canola Pressed from rapeseed, a relative of the mustard plant. High in healthful monounsaturated fat, this bland oil is recommended for general cooking and baking; however, it can smell unpleasant at high temperatures required for frying.

Olive Pressed from the fruit of the olive tree and high in monounsaturated fat. Extra-virgin olive oil is produced from the first press of the olives without the use of heat or chemicals. It has a clear green or brownish hue and a fruity, even slightly peppery flavor. Olive oils labeled "mild," "light," "pure," or simply "olive oil" are not as fragrant as extra-virgin.

Peanut Pressed from peanuts, which give the oil a hint of rich, nutty flavor, unless it is a refined version. It is often used for stir-frying, in salad dressings, and in dipping sauces for a variety of Asian dishes.

Safflower Flavorless oil pressed from safflower seeds. It has a high smoke point and is high in polyunsaturated fat.

Walnut Deep brown oil carrying the rich taste of the nuts from which it is pressed. It is used in small amounts in dressings and sauces. Because of its low smoke point, it is not recommended for high-heat cooking. Refrigerate nut oils after opening, as they turn rancid quickly.

PANKO Japanese bread crumbs made from wheat flour. The coarse flakes are used to coat foods before cooking, giving them a light, crunchy coating.

PROSCIUTTO Unsmoked, uncooked Italian ham that is seasoned, cured with salt, and air-dried. Although treated with a minimum of salt, prosciutto can be eaten without cooking. The most prized prosciutto is aged up to 2 years and is produced in Parma in the Italian region of Emilia-Romagna. The flavor of the meat is so distinctive that only a little is needed to season a recipe. Typically sliced paper thin, it is best when served raw or only lightly cooked, since longer cooking can toughen the meat.

QUINOA Nutritious quinoa (pronounced KEEN-wa) dates to the time of the Incas of Peru, who called this staple "the mother grain." Although cooks treat it like a grain, it is actually the seed of a leafy plant distantly related to spinach. The quick-cooking seeds look like spherical sesame seeds. When steamed, quinoa has a mild taste and a light, slightly chewy texture well suited to making pilafs, baked dishes, and salads. Quinoa should be rinsed thoroughly before cooking to remove a naturally occurring residue that has a bitter taste. A great source of protein, vitamins, and minerals, quinoa contains all of the essential amino acids.

RICE Seeds of a species of grass, of which more than 40,000 distinct varieties have been identified. The most universally eaten of all grains, rice contains virtually no fat and is high in complex carbohydrates, low in sodium, and cholesterol and gluten free. White rice, regardless of grain shape or size, has had the husk, bran, and germ removed. This process also removes fiber, vitamins, and minerals. Enriched or converted rice has added calcium, iron, and some B vitamins; brown rice is the richest in most nutrients.

Arborio Variety of medium-grain rice whose grains have a high surface-starch content. When the rice is simmered and stirred, the starch dissolves and contributes a creamy texture to the classic Italian dish risotto and other recipes. Arborio rice, traditionally grown only in Italy, is now cultivated in the United States.

Basmati Long-grain rice with a sweet, nutlike taste and perfume. Grown primarily in India, Iran, and the United States, and ideal for use in pilafs. Brown and white varieties are available.

Brown Term referring to any rice that has not been processed by milling or polishing and therefore has its brown hull still intact. As a result, brown rice takes longer to cook than comparable white rice. It also has a chewier texture and more robust taste. Short-, medium-, and long-grain brown rice varieties are available.

Carnaroli Italian variety with characteristics similar to those of Arborio, above, for which it may be used as a substitute.

Jasmine Cultivated in Thailand and also in the United States, this long-grain rice variety has a sweet floral scent.

White, long-grain Any white rice variety with grains three to five times longer than they are wide. The cooked grains separate and are generally fluffy. Commonly used in pilafs and as an accompaniment to main dishes.

RICE STICK NOODLES, DRIED Made from rice flour and water and sold in clear plastic packages. Used in summer rolls and other Asian dishes, as are rice vermicelli, below.

RICE VERMICELLI Consisting of rice flour and water. Often round rather than flat and produced in various widths. These dried noodles are packaged in small bundles tied with ribbon.

SAKE Japanese rice wine typically drunk but also often used as a seasoning.

SALT The most basic and ancient of seasonings. Varieties include table salt, sea salt, and kosher salt. Table salt usually contains added iodine along with additives that prevent it from caking so that it flows freely. Sea salt, by contrast, rarely has additives, and contains more minerals than table salt. It is produced naturally by evaporation, with the taste of each variety reflecting the location where it was made. Available in coarse or fine grains that are shaped like hollow, flaky pyramids, sea salt adheres better to foods and dissolves more quickly than table salt. Many cooks prefer kosher salt, the type used in the recipes in this book. Its large, coarse flakes are easy to handle, and it usually contains no additives or preservatives. Kosher salt can be used more liberally since it does not taste as salty as regular table salt.

SESAME SEEDS Tiny flat seeds that range in color from white to tan to black and provide some protein and polyunsaturated fat. Added to a recipe or sprinkled over a finished dish to contribute a nutty flavor and subtle texture. Widely used in Asian, African, Middle Eastern, and Latin American cuisines.

SOUR CREAM Cream to which a special bacterial culture has been added to produce lactic acid, which sours the cream. With its distinctive, clean tang and velvety texture, sour cream adds a luxuriant touch to both savory and sweet dishes. Light sour cream has about 40 percent less fat than regular sour cream. Nonfat sour cream is made from skim milk solids and is thickened with added stabilizers.

SOY SAUCE, REDUCED-SODIUM Popular Asian seasoning made from fermented soybean meal and wheat. Reduced-sodium soy sauce, while still high in sodium, has about half the sodium of regular soy sauce, with popular brands containing slightly more than 1,000 milligrams of sodium per tablespoon.

SQUID Also known by its Italian name, calamari. Falling under the broad category of shellfish, it is a member of the cephalopod class in the mollusk family. Its chewy texture and sweet, mild flavor takes well to a wide range of preparations. When buying fresh squid, select those that are shiny and firm, with clear eyes and a delicate ocean smell. The membrane that covers the squid should be gray. Key nutrients found in squid include riboflavin, niacin, vitamins B_{12} and E, and zinc. Many fishmongers sell squid already cleaned.

To clean squid, pull the head and tentacles from the body, or pouchlike part, of the squid. The innards, including the ink sac (which you want to avoid breaking), should come away with the head. Next, reach into the pouch and remove the long, plasticlike quill, or transparent spine, and discard it. Finally, cut off the tentacles from the rest of the head just below the eyes and discard the head and innards. Squeeze the cut end of the tentacles to remove the hard, round "beak" at the base and discard it. Rinse the body, removing the gray membrane.

SWEET ONIONS Fresh onions with mild, sweet, and juicy flesh that results from the soil and climate where the onions are grown. Varieties are named for their place of origin. Maui onions from Hawaii and Vidalia onions from Georgia come into season during spring; Walla Walla onions from Washington, during late summer. Onions contain the phytochemicals allicin and sulforaphane, which are thought to reduce the risk of several types of cancer.

SWEET POTATOES Large, edible roots. The darker-skinned variety, with dense, orange flesh that is sweet, is often labeled "yam" in American markets. Rich source of beta-carotene, vitamin C, and potassium, and a good source of fiber.

TAMARI SAUCE Seasoning made from soybeans. Thicker than Chinese-style soy sauce, with a more intense flavor.

THAI BASIL Popular herb in Thai cooking. The leaves are darker (red or purple tinged) than those of regular sweet basil, and their flavor is more biting.

THAI FISH SAUCE Made from salted and fermented fish. Also known as *nam pla*, the Thai variety of fish sauce has an especially intense aroma and taste. The amber-colored liquid is sold in bottles.

TOFU Mild-flavored, ivory-colored tofu, made from curdled soy milk, is rich in protein and is easily digestible. Also known as bean curd, it comes in varying densities and is labeled "firm," "soft," or "silken." Sold in blocks packed in water or in aseptic packaging, tofu should be drained, rinsed, and then drained again before use. When storing tofu, change the water daily to help keep it fresh. Other forms of tofu, such as smoked, are also available. Tofu is often fortified with calcium. It is naturally low in calories and sodium, high in protein, and cholesterol free, making it a particularly healthy food choice.

TOMATO PASTE Dense purée made from slow-cooked tomatoes that have been strained and reduced to a deep red concentrate. It has a low acid and high sugar content. Tomato paste is sold in tubes, tins, and jars.

TOMATO SAUCE Thinner purée than tomato paste, above, with salt and other seasonings added. Tomato sauce is ready to use in recipes, often as a base for sauces. Look for high-quality, low-sodium products. Many cooks prefer Italian sauces and those made from organic tomatoes. Like tomato paste, tomato sauce is rich in the antioxidants lycopene and vitamins C and A, and is a good source of potassium.

TOMATOES, PLUM Egg-shaped tomatoes, also known as Roma tomatoes. This variety has meaty, flavorful flesh prized particularly for making sauce. When buying plum tomatoes, choose those that are fragrant. For canned plum tomatoes or those packaged in aseptic boxes, look for brands low in sodium and other additives. Italian varieties are often the best quality. Tomatoes are rich in vitamins C and A, and also contain lycopene, a powerful antioxidant that may help lower the risk of prostate cancer and cardiovascular disease. Lycopene also enhances the body's absorption of beta-carotene.

TOMATOES, SUN-DRIED Dehydrated plum (Roma) tomatoes sold dried (labeled "dry packed") or packed in oil. Dry-packed tomatoes must be reconstituted in hot water before use. They contain virtually no fat (compared with oil packed) and are naturally low in calories and sodium. Tomatoes are rich in vitamin A, as well as vitamin C and lycopene, both of which are antioxidants. Research shows antioxidant-rich foods may help keep the immune system healthy and lower the risk of some cancers and other diseases, such as diabetes.

TUNA, SUSHI-GRADE Very fresh and clean-tasting fish that can be eaten raw. It may be labeled sushi- or sashimi-grade at fish markets. Tuna is a high-quality protein source rich in beneficial omega-3 fatty acids.

VINEGARS Many types are available, made from a variety of red or white wines or, like cider vinegar and rice vinegar, from fruits and grains. Vinegars are further seasoned by infusing them with fresh herbs, fruit, garlic, or other flavorful ingredients. All offer a healthful, low-fat way to season a range of foods.

Balsamic Aged vinegar made from unfermented grape juice of white Trebbiano grapes. Aged briefly, for only 1 year, or for as long as 75 years, the vinegar slowly evaporates and grows sweeter and mellower. Balsamic vinegar is a specialty of Italy's Emilia-Romagna region, chiefly the town of Modena.

Red wine Pantry staple carried in most supermarkets. Varietal wine vinegars are available in some specialty-food stores.

Rice Produced from fermented rice and widely used in Asian cuisines. It adds a slight acidity to cooked dishes and makes an excellent dressing for delicate greens.

Sherry Full-bodied vinegar possessing a nutty taste. It is especially good on vegetables and in salad dressings.

Tarragon Made by steeping fresh tarragon in vinegar, resulting in a vinegar infused with the herb's sweet, aniselike flavor.

WASABI Root of a Japanese plant that is grated to produce a potent seasoning resembling prepared horseradish. Green wasabi powder, sold in small tins or envelopes, is mixed with water to form a paste. Ready-to-use wasabi paste comes in tubes. Wasabi is often mixed with soy sauce and served as a condiment.

Nutrients at Work

Some nutrients require others for optimal absorption, but excess amounts may interfere with absorption and cause a deficiency. The best way to get all the nutrients you need is to eat a varied diet. If you have special nutrient needs, consult your doctor or a registered dietitian.

Humans need more than forty nutrients to support life. Many foods are good sources of many different nutrients, but no food provides everything. By eating whole foods and by eating a variety of foods, you are likely to consume a wide range of important nutrients.

A *balanced* multivitamin-mineral supplement or a fortified cereal that does not exceed 100 percent of the daily need for any nutrient is a safe addition to your diet. Many of the individual nutrient supplements people take (without medical advice) are unnecessary. Some actually can be harmful by creating nutrient imbalances, causing toxicity, or interacting with medications.

Until recently, nutrition experts recommended the distribution of macronutrients (carbohydrates, protein, and fat) in a well-balanced diet to be 55 percent of calories from carbohydrates, 15 percent of calories from protein, and 30 percent of calories from fat. As we have learned more about individual health needs and differences in metabolism, we have become more flexible in determining what constitutes a healthy diet. The table below shows macronutrient ranges recommended in September 2002 by the Institute of Medicine, part of the U.S. National Academies. These ranges are more likely to accommodate everyone's health needs.

Nutrition experts have also determined guidelines for micronutrients (vitamins and minerals), which are required in smaller amounts than macronutrients. Information on these nutrients begins on page 288.

MACRONUTRIENTS

NUTRIENTS AND FOOD SOURCES	FUNCTIONS	RECOMMENDED %, DAILY CALORIES AND GUIDANCE
Carbohydrates COMPLEX CARBOHYDRATES ■ Grains, breads, cereals, pastas ■ Dried beans and peas, lentils ■ Starchy vegetables (potatoes, corn, green peas)	■ Main source of energy for the body ■ Particularly important for the brain and nervous system ■ Fiber aids normal elimination	45–65% ■ Focus on complex carbohydrates, especially legumes, vegetables, and whole grains (brown rice; whole-grain bread, pasta, and cereal). ■ Many foods high in complex carbohydrates are also good fiber sources. Among the best are bran cereals, canned and dried beans, dried fruit, and rolled oats. Recommended daily intake of fiber for adults under age 50 is 25 g for women and 38 g for men. For women over age 50, intake is 21 g; for men, 30 g.
SIMPLE CARBOHYDRATES ■ Naturally occurring sugars in fruits, vegetables, and milk ■ Added sugars in soft drinks, candy, baked goods, jams and jellies, etc.	■ Provide energy	■ Limit added sugar to control calories. ■ Fruit and vegetables have naturally occurring sugars but also have vitamins, minerals, and phytochemicals.
Protein ■ Foods from animal sources ■ Dried beans and peas, nuts ■ Grain products	■ Builds and repairs cells ■ Regulates body processes by providing components for enzymes, hormones, fluid balance, nerve transmission, etc.	10–35% ■ Choose lean sources such as dried beans, soy, fish, poultry, lean cuts of meat, and low-fat dairy products most of the time. Egg yolks are rich in many nutrients but also high in cholesterol; limit to 5 per week.

Source: Institute of Medicine. *Dietary Reference Intakes for Energy, Carbohydrates, Fiber, Fat, Protein and Amino Acids (Macronutrients),* 2002.

NUTRIENTS AND FOOD SOURCES	FUNCTIONS	RECOMMENDED %, DAILY CALORIES AND GUIDANCE
Fats All fats are mixtures of saturated and unsaturated (polyunsaturated and monosaturated) types. Canola oil is the most unsaturated fat commercially available, but even it is 6% saturated fat. Coconut oil is the most saturated fat available, but is approximately 8% unsaturated.	■ Supplies essential fatty acids needed for various body processes and to build cell membranes, particularly of the brain and nervous system ■ Transports certain vitamins ■ Polyunsaturated (PUFA) and monounsaturated (MUFA) promote cardio-vascular health	20–35% ■ Experts disagree about the ideal amount of total fat in the diet. Some say more is fine if it is heart-healthy fat; others recommend limiting total fat. Virtually all experts agree that saturated fat, trans fats, and cholesterol, all of which can raise LDL cholesterol, should be limited. ■ If you have high triglycerides, talk with your physician about taking daily supplements of 2–4 g of EPA, eicosapentaenoic acid, and DHA, docosahexaenoic acid—both of which are omega-3 fatty acids.
PRIMARILY SATURATED ■ Foods from animal sources (meat fat, butter, cheese, cream) ■ Coconut, palm, palm kernel oils	■ Raises blood levels of "bad" (LDL) cholesterol	■ Limit saturated fat. ■ Substitute PUFA or MUFA for saturated fat when possible.
PRIMARILY POLYUNSATURED (PUFA) ■ Omega-3 fatty acids: herring, salmon, mackerel, lake trout, sardines, swordfish, nuts, flaxseed, canola oil, soybean oil, tofu ■ Omega-6: vegetable oils such as corn, soybean, and safflower (omega-6 fats are abundant in the American diet.)	■ Reduces inflammation; influences blood clotting and blood vessel activity to improve blood flow	■ Eat fish at least twice a week. ■ Substitute PUFA for saturated fat or trans fat when possible.
PRIMARILY MONOUNSATURATED (MUFA) Olive oil, canola oil, sesame oil, avocados, almonds, chicken fat, some margarines	■ Raises blood levels of "good" (HDL) cholesterol	■ Substitute MUFA for saturated fat or trans fat when possible.
DIETARY CHOLESTEROL Foods from animal sources (egg yolks, organ meats, cheese, fish roe, meat)	■ A structural component of cell membranes and some hormones	■ The body makes cholesterol, and some foods contain dietary cholesterol. U.S. food labels list cholesterol values.
TRANS FAT Processed foods, baked goods, margarine and shortening	■ Raises blood levels of "bad" (LDL) cholesterol	■ All U.S. food labels will list trans fat by 2006.
PLANT STEROLS (STANOLS) Added to margarines and salad dressings; naturally present in vegetable oils	■ Inhibit cholesterol absorption	■ U.S. food labels list stanols when added to foods.

MICRONUTRIENTS

FAT-SOLUBLE VITAMINS AND FOOD SOURCES	FUNCTIONS	DAILY RECOMMENDED INTAKES FOR ADULTS*
Vitamin A Dairy products, deep yellow-orange fruits and vegetables, dark green leafy vegetables, liver, fish, fortified milk, cheese, butter	■ Promotes growth and healthy skin and hair ■ Helps build strong bones and teeth ■ Works as an antioxidant that may reduce the risk of some cancers and other diseases ■ Helps night vision ■ Increases immunity	700 mcg for women 900 mcg for men
Vitamin D Fortified milk, salmon, sardines, herring, butter, liver, fortified cereals, fortified margarine	■ Builds bones and teeth ■ Enhances calcium and phosphorus absorption and regulates blood levels of these nutrients	5–10 mcg
Vitamin E Nuts and seeds, vegetable and seed oils (corn, soy, sunflower), whole-grain breads and cereals, dark green leafy vegetables, dried beans and peas	■ Helps form red blood cells ■ Improves immunity ■ Prevents oxidation of LDL cholesterol ■ Works as an antioxidant that may reduce the risk of some cancers	15 mg
Vitamin K Dark green leafy vegetables, liver, carrots, asparagus, cauliflower, cabbage, wheat bran, wheat germ, eggs	■ Needed for normal blood clotting ■ Promotes protein synthesis for bone, plasma, and organs	90 mcg for women 120 mcg for men

WATER-SOLUBLE VITAMINS

	FUNCTIONS	DAILY RECOMMENDED INTAKES FOR ADULTS*
B vitamins Grain products, dried beans and peas, dark green leafy vegetables, dairy products, meat, poultry, fish, eggs, organ meats, milk, brewer's yeast, wheat germ, seeds	■ Help the body use carbohydrates (biotin, B_{12}, niacin, pantothenic acid) ■ Regulate metabolism of cells and energy production (niacin, pantothenic acid) ■ Keep the nerves and muscles healthy (thiamin) ■ Protect against spinal birth defects (folate) ■ Protect against heart disease (B_6, folate)	■ B_6: 1.3–1.5 mg ■ B_{12}: 2.4 mcg (B_{12} is found only in animal-based food sources; vegetarians need supplements.) ■ Biotin: 30 mcg ■ Niacin: 14 mg niacin equivalents for women; 16 mg for men ■ Pantothenic acid: 5 mg ■ Riboflavin: 1.1 mg for women; 1.3 mg for men ■ Thiamin: 1.1 mg for women; 1.2 mg for men
Vitamin C Many fruits and vegetables, especially citrus fruits, broccoli, tomatoes, green bell peppers (capsicums), strawberries, melons, potatoes, papayas	■ Helps build body tissues ■ Fights infection and helps heal wounds ■ Helps body absorb iron and folate ■ Helps keep gums healthy ■ Works as an antioxidant	75 mg for women 90 mg for men

Sources: Institute of Medicine reports, 1999–2001

*mcg=micrograms; mg=milligrams

MICRONUTRIENTS

MINERALS** AND FOOD SOURCES	FUNCTIONS	DAILY RECOMMENDED INTAKES FOR ADULTS*
Calcium Dairy products (especially hard cheese, yogurt, and milk), fortified juices, sardines and canned fish eaten with bones, shellfish, tofu (if processed with calcium), dark green leafy vegetables	■ Helps build bones and teeth and keep them strong ■ Helps heart, muscles, and nerves work properly	1,000–1,200 mg
Iron Meat, fish, shellfish, egg yolks, dark green leafy vegetables, dried beans and peas, grain products, dried fruits	■ Helps red blood cells carry oxygen ■ Component of enzymes ■ Strengthens immune system	18 mg for women 8 mg for men
Magnesium Nuts and seeds, whole-grain products, dark green leafy vegetables, dried beans and peas	■ Helps build bones and teeth ■ Helps nerves and muscles work properly ■ Necessary for DNA and RNA ■ Necessary for carbohydrate metabolism	310–320 mg for women 400–420 mg for men
Phosphorus Seeds and nuts, meat, poultry, fish, dried beans and peas, dairy products, whole-grain products, eggs, brewer's yeast	■ Helps build strong bones and teeth ■ Has many metabolic functions ■ Helps body get energy from food	700 mg
Potassium Fruit, vegetables, dried beans and peas, meat, poultry, fish, dairy products, whole grains	■ Helps body maintain water and mineral balance ■ Regulates heartbeat and blood pressure	2,000 mg suggested; no official recommended intake
Selenium Seafood, chicken, organ meats, brown rice, whole-wheat (wholemeal) bread, peanuts, onions	■ Works as an antioxidant with vitamin E to protect cells from damage ■ Boosts immune function	55 mg
Zinc Oysters, meat, poultry, fish, soybeans, nuts, whole grains, wheat germ	■ Helps body metabolize proteins, carbo-hydrates, and alcohol ■ Helps wounds heal ■ Needed for growth, immune response, and reproduction	8 mg for women 11 mg for men

** The following minerals are generally sufficient in the diet when the minerals listed above are present: chloride, chromium, copper, fluoride, iodine, manganese, molybdenum, sodium, and sulfur. For information on fucntions and food sources, consult a nutrition book.

Nutritional Values

The recipes in all eight chapters, as well as the twenty basic recipes on pages 270–75, have been analyzed for significant nutrients. Using these calculations, along with the other information in this book, you can create meals that have the optimum balance of nutrients.

Having the following nutritional values at your fingertips will help you plan healthful meals. Keep in mind that the calculations reflect nutrients per serving unless otherwise noted. Not included in the calculations are ingredients that are optional or added to taste, or those that are suggested as an alternative or substitution in the recipe, recipe note, or variation. For recipes that yield a range of servings, the calculations are for the middle of that range. Many recipes call for a specific amount of salt and also suggest seasoning food to taste; however, if you are on a sodium-restricted diet, it is prudent to omit salt. If you have particular concerns about salt intake or other nutrient needs, you should consult your doctor or a registered dietitian.

The numbers for all nutritional values have been rounded using the guidelines required for reporting nutrient levels in the "Nutrition Facts" panel on U.S. food labels.

APPETIZERS		CALORIES (KILOJOULES)	PROTEIN/ GM	CARBOHY-DRATES/GM	TOTAL FAT/GM	SATURATED FAT/GM	CHOLES-TEROL/MG	DIETARY FIBER/GM	SODIUM/ MG
p. 37	Goat Cheese Tartlets with Cranberry–Red Onion Compote (per tartlet)	100 (420)	3	17	3.5	1.5	5	1	160
p. 38	Grilled Vegetable Antipasto	100 (420)	5	14	4.5	.5	0	6	95
p. 41	Creamy Herb Dip with Crudités	35 (145)	1	6	1	0	0	0	140
p. 42	New Potatoes Stuffed with Fines Herbes	50 (210)	5	6	0	0	0	2	200
p. 43	Red Bean Purée with Pita	80 (340)	3	13	1.5	0	0	2	70
p. 44	Mussels with Fresh Herbs	90 (380)	12	6	2.5	.5	30	1	420
p. 45	Smoked Salmon with Mustard-Horseradish Sauce	90 (380)	11	3	2.5	.5	15	0	1,760
p. 46	Tuna Tartare	120 (500)	15	3	5	1	20	1	560
p. 49	Grilled Shrimp with Tomato-Quinoa Salsa	160 (670)	19	13	4	.5	125	2	250

SOUPS AND STEWS		CALORIES (KILOJOULES)	PROTEIN/ GM	CARBOHY-DRATES/GM	TOTAL FAT/GM	SATURATED FAT/GM	CHOLES-TEROL/MG	DIETARY FIBER/GM	SODIUM/ MG
p. 54	Chilled Potato and Leek Soup	190 (800)	6	33	5	3	10	3	620
p. 55	Butternut Squash Soup	120 (500)	4	30	.5	0	0	4	250
p. 56	Tuscan Bean Soup	170 (710)	8	27	4	.5	0	4	310
p. 58	Black Bean Stew	230 (970)	13	44	1	0	0	8	250
p. 59	Sweet Green Pea Soup	130 (550)	5	19	4	.5	0	5	100
p. 61	Roasted Tomato Bisque	90 (380)	3	17	2.5	.5	0	4	640
p. 63	Corn Chowder	120 (500)	5	18	3.5	1	5	3	180

SOUPS AND STEWS CONT.	CALORIES (KILOJOULES)	PROTEIN/ GM	CARBOHY- DRATES/GM	TOTAL FAT/GM	SATURATED FAT/GM	CHOLES- TEROL/MG	DIETARY FIBER/GM	SODIUM/ MG
p. 64 Kale and Potato Soup	200 (840)	12	35	3	1	5	6	290
p. 66 Fish Stew with Fennel and Saffron	220 (920)	25	19	6	1	50	4	510
p. 69 Italian Shellfish Stew	470 (1,970)	50	37	13	2	290	4	630

SALADS	CALORIES (KILOJOULES)	PROTEIN/ GM	CARBOHY- DRATES/GM	TOTAL FAT/GM	SATURATED FAT/GM	CHOLES- TEROL/MG	DIETARY FIBER/GM	SODIUM/ MG
p. 74 Belgian Endive, Apple, and Walnut Salad	250 (1,050)	3	22	18	1.5	0	5	250
p. 75 Green Bean and Yellow Tomato Salad with Mint	110 (460)	3	12	7	1	0	3	260
p. 76 Beet and Stilton Salad with Orange Vinaigrette	190 (800)	7	12	13	5	15	2	600
p. 78 Carrot and Jicama Salad with Lime Vinaigrette	100 (420)	1	12	6	.5	0	5	220
p. 79 Tomato and Cucumber Salad	140 (590)	4	10	10	3	10	3	410
p. 80 Couscous Vegetable Salad	190 (800)	5	26	7	1	0	3	280
p. 82 Edamame and Orange Salad	230 (970)	12	20	12	1.5	0	8	65
p. 83 French-Style Potato Salad	110 (460)	3	10	7	1	0	4	240
p. 84 Spinach, Tomato, and Corn Salad	190 (800)	3	16	15	2	0	5	320
p. 87 Cannellini Bean, Fennel, and Shrimp Salad	350 (1,470)	29	36	11	1.5	150	7	380
p. 89 Salmon, Red Potato, and Asparagus Salad	410 (1,720)	28	16	27	4.5	70	6	340
p. 90 Chicken, Roasted Red Pepper, and Green Bean Salad	300 (1,260)	23	15	18	2.5	50	2	330
p. 93 Thai Beef Salad	320 (1,340)	30	12	16	6	70	2	540

MAIN DISHES		CALORIES (KILOJOULES)	PROTEIN/ GM	CARBOHY- DRATES/GM	TOTAL FAT/GM	SATURATED FAT/GM	CHOLES- TEROL/MG	DIETARY FIBER/GM	SODIUM/ MG
p. 99	Roasted Vegetables with Warm Lemon Dressing	230 (970)	9	33	8	1	0	7	440
p. 100	Spinach and Roasted Red Pepper Lasagna	360 (1,510)	23	43	12	5	25	7	1,020
p. 103	Wild Mushroom Risotto	370 (1,550)	12	59	9	2	5	6	800
p. 104	Whole-Wheat Pasta with Broccoli Rabe	410 (1,720)	18	73	8	1	0	11	770
p. 105	Pasta with Tomatoes, Arugula, and Goat Cheese	390 (1,640)	13	68	7	2	5	3	840
p. 106	Spicy Scallops with Vegetable-Rice Pilaf	340 (1,430)	20	48	7	1.5	30	2	520
p. 108	Stir-Fried Shrimp with Snow Peas and Mushrooms	160 (670)	20	6	6	1	140	1	180
p. 111	Grilled Halibut with Mango Salsa	220 (920)	24	20	4	.5	35	1	290
p. 112	Salmon with Ginger and Lime	320 (1,340)	26	8	21	6	90	0	1,100
p. 115	Salmon with Green Lentil Ragout	450 (1,890)	39	41	15	3	70	7	370
p. 117	Sicilian-Style Swordfish and Spaghetti	550 (2,310)	34	76	13	2	40	5	1,490
p. 118	Spice-Crusted Tuna	210 (880)	30	1	9	2	50	1	50
p. 119	Oven-Crisped Chicken	240 (1,010)	33	11	6	1	75	1	380
p. 120	Chicken Breasts Stuffed with Prosciutto and Jarlsberg Cheese	330 (1,390)	38	24	8	3	80	1	850
p. 122	Coq au Vin	280 (1,180)	39	20	4.5	1	85	5	430
p. 125	Eggplant Cannelloni	360 (1,510)	28	28	15	6	55	3	670
p. 126	Roasted Turkey Breast	240 (1,010)	54	0	1	.5	150	0	140
p. 128	Spinach-Stuffed Turkey Meat Loaf	260 (1,090)	32	17	7	2	70	3	800
p. 131	Cider-Braised Pork Chops with Apples	250 (1,050)	24	14	10	2	65	2	480
p. 132	Pork Tenderloin with Fennel and Bell Peppers	280 (1,180)	36	14	9	2	100	4	1,010

MAIN DISHES CONT.		CALORIES (KILOJOULES)	PROTEIN/ GM	CARBOHY- DRATES/GM	TOTAL FAT/GM	SATURATED FAT/GM	CHOLES- TEROL/MG	DIETARY FIBER/GM	SODIUM/ MG
p. 134	Beef Bourguignon with Noodles	480 (2,020)	40	36	19	5	140	2	620
p. 137	Grilled Beef Fillets with Mushrooms and Red Wine Sauce	310 (1,300)	30	8	17	5	80	2	290
p. 138	Grilled Beef with Salsa Verde	240 (1,010)	23	1	15	5	60	0	720
p. 141	Bread Crumb-Crusted Rack of Lamb with White Beans	530 (2,230)	44	65	10	3	65	11	560
p. 142	Medallions of Venison with Cranberry-Port Sauce	350 (1,470)	35	19	14	5	135	.5	580

SMALL PLATES		CALORIES (KILOJOULES)	PROTEIN/ GM	CARBOHY- DRATES/GM	TOTAL FAT/GM	SATURATED FAT/GM	CHOLES- TEROL/MG	DIETARY FIBER/GM	SODIUM/ MG
p. 149	Pizza with Caramelized Red Onions, Olives, and Feta Cheese	290 (1,220)	9	38	12	5	25	3	740
p. 150	Pizza with Potatoes, Mushrooms, and Tomato- Basil Pesto	270 (1,130)	10	40	8	2	5	5	550
p. 152	Fish Tacos with Tomato and Orange Salsa	200 (840)	14	20	7	1.5	35	3	440
p. 155	Vegetable Melts on Garlic Toast	360 (1,510)	14	34	21	5	20	6	460
p. 156	Lahvosh Filled with Goat Cheese, Walnuts, and Dried Figs	350 (1,470)	16	37	17	9	25	4	540
p. 159	Roasted Red Pepper and Mozzarella Sandwiches	590 (2,480)	20	60	32	7	45	6	550
p. 160	Portobello Burgers	220 (920)	6	24	12	2	0	4	190
p. 163	Ahi Tuna and Cucumber Sandwiches with Tapenade	530 (2,230)	30	57	21	3	60	5	790
p. 164	Tomato, Onion, and Goat Cheese Sandwiches	410 (1,720)	16	57	14	5	35	7	670
p. 166	Buckwheat Crepes with Mushrooms	260 (1,090)	12	28	13	3	110	3	420
p. 169	Vietnamese-Style Summer Rolls with Dipping Sauce	300 (1,260)	10	66	0	0	55	3	320
p. 170	Spinach Custard with Gruyère Topping	160 (670)	10	8	10	3.5	120	2	330

SIDE DISHES		CALORIES (KILOJOULES)	PROTEIN/ GM	CARBOHY-DRATES/GM	TOTAL FAT/GM	SATURATED FAT/GM	CHOLES-TEROL/MG	DIETARY FIBER/GM	SODIUM/ MG
p. 176	Roasted Asparagus with Toasted Bread Crumbs	70 (290)	3	7	4	.5	0	1	70
p. 178	Three-Pepper and Sweet Onion Roast with Kalamata Olives	150 (630)	3	21	7	1	0	5	310
p. 181	Roasted Tomatoes with Cannellini Beans and Capers	230 (970)	13	37	4.5	.5	0	7	240
p. 182	Eggplant with Tomatoes, Ricotta, and Parmigiano-Reggiano	110 (460)	5	10	6	2	10	2	290
p. 185	Artichokes Vinaigrette	140 (590)	3	10	11	1.5	0	5	210
p. 186	Roasted Carrots with Orange Zest and Cinnamon	80 (340)	1	11	4	.5	0	3	160
p. 187	Stir-Fried Spinach with Garlic and Lemon Zest	70 (290)	5	6	4	.5	0	4	160
p. 188	Stir-Fried Baby Greens with Ginger and Garlic	50 (210)	1	4	3	0	0	1	45
p. 190	Broccoli with Red Pepper Flakes and Garlic Chips	90 (380)	3	6	7	1	0	3	150
p. 191	Cauliflower with Orange Zest and Green Onion	50 (210)	2	4	4	.5	0	2	135
p. 193	Maple-and-Soy-Glazed Acorn Squash	170 (710)	2	40	1.5	0	0	9	280
p. 194	Zucchini and Red Onions with Mint	70 (290)	3	9	4	.5	0	2	130
p. 195	Steamed Sugar Snap Peas with Black Sesame Seeds	70 (290)	3	8	2	.5	0	3	30
p. 196	Stir-Fried Green Beans with Tamari Almonds	140 (590)	4	10	9	1	0	3	790
p. 199	Roasted Mushrooms, Potatoes, and Green Beans	90 (380)	4	10	4.5	1	5	3	150
p. 200	Goat Cheese and Potato Gratin	180 (750)	8	24	7	3.5	15	2	200
p. 202	Mashed Yukon Gold Potatoes	140 (590)	6	16	6	4	20	6	160
p. 203	Roasted Russet Potatoes with Parsley and Garlic	60 (250)	2	5	3.5	.5	0	2	250

SIDE DISHES CONT.		CALORIES (KILOJOULES)	PROTEIN/ GM	CARBOHY- DRATES/GM	TOTAL FAT/GM	SATURATED FAT/GM	CHOLES- TEROL/MG	DIETARY FIBER/GM	SODIUM/ MG
p. 205	Roasted Sweet Potatoes with Cumin and Cilantro	120 (500)	1	20	4	.5	0	2	260
p. 206	Sweet Potato and Cranberry Hash	190 (800)	2	33	6	3.5	16	5	140
p. 207	Lemon Orzo with Parsley	220 (920)	6	38	4.5	2.5	10	1	180
p. 208	Sesame Brown Rice	200 (840)	4	39	3.5	.5	0	2	250
p. 209	Quinoa with Dried Cranberries and Toasted Pecans	260 (1,090)	8	34	12	1	0	4	250
p. 210	Spiced Basmati Rice Pilaf	280 (1,180)	7	42	12	1	0	1	270
p. 213	Baked Polenta with Mushrooms	180 (750)	7	25	5	2	5	2	210

DESSERTS		CALORIES (KILOJOULES)	PROTEIN/ GM	CARBOHY- DRATES/GM	TOTAL FAT/GM	SATURATED FAT/GM	CHOLES- TEROL/MG	DIETARY FIBER/GM	SODIUM/ MG
p. 219	Chocolate-Cherry-Almond Biscotti (per cookie)	50 (210)	1	9	1.5	0	10	.5	40
p. 221	Oatmeal-Raisin Cookies (per cookie)	80 (340)	1	14	2	.5	0	1	40
p. 222	Chocolate Meringues (per cookie)	30 (125)	.5	7	0	0	0	0	15
p. 224	Glazed Lemon Loaf	210 (880)	3	36	6	0.5	35	.5	90
p. 227	Angel Food Cake with Mocha Sauce	250 (1,050)	5	56	1.5	1	0	0	90
p. 228	Key Lime Chiffon Pie	230 (970)	6	41	5	1	80	.5	160
p. 230	Three-Berry Cobbler	310 (1,300)	4	61	7	4	15	7	410
p. 233	Cinnamon-Raisin Bread Pudding with Maple Sauce	500 (2,100)	12	96	8	3	140	2	370
p. 235	Baked Apples Filled with Apricots and Figs	480 (2,020)	3	125	1.5	0	0	10	20
p. 236	Cranberry-Apple Crisp	290 (1,220)	2	56	6	4	15	4	20
p. 237	Swirled Melon Soup	140 (590)	1	30	0	0	0	2	20
p. 239	Summer Fruit Parfaits	270 (1,130)	6	62	.5	0	0	3	80
p. 240	Chocolate Sorbet	290 (1,220)	2	67	4	2	0	0	70

DESSERTS CONT.		CALORIES (KILOJOULES)	PROTEIN/ GM	CARBOHY- DRATES/GM	TOTAL FAT/GM	SATURATED FAT/GM	CHOLES- TEROL/MG	DIETARY FIBER/GM	SODIUM/ MG
p. 241	Peach-Mango Sorbet	190 (800)	1	49	.5	0	0	2	20
p. 242	Tropical Fruit Kabobs with Rum Sauce	210 (880)	2	53	1	0	0	3	10
p. 244	White Wine–Poached Pears	270 (1,130)	1	70	1	0	0	4	10
p. 245	Red Wine–Poached Pears	230 (970)	1	60	1	0	0	4	10
p. 246	Very Chocolate Mousse	230 (970)	7	31	11	5	0	1	60

BREAKFASTS		CALORIES (KILOJOULES)	PROTEIN/ GM	CARBOHY- DRATES/GM	TOTAL FAT/GM	SATURATED FAT/GM	CHOLES- TEROL/MG	DIETARY FIBER/GM	SODIUM/ MG
p. 253	Fresh Corn and Cornmeal Muffins (per muffin)	190 (800)	5	28	7	1	40	1	340
p. 254	Date-Apple Oat Bran Muffins (per muffin)	210 (880)	4	35	7	1	20	2	250
p. 256	Banana-Buttermilk Muffins (per muffin)	190 (800)	4	29	7	1	20	2	210
p. 259	Ricotta-Lemon Pancakes	290 (1,220)	14	37	10	4	180	5	250
p. 260	Waffles with Strawberry and Honey Sauce	500 (2,100)	14	96	11	5	125	6	690
p. 263	Multigrain Yeast Bread (per slice)	140 (590)	5	25	3	1	15	2	200
p. 264	Roasted Red Pepper, Spinach, and Feta Omelet	260 (1,090)	15	8	19	5	430	0	290
p. 266	Scrambled Eggs with Tomato, Cheddar, and Basil	180 (750)	12	3	13	4	310	1	380
p. 269	Mango–Yogurt Smoothies	200 (840)	7	44	.5	0	0	1	90

BASIC RECIPES		CALORIES (KILOJOULES)	PROTEIN/ GM	CARBOHY- DRATES/GM	TOTAL FAT/GM	SATURATED FAT/GM	CHOLES- TEROL/MG	DIETARY FIBER/GM	SODIUM/ MG
p. 270	Rich Chicken Stock (per 1 cup/8 fl oz/250 ml)	30 (125)	3	3	1	.5	5	0	90
p. 270	Roasted Vegetable Stock (per 1 cup/8 fl oz/250 ml)	40 (170)	1	6	1	0	0	1	20
p. 271	Spicy Tomato Sauce (per 1/2 cup/4 fl oz/125 ml)	30 (125)	1	5	1.5	0	0	1	230
p. 271	Lean Béchamel Sauce (per 1/4 cup/2 fl oz/60 ml)	30 (125)	2	3	1	0	0	0	100
p. 271	Roasted Garlic	30 (125)	1	4	1	0	0	0	65
p. 272	Tomato Chutney (per 1/4 cup/2 fl oz/60 ml)	80 (340)	1	20	0	0	0	1	10
p. 272	Gremolata (per 1 tablespoon)	2 (8)	0	0	0	0	0	0	0
p. 272	Preserved Lemons (per 1/8 lemon)	10 (40)	0	1	0	0	0	1	460
p. 272	Tzatziki (per 1/4 cup/2 fl oz/60 ml)	40 (170)	2	3	2	1	5	.5	160
p. 273	Yogurt Cheese	50 (210)	5	2	15	0	5	0	40
p. 273	Pico de Gallo (per 2 tablespoons)	35 (145)	0	2	0	0	0	.5	125
p. 273	Aioli (per 1 tablespoon)	25 (105)	0	4	1	0	0	0	180
p. 273	Buttermilk, Yogurt, and Herb Dressing (per 2 tablespoons)	30 (125)	2	2	1.5	0	0	0	120
p. 274	Citrus-Mustard Dressing (per 2 tablespoons)	130 (550)	0	0	1.5	2	0	0	300
p. 274	Green Goddess Dressing (per 2 tablespoons)	40 (170)	3	5	1	.5	5	.5	290
p. 274	Honey and Cider Vinaigrette (per 2 tablespoons)	70 (290)	0	20	0	0	0	0	240
p. 274	Lime-Ginger Vinaigrette (per 2 tablespoons)	160 (670)	0	1	18	1	0	0	240
p. 274	Herb and Cheese Croutons (per 1/4 cup/2 oz/60 g)	50 (210)	2	7	1	.5	0	1	130
p. 275	Candied Lemon Peel	25 (105)	0	6	0	0	0	0	0
p. 275	Raspberry Sauce (per 2 tablespoons)	15 (60)	0	4	0	0	0	.5	0

Index

OXMOOR HOUSE INC.

Oxmoor House®

Oxmoor House books are distributed by Sunset Books
80 Willow Road, Menlo Park, CA 94025
Telephone: 650-321-3600 Fax: 650-324-1532
Vice President/General Manager: Rich Smeby
Director of Special Sales: Gary Wright

Oxmoor House and Sunset Books are divisions of
Southern Progress Corporation

WILLIAMS-SONOMA, INC.
Founder & Vice-Chairman: Chuck Williams

WELDON OWEN INC.
Chief Executive Officer: John Owen
President: Terry Newell
Chief Operating Officer: Larry Partington
Vice President International Sales: Stuart Laurence
Creative Director: Gaye Allen
Associate Creative Director: Leslie Harrington
Publisher: Hannah Rahill
Series Editor: Jennifer Newens
Managing Editor: Judith Dunham
Copy Editor: Sharon Silva
Assistant Editor: Donita Boles
Photography Director: Nicky Collings
Designer: Charlene Charles
Production Director: Chris Hemesath
Color Specialist: Teri Bell
Production and Shipping Coordinator: Libby Temple
Proofreader: Desne Ahlers
Indexer: Ken DellaPenta
Photographers: Jeff Tucker and Kevin Hossler
Food Stylist: Randy Mon
Assistant Food Stylist: Leslie Busch

ACKNOWLEDGMENTS
Mary Abbott Hess appreciates the support of members of Food &
Culinary Professionals, the practice group of culinary experts within
the dietetics profession. Special thanks go to Jane Grant Tougas for
her collaboration on this book.
    Jeff Tucker and Kevin Hossler thank Champ De Mar, San Francisco;
Steve Mcguire and Eileen Morgan; Nancy White; Rubylane.com; and
Chrome Works, San Francisco, for their assistance.
    Information in the Guide to Produce by Color on page 14 has been
adapted from the educational materials of the Produce for Better
Health Foundation at www.5aday.com.
    Weldon Owen thanks Lynne S. Hill of Hill Nutrition Associates Inc.
for providing the nutrient values; Vené Franco for providing the glos-
sary text; and Linda Bouchard, Jody Ginsberg, Karen Kemp, and Joan
Olson for their production assistance.

THE ESSENTIALS SERIES
Conceived and produced by
WELDON OWEN INC.
814 Montgomery Street, San Francisco, CA 94133
Telephone: 415-291-0100 Fax: 415-291-8841

In Collaboration with Williams-Sonoma, Inc.
3250 Van Ness Avenue, San Francisco, CA 94109

A WELDON OWEN PRODUCTION
Copyright © 2003 Weldon Owen Inc.
and Williams-Sonoma, Inc.

First printed in 2003
10 9 8 7 6 5 4

ISBN 0-8487-2864-5

Printed by Midas Printing Limited
Printed in China